I Have Not Seen Mandu

A Fractured Soul-Memoir

Swadesh Deepak

Translated by Jerry Pinto

SPEAKING TIGER

SPEAKING TIGER BOOKS LLP
125A, Ground Floor, Shahpur Jat, near Asiad Village,
New Delhi 110049

First published in Hindi by Rajkamal Prakashan 2003
First published in English by Speaking Tiger Books 2021

ISBN: 978-93-90477-58-6
eISBN: 978-93-90477-59-3

10 9 8 7 6 5 4 3 2 1

Typeset in Sabon Roman by SÜRYA, New Delhi
Printed at Shree Maitrey Printech Pvt. Ltd., Noida

Author and playwright Swadesh Deepak was born in Rawalpindi on 6 August 1942. After his MA in English Literature, he taught for a long time at the Gandhi Memorial National College, Ambala Cantonment. Following a period of illness from 1991 to 1997, when he had little contact with anyone other than his family and close friends, he made a momentous return to the world of letters with an autobiographical account of his illness, *Maine Mandu Nahin Dekha*, and the play *Sabse Udaas Kavita*. He received the Sangeet Natak Akademi Award in 2004. He has a total of 15 published books to his name including short-story collections such as *Tamasha*, *Baal Bhagwan* and *Kisi Ek Pedh Ka Naam Lo* and hugely successful plays such as *Court Martial* and *Kaal Kothri*.

In 2006 he left home for a walk and never returned. He has been missing ever since.

Jerry Pinto is the author of *Murder in Mahim* (2017) and *Em and the Big Hoom* (2012; winner of the Hindu Prize and the Crossword Book Award), and the non-fiction book *Helen: The Life and Times of an H-Bomb* (2006; winner of the National Award for the Best Book on Cinema). His other books include *Asylum and Other Poems*, *Surviving Women*, *A Bear for Felicia*, *Monster Garden*, *When Crows Are White* and, as editor, *A Book of Light: When a Loved One Has a Different Mind*, *Reflected in Water: Writings on Goa*, *The Greatest Show on Earth: Writings on Bollywood*, *Bombay, Meri Jaan: Writings on Mumbai* (with Naresh Fernandes) and *Confronting Love: Poems* (with Arundhathi Subramaniam). He has also translated (from Marathi) Daya Pawar's classic autobiography *Baluta* and Baburao Bagul's *When I Hid My Caste* (*Jevha Mee Jaat Chorli Hoti*), and the memoirs *I Want to Destroy Myself* (*Mala Udhvasta Vhachay*) by Malika Amar Shaikh and *I, the Salt Doll* (*Mee Mithaachi Baahuli*) by Vandana Mishra. Jerry Pinto also teaches journalism at the Sophia Institute of Social Communications Media in Mumbai and is on the board of directors of Meljol, which works in the sphere of child rights. In 2016, Jerry Pinto was awarded the Windham-Campbell Prize and the Sahitya Akademi Award.

Caveat:

Where you think fit, add the word 'perhaps'.
For some unsettled memories are fractured.

Writer's dedication:

This book is for Soumitra Mohan.

Translator's dedication:

To all those who have suffered from mental distress
and to all those who have loved them.

Sequence

Translator's Introduction

In some ways, my journey to the translation of this book began when I was a young man who found that he was not the only person in the world with a bipolar mother. I began to read psychological literature with the avidness with which other boys read pornography. A friend's father evicted Krafft-Ebing's *Psychopathia Sexualis* from his library and it came my way. I read Freud's *The Interpretation of Dreams* and Jung's *Man and His Symbols* and some bits and bobs of Adler. I read *I Never Promised You a Rose Garden* by Hannah Green (real name Joanne Greenberg) and *Sybil* by Flora Rheta Schreiber and *The Three Faces of Eve* by Corbett H. Thigpen and Hervey M. Cleckley. I read Mary Barnes, writing with Joseph Berke—*Two Accounts of a Journey Through Madness*—and I read *Darkness Visible: A Memoir of Madness* by William Styron. I read *One Flew Over the Cuckoo's Nest* by Ken Kesey and *The Bell Jar* by Sylvia Plath. Sublime, ridiculous—it did not matter. Some of these books became part of my permanent library at home; some of them went back to the libraries from which they came. Through it all, there wasn't much out of India. I didn't expect there to be: I grew up in the 1970s when the whole notion of mental ill-health was to be swept under the carpet. People just didn't talk about it. (And even today, most of Middle India won't.)

I don't think I was consciously preparing to write *Em and the Big Hoom*, a novel that was based on the experiences of four love-battered Pintos, one of whom was bipolar. I have always maintained that the novel was ninety per cent fact and ninety per cent fiction. If you know your Venn diagrams, you will know that this allows the reader comfortable space to make her own decisions about the book. Out of *Em and the Big Hoom* grew *A Book of Light: When a Loved One Has a Different Mind*, an anthology of carers' experiences of living with those whose minds were in some way different. I was running a final edit on it when Nirupama Dutt, a fine Punjabi poet and contributor to the book, called and asked if I knew of a writer called Swadesh Deepak.

I try to keep up but India lives and writes and reads in several simultaneous worlds. I confessed that it seemed familiar but I couldn't really remember.

'*Court Martial*?'

Of course. I had read her translation of the play somewhere; I remember thinking that the writer came out swinging sledgehammers; that it was a male play, drenched in testosterone, but then it was set in the army.

'You do know what happened to him?'

I had to admit I didn't.

Nirupama filled me in. Swadesh Deepak had written one of the most famous plays of his time; it is still performed across the country, in Delhi, in Mumbai, in Kolkata. Then he had had a breakdown. He found himself without words—the ultimate Hell for a writer. He had tried to kill himself by setting himself on fire and ended up in a hospital, where the authorities had found it difficult to decide whether he belonged in the Burns Unit or the Psychiatric Ward. The road to recovery was long and hard, but finally Swadesh Deepak made it. By then, he had lost his job as a teacher of English literature to post-graduate students and he had exiled himself from his friends, but he had not lost his family. They stood by him with a love that was both bewildered and beleaguered.

As he recovered, his friends refused to let him remain in isolation. They invaded him in the kindest possible way, led by the redoubtable Krishna Sobti and assisted by Vikas Rai.

Finally, Swadesh Deepak had begun to write again, finishing a couple of plays and writing *Maine Mandu Nahin Dekha: Khandit Jeevan ka Collage*, a first-hand account of his descent into madness and his return therefrom. The book came out, it was well-received, even celebrated and then early one morning, tormented again by his demons, Swadesh Deepak got up, went out for a walk and never returned.

How do you respond to such a story?

But Nirupama was continuing.

'His son, Sukant, would like to write for the anthology,' said Nirupama. 'Would you be interested?'

Needless to say, I was.

A couple of weeks later, the piece came in. It was written with sensitivity, honesty and rare self-implication. I edited it lightly and sent *A Book of Light* off to Ravi Singh. But the name continued to sound inside my head: *Maine Mandu Nahin Dekha*.

At around this time, I was helping Jehangir Sabavala's widow Shirin sort out the material she was going to hand over to the archives of the Chhatrapati Shivaji Maharaj Vastu Sangrahalaya, Mumbai (the institution formerly called The Prince of Wales Museum, Bombay), and in the middle of all the letters and the files, I came upon a copy of *Maine Mandu Nahin Dekha*. The cover featured a painting by Jehangir Sabavala. The Punjabi writer of Hindi from Ambala and the elegant Parsi painter from Mumbai had kept up a correspondence over the years.

I borrowed the book with Shirin's permission. On the way home, I opened it idly. By the time I got home, half an hour later, I was hooked. I had never read anything like it. The opening sequence was a long scene in which Swadesh Deepak, newly recovered, newly liberated from the Psychiatric Ward, comes to Delhi to make his literary re-entry. He is to have dinner at Nirmal Verma's house and suddenly, I, the reader, was a fly on the wall as the cream of Delhi's Hindi literati chatted with each other, late into the night. Since it is also a book about writing, you get to listen in as the noted poet and editor Giridhar Rathi and Deepak discuss the genesis of the book; which means you now have an insight into its prehistory.

But I could also see why Swadesh Deepak had chosen to

call it a 'fractured collage'. I could see—no, I could smell his uncertainty, the gingerly handling of words. I could sense the illness underneath; it had not gone away, it was biding its time. Everything was just a beat off. It is to the credit of the editors at Rajkamal that no one sought to smoothen this out, to clean it up.

I thought of the beautifully polished work that is *Darkness Visible: A Memoir of Madness*. Yes, I was there, William Styron tells us, yes, I was but I am back now. I am a writer at the height of my powers. Swadesh Deepak's words carry all the scars of who he was and what his illness had made of him. I could not tell, for instance, whether his misogyny was part of his illness or part of his character. When he says that he cannot befriend a woman because he has had a hatred of them since the time he was born, is it his illness speaking? Or is it the voice of a man who likes to shock? Or a confession? I could not tell. At other points he displays a communal streak: judging people by surnames. He body-shames others when he is in a rage. Is this one of the 'grenades'—a metaphor he uses for his own savagery—or is it him?

His voice echoes from the bottom of a well.

I hate it when people talk about instant classics but I have not read anything like this, so completely naked, so dependent on the kindness of strangers, so raw.

I read the whole book in two or three days. Few books have this effect on me. I was then in the middle of reading several other books. (I always am. I cannot read one book at a time. I need fiction and non-fiction and poetry and something that smells non-Anglophone all at once.) But *Maine Mandu Nahin Dekha* spoke with an urgency I had not felt since I was reading *Baluta* by Daya Pawar.*

* *Baluta* by Daya Pawar (Speaking Tiger, 2015). Translated by Jerry Pinto.

I was on Facebook then, and the day after I finished I messaged Sukant Deepak and suggested that he translate the book. He said he couldn't because it was too personal, and before I could even think of what I was writing, I had keyed in 'Then may I do it?'

Sukant Deepak is a kind young man. He did not say what anyone else in his position might say. 'You're from Mumbai, do you even speak Hindi?' 'You translate from Marathi, are you up to this?' He simply agreed. This was a huge act of faith and I record it as such. I can only hope that I have been worthy of it.

Now I began a second reading of the book, watching myself read, and trying out tones in my head. That some of it was in Punjabi did not worry me much. For that, I could have recourse to Ravi Singh, my editor and publisher, Nirupama Dutt and Sukant Deepak. But what was worrisome was that one of the symptoms of Swadesh Deepak's manic episodes was the tendency to break out into English. Here was a professor of English who had been silenced by a 'seductress'—I use the word he uses. He has insulted her in public and she takes revenge by silencing him. The sedge is withered from the lake, and no birds sing. One can see why Helen of Troy comes to mind, why he wanders in Eliot's 'The Waste Land', why Maud Gonne (who spurned W.B. Yeats) features in the book. You can also tell that this is no easy set of references; this speaks to a deeper malaise that Deepak, writer in Hindi, teacher of English, small-town resident and playwright, must constantly be aware of. To him, English is a 'language of lies'. Or at least to the Swadesh Deepak we meet here. For it seems also to be the language from which he draws his references, and anyone who has sought one knows it is to express something deep within that may have been said before. How then can this be the language of lies for him? Once again, I don't know. Perhaps the best way to look at the relationship between Swadesh Deepak and English as a language is as a reflection of the ambivalence many feel for the language of power and the power of the language. If you consider Deepak's play *Kaal Kothri*,* we have the figure of the Culture Commissioner, Kishorechand Sharma, a poet who writes in English, a straw man who represents all the fears and hurts Deepak might have otherwise been unable to express.

But in translating his book into English, I needed a way to work around this. I have come up with a way of signalling the English in the original: I have used a different font to indicate these relapses. Where he has quoted English poetry, I have stuck to his renderings of the lines, mangled perhaps out of choice, perhaps by his ailment. But I have tried to keep the line lengths and punctuation as in the originals even where he has departed from them and offered the correct versions as footnotes.

And one might also note that the Swadesh Deepak we meet here turns his guns on Hindi and Hindi writers with as much violence. Perhaps language itself was the betrayer, the seductress who had given him so much pleasure and then simply refused to respond for seven long years.

I wish this book could have had a happy end. I wish we could put it down and think of Swadesh Deepak in his house in Ambala, working on his next play. But that's not how things work out. We don't know where he is but there is this magnificent book that he has left us, its flaws the source of its strength. It is a document of rare honesty: when he falls in the shit, quite literally, he will not spare you. And he records with clarity and intelligence the effect his illness has on his family.

Their journey is as real and as moving: his wife Geeta who is savage in her misery at the ruin of her husband; his

* *Kaal Kothri* has been translated as *Dungeon* by Jerry Pinto and is forthcoming from Speaking Tiger in a volume of Deepak's plays, *Court Martial and Other Plays*.

daughter Parul who is a firebrand in his defence; and finally Sukant, who began to spend time in the Psychiatric Ward with a maturity far beyond his years. And so perhaps it is not wrong to say that the last chapter of this book appears in *A Book of Light*, in the section called 'Papa Elsewhere' by Sukant Deepak. It begins with the image of a boy, lying in bed, trying to sleep. His father, having recently returned from hospital, is outside the door, knocking. The boy has an iron rod under his bed. He loves his father; his father loves him. The rod is 'just in case'.

That's also how it can be.

It was said of Swadesh Deepak that he hunted his characters with a gun. I suspect that in this book, he has turned his weapon on his readers.

You have been warned.

Jerry Pinto
Mumbai
May 2021

There Is No Bridge Here

(In place of an introduction)

Calcutta. The eleventh month of 1991.

Mayavini has hammered a nail into my head. I found out later, very much later. My world went from Glorious Technicolor to monochrome, diseased and ugly. My river was lost. There was no bridge for me anywhere.

For about seven years I was the prisoner of a mental illness. Those who suffer from this disease have terrifying dreams and their responses are violent and full of hate. At worst, strangers attack you as do the people who know. The latter give you no support or encouragement. The mentally ill are branded by society.

Seven years. The seasons have no effect. Thinking stops so feeling stops. When fire was chewing up my clothes—dhoo, dhoo-dhoo—and my body was burning, the domestic help Sultan saved me. Later he told me he found me sitting in a chair, smoking a cigarette.

Once your mind shuts down, you do not feel the heat, you do not feel the cold.

I spent five months at the Post-Graduate Institute of Medical Education and Research,* Chandigarh, as a patient shared by the Burns Unit and the Psychiatric Ward. Despite many grim predictions and evil omens, I left the hospital in February 1995. And then began the difficult time of re-entry. My heart and my brain lead me in different directions, neither listening to the other.

Immediately after recovering, I wrote the play *Sabse Udaas Kavita* ('The Saddest Poem'). But despite the advice of friends, I could not write about my seven-year-long experiences. I was afraid. Dr Pratap Sharan told me not to

---

* This institution is referred to as PGI in the rest of this book.

push it. Many years later hazy and fractured memories began to return, but not in sequence. I began to make notes. What I could not remember accurately, I salvaged by talking to my family and the people at the hospital. My armoury began to fill again. I thought memories dry out in the sun; I was wrong. Memory lives in the soul and therefore it is immortal. The first part of this appeared in *Kathadesh*, November 2001; the last in May 2003. I finished it in the intervening period.

Books like these are not written for praise. When you have been mad, your memories are of insult and contumely. First, I had to make the ethical decision that nothing would be hidden.

I Have Not Seen Mandu is not a history of the external world. Nor is it a paper written for a medical journal. It is a soul-memoir, a fractured one. When it began to rain inside me, my memories turned green and fresh. Since memory came in flashes, I used the collage mode, juxtaposing various time zones. For all the years that my soul was in chains, I was addicted to the speaking of English. Dr Bahry's *English–Hindi Dictionary* was very handy!

There is much more to write. I abandoned this midway. How long can one talk of one's sorrows? The dark shadow of this disease never completely evaporates. My dilemma is best summed up in Horatio's words after Hamlet's death: The rest is silence.

Swadesh Deepak
Ambala
3 June 2003

1. A Late Night with Nirmal Verma

'All desires are not evil.'
—Katyayani

PLACE: NEW DELHI
SHEILA SANDHU'S HOUSE

Nirmal Verma said: Swadeshji, you have recovered completely. Your eyes have that old shine in them.

At first I thought: Perhaps Nirmal Verma said this to encourage me. Then I remembered that his observation is always true and he never lies and I actually felt happier, a little happier, the unafraid happiness one feels when emerging from darkness into light.

This he said at Sheila Sandhu's home, where in the winter of 1996, a few of us had gathered on a cold night.

I had spent seven years in a dark deep pit. Slowly I had forgotten how to use language. But I kept chatting to the darkness; in the language of the darkness. A soul in a constant state of unrest learns strange, unique languages. These words are not to be found in any dictionary.

When it becomes apparent that the disease is incurable, everyone abandons you, both your friends and your lovers. Only two people stood at the mouth of the pit—my wife Geeta and my friend Vikas Narayan Rai. But it was I who had to make the leap that would bring me out.

For seven years, I did not make the leap and did not come out. I was swimming in a river of acid. But one day I tried a little hop and Geeta and Vikas reached for me and hauled me out. They brought me to a great big hospital in Chandigarh. The hospital in which the doctors were gods descended from the Heavens and the nurses were Florence Nightingales. It was only when I emerged from the Intensive Care Unit, after defeating death which had been within touching distance, that they found out that their patient was the author Swadesh Deepak. Their love cascaded over me like a stream that has burst its banks. I do not know why doctors develop a personal affection for their author-patients despite being taught that they should keep a safe distance, so that they will not be personally affected if they die.

They were surprised that I always spoke in English. When it is an incurable disease we generally forget even the mother tongue, for one lives in a land of forbidden memories. That's when we withdraw to a foreign dream world.

I came home. I had now begun to be frightened of light. After seven years of living in a bottomless pit, light seemed to be a warrior of the enemy camp. I stopped going out of my room. Geeta and Vikas were afraid that this was a second attack from which God himself would not be able to rescue me. If one remains in warrior mode all the time, then with the body, the soul force too shrinks and weakens. Vikas trusts what I say. He does not argue nor does he offer frivolous advice in the manner of frivolous friends—Swadesh, keep the faith! You will get well soon! As if faith were a mistress to be kept. Faith can also be eroded when the body is being stimulated through the modern medical machinery. Your body flies up three feet in the air when you're given electric shocks. This 'encouraging' advice marks the giver as an outsider. For me everything had become frightening, disgusting—in a word, macabre.

Vikas: Let's go for a walk. Doctor's orders too, I think.

Swadesh: No, I'm frightened.

Vikas: That's natural. You haven't emerged from your room for seven years.

A small burst of happiness. Someone who accepts what I say as truth instead of lecturing me.

Swadesh: What will I do in Delhi?

Vikas: You have so many friends there. You can meet Krishna Sobti, Sheila Sandhu, Soumitra Mohan, Nirmal Verma. Meet them, talk to them, you'll feel better.

Vikas is from Allahabad; he is steeped in literature. It is a familiar world for him. I agreed to go. On the blank screen of my heart, the memories of some people, their kind worlds, began to appear. When we were leaving, Geeta said to him—Don't let him go anywhere alone... Vikas is never surprised, by things or people. This time he was. He knew everything about my condition. So why these orders? But he does not argue over little things. His responses are as short as he is tall. He said—Sure.

And so ended my seven-year exile from Delhi. I was a little scared. How would my acquaintances behave with me? Would they dig around? They might. They might even laugh.

For I was stuck in the past and struggling to arrive in the present. I was awake but asleep as well. My body told me nothing—nothing of its pains, nothing of its discomforts; and my soul and I were not on talking terms. I was living in an unfamiliar world.

We arrived at Kaka Nagar, Delhi. I got out of the car. Both sides of the street were deserted, empty. No children playing, no cycle-toting vegetable vendors, no working-class men or women. I took a leap backwards. The film began to rewind. Seven years ago, in a metropolis. My play *Court Martial* was playing there. I was staying in a deserted area. That beautiful Mayavini saw the play and then turned into a seductress. On 20-02-2000, Nirmal Verma asked me over the phone how he could render the word 'seductress' in Hindi. I advised him to use the English word; Hindi has no seductresses. She court-martialled me and handed down a seven-year sentence because I had dared to take her on. And a witch, a beautiful witch, can never stand any opposition.

When she falls in love, she takes your soul into her paws and devastates it. Don't believe me if you don't want to. I know this at my own cost.

I asked Vikas: Why are the streets so empty?

Vikas: High-ranking IAS and IPS officers live here. You won't see them in their houses, never mind the streets.

Swadesh: What sort of name is Kaka Nagar?

Vikas: In Punjab, we call children 'Kaka'. These are also children. Innocent ignorant children who live in their own untouched world.

Two people came down to the car. From the way they thumped their feet to attention, I could tell they were plain-clothes policemen. Vikas had got me two bodyguards.

After lunch Vikas asked: Do you have to take pills in the afternoon?

I nodded.

Vikas: Take them then.

I did.

Vikas: Now try and sleep. I'll be back from the office by four. These two will be somewhere around your room.

I slept for two solid hours. After many years the seductress did not come into the room, did not sit on the chair by the bed and make conversation, waiting for her demon lover. I was happy. I was free. No. The policemen stationed outside must have frightened her off. The entire nation is terrified of the police, trembles in fear of it, so how would she dare?

Vikas called: Awake?

Yes. Actually he knows that I can sleep while awake, that I am a neonate who needs his eighteen to twenty hours a day.

—Watch TV.

—No.

Vikas hung up. He knows I have acquired the art of talking to myself. It makes no difference whether I am alone or someone is with me. My new son had been born—this was the play *Jalta Hua Rath* ('The Burning Chariot'), but he could not write nor speak as yet. I thought of Ebrahim Alkazi. When he read a draft, he had turned sad and asked: Why are you so cruel? Why is there so much darkness? I will do this play. At that time I did not tell him I was standing at the mouth of a tunnel of darkness. And then I took the leap and for seven years I lived a subterranean existence. Perhaps Sheila Sandhu told him that now Swadesh would not be back. Everyone had given up hope of my return.

A tinkling, a clattering on the windowpanes. I thought the wind was feeling cold and was knocking to come in. Then it became a hunter. My body shrank into itself. The hunters had arrived. One pressed his face against the windowpane. His face was blurred. He turned transparent, reading something. I understood: my last letter which in reality was a translation of Eliot's lines:

> That corpse you planted last year in your garden,
> Has it begun to sprout? Will it bloom this year?
>
> ('The Waste Land')

We were outside Sheila Sandhu's house. It was late. I gave Vikas the wrong address. Then in my own exoneration I said, I knew the address but not the way. Vikas said: No problem. The entire nation does not know the way. So what if you forget?

Yesterday I called Sheilaji in the evening. When she recognized my voice, she was delighted.

—Where are you calling from?

—Delhi.

—Who brought you?

—Vikas Rai.

—I was thinking of coming to Ambala to meet you. Some of my relatives from Canada are here. I took them to see *Court Martial*. They're longing to meet you.

—Happy to meet them.

—Give the phone to Vikas.

Only Sheilaji knows all about my seven-year exile. And she had hidden it from everyone. She had a mysterious relationship with Geeta.

Geeta told Sheilaji about my go-went-gone. She let no one visit me because I have a hatred of well-wishers. Seeing one, I would retreat into a dark corner of my pit.

We were in the big hall. Sheilaji had called many people. I recognized Soumitra Mohan, I recognized Nirmal Verma but I did not recognize the woman sitting next to him, a woman who had escaped the covers of a book and had gone from being a dignified girl to being a woman. I offered Sheilaji a Namaste but she reprimanded me with: Is that the way to greet me, Swadesh? She spread her arms as a mother bird would spread her wings. I melted into them and the intervening seven years vanished. I stopped by Soumitra. He knows me inside out, this friend of mine. His advice—Don't get involved. Vikas sat down by Soumitra and said—Let's not talk about illness.

The woman out of the book moved a bit. I sat down by Nirmal Verma. He took both my hands in his and said—Swadeshji, you have recovered completely. Your eyes have that old shine in them.

When Nirmal says something, writes something, words become pure, for there is no agenda behind them. This gift comes only when one has gone through severe practices; through sadhana alone comes the gift of words that wash away sorrow. The listener, the reader is purified. Catharsis.

Next to him, the dignified girl who had become a woman said: Swadeshji, don't you know me? I'm Gagan Gill. We spent some time together in Bhopal, with Manzoor Ahtesham. A memory that had been crouching behind a tree jumped out. Then she had seemed like a dislocated girl. A refugee. As if she had come to this country in times of distress looking for some humble place to stay. And now! In a sari. Lovely. A bindiya on her forehead. On her face, a deep grace. I looked again. She looked like a woman from a Satyajit Ray film. One of those in which Madhabi Mukherjee acted.

Swadesh: You had an English friend with you?

Gagan: What was her name?

Gagan asked me, as if trying to jog the memory of a child in the Upper Kindergarten. I shook my head.

Gagan: Who was she now? She became your friend.

I: You recited a poem to her.

Gagan: Which one?

I: The one about bangles.

Gagan: Try to remember. What was her name?

I shook my head.

Gagan: Don't worry. 'Ek Ichchha Choodiyon Mein' ('A Wish Amidst the Bangles'). Now tell me, which one did you recite?

I: I don't even write poetry.

Gagan: Not your own. Sylvia Plath's. You knew many of her poems by heart. About death and art.

Pachmarhi. The wind like a revolutionary army. Manzoor explained that the wind is manufactured all day and then locked up in a room. In the evening, they open the doors and then many of the wind's rebel platoons come rushing out. One of these soldiers put his spear on my neck and I was reminded of Sylvia Plath, in those days an obsession with me. I recited the lines.

Dying
Is an art, like everything else.
I do it exceptionally well.

('Lady Lazarus')

Gagan was delighted, as with an upper KG child who has passed a test. Sheila Sandhu introduced a healthy and well-dressed woman sitting next to her—Dr Nirmala Jain. Hindi Head. A very good critic. Sheilaji said 'Head'; she does not use useless words like vibhag-adhyaksha.

I was not a bit surprised that her name was Nirmala Jain. Head of the Department of Hindi, a critic too. I was surprised that she did not write poetry, for the Heads of Hindi Departments are always poet-critics, some of whom even threaten to write novels. This is why they look down on writers. They have the weapons of literature. When they feel so inclined, they can deploy them. They are often very clever but are they wise? Someone said: Education comes but wisdom lingers. These doctors of literature know that I do not know these things, nor have I read them. She attacked.

Dr Jain: Sheilaji has left Rajkamal. Now she works with Ashok Maheshwari.

This was the moment in which I learned that Sheilaji had left Rajkamal.

Sheilaji: Swadesh. I didn't think it was important enough to tell you when you were ill.

Sheilaji always does the right thing.

Dr Jain: Now Rajkamal's style of functioning has changed. They have a committee of editors who vote on books to publish. Two of your manuscripts are with them. What should be done with them?

There is always a hand-grenade lodged in my head; in a moment it was in my hand. In the five months I was in the hospital, the doctors had removed the pin. No explosion. Dr Nirmala Jain, Head of the Department of Hindi, did not seem to know that manuscripts are either returned or published. There is no question of what to do with them.

Besides, I had given these two plays to Sheilaji. I gave her whatever I wrote—poor Dr Nirmala Jain! She sought to frighten me. To patronize me. How could she know that the pin was out of my hand-grenade?

—Burn them.

Dr Nirmala Jain reacted as if struck by lightning for the next three hours; she took no part in the conversation. Ashok Maheshwari was not to blame in any of this but these two plays were published by Vani.

Sheilaji's Canadian relatives said many good things about *Court Martial*. But I grew uneasy. I like praise in letters. I can't deal with it face to face.

What had that seductress said?

—You are the most handsome but the most arrogant man I have ever seen.

I knew this. In front of scores of people I abused her in English.

—Why are you so angry?

—I see a beautiful woman and I become her enemy. I hurt her.

—You do not know my powers. I will come to your home. Let's see how long you can stay angry.

I thought she was goading me. Every afternoon she would visit me in my bedroom and in the next seven years she would tame me. How could I know that she could disembody herself? First she took language from me. Then my pen. Then my right hand died, the hand in which I hold my pen. I was disarmed, defenceless, but not yet defeated for the doctors could not find the disease. I knew the enemy. But why would I tell them? They would mock me. All except Nirmal Verma.

I made the mistake of thinking of her as the embodiment of lust because she wanted to take me to Mandu. To the palace of Rani Roopmati and Baz Bahadur. I refused, using English abuse. I was very proud of my appearance then. I had forgotten Shakespeare's lines: 'Hell hath no fury like a woman scorned'.

I made the mistake of thinking of her as a woman. By the time I discovered she was Mayavini, it was too late.

I had crossed the borders of time. Past and present were at one place. My memories kept moving from their predetermined places.

I began to turn from a man into a chunk of meat on that summer afternoon when she arrived in my home for the first time and sat down on the chair by my bed without so much as a by-your-leave or greeting. Her head was covered in a white sari; she began to sing a dirge. I did not stop her tears. A man tough in his dealings with women, that's Swadesh Deepak for you. It was only when I realized the dirge was for my death that I screamed. I got to the balcony from the bed. She said: I'll come every day. My armour began to crack. That day she escorted me to the door. I stopped her from coming to the station. We were standing between two marble lions. She opened her purse. She put on a pair of gold-framed spectacles. Now she did not look serious, she looked sexy. Blood began to thunder in my ears. A cannonball of wind, hidden behind a pillar, rose like a small dust-devil and attacked her. It wanted to pull her sari off her. I took hold of her pallu, the part near her neck. I was shocked to see that her neck was as fair as her throat.

Had I begun to be attracted to her? Yet I did not look back even once as I left.

She had started me off on the road towards a deep, bottomless, black pit. She was a seductress. She was Mayavini. But how could I have known that? I had begun to change into a soul with no rest.

Nirmal said: Swadesh, you used to write me letters. You could have come to see me at least once.

Sheila: He didn't want to meet anyone. He did not want any sympathy. After all, he sees himself as a solitary hero. Geeta would keep me informed over the phone.

Nirmal: No one went to see him?

Sheila: Krishnaji went. Who can stop her?

I have never told Sheilaji this but I call her 'Jarnail' to myself. Where does the English word General have the power and command of the Hindi 'Jarnail'? She sizes up a situation quickly, makes a decision immediately and swings into action. I sometimes feel that if she were Prime Minister, she would run the country with as much effortless discipline as she runs Rajkamal. Geeta and she had some kind of secret entente.

After she understood everything, she told everybody that if anyone came to visit me, I got disturbed. 'So many times I have tried to get it across to him: this sort of anger does you no good.' But why would I listen to her. The dark bottomless pit was written into my destiny.

And the reason for that was my blind reasonless anger at Mayavini.

Nirmal: Did anyone write?

Swadesh: Yes. Rajendra Yadav wrote to Geeta. His literary network is very strong even though I don't think I've met him in twenty years.

Gagan Gill: When we were in Bhopal together, you didn't speak with me.

Swadesh: How could I? You had your English friend Jane with you.

Manzoor Ahtesham is a naughty child too. He said—Look, Swadesh, the three of us will speak in Hindi. Jane doesn't know any. You're the Englishwala. You'll have to give her the gist of what we say. After all, 'Our guest is as our God.' So I spent the next three days telling her the names of trees and birds and summaries of the conversations. I couldn't talk to anyone.

Sheila: Manzoor is Manzoor.

Swadesh: Gagan, do you remember how one day you burst into tears for no reason at all? Manzoor told me I should calm you down. So I opened my tiffin box and said—

Gagan: You said: 'If you're hungry, eat something; don't cry.' Right?

Swadesh: Whenever I cried, my mother assumed I was hungry. She'd give me something to eat and I would stop.

Gagan: That worked for me too. Okay. May I ask you something? Why did you keep reciting Sylvia Plath to us?

Swadesh: In those days, Sylvia had drilled a hole in my soul.

Gagan: And you had a heated discussion with Manzoor over Nirmal in Pachmarhi. How did that begin?

I was silent for a moment. From Sheilaji's house, I went to Pachmarhi. But unstable memories can do that, they change space and time. I remember the hammering of the breeze but...Gagan Gill is a poet through and through, a total poet. So her memory is very sharp. She helped me now—I remember it was about *Ek Chitda Sukh*.*

Yes. I had said that *Ek Chitda Sukh* was dear to me because it begins outside and then turns inward. The first novel on theatre people in Hindi. Nirmal is never cruel to any of his characters, so that even the girl writing her diary is a character in the round. When I had finished reading it, a whistling began, a long and wounded sound.

Manzoor felt that Nirmal had deliberately left some gaps in the novel.

I may have got a little excited: A genuine writer has total faith in the intelligence of the reader. So he leaves some spaces for them to fill. As in a play.

Manzoor: You're right. But why are you so excited?

Swadesh: Because Nirmal is every woman's favourite writer.

Manzoor: And you are the girls' favourite.

The guffawing of five people frightened the wind; she retreated to her room. Pachmarhi fell silent. And I began to translate for Jane. Should I ask Nirmal, should I tell him or not? Sukant, my son, said I should. What I wanted to ask was not personal but I was still frightened. He might be offended. This is because I have neither the good fortune nor the courage to call Nirmal Verma my friend. We have never met by appointment. We've met by coincidence over the last thirty years—at Triveni, at the Shri Ram Centre and once at some good hotel, that too when Nirmal was with a friend who had taken us there. People were sitting at their tables, drinking beer or gin. I drank neemboo paani. Nirmal was surprised but said nothing.

Two girls in cotton saris were sitting apart. Nirmal's friend said—They are call girls.

---

* *Ek Chitda Sukh* was translated by Kuldip Singh and published under the title *A Rag Called Happiness* (Penguin, 1993).

Nirmal said: Then call them.

This side of Nirmal—in which he took pleasure in jokes—was new to me. By then the two girls had been joined by two drinkers and the picture was complete. I asked Nirmal: Which is your best book?

Nirmal looked at me. He wanted to know the reason I was asking. He understood that I was not making small talk.

He said: The hope of writing one's best book is what keeps one alive.

I was humbled by this. Like any other common friend, he could have talked for hours on his work. Such humility is rare in the literary world. Although English music was playing, I remembered Eliot's line: 'Humility is endless.'*

By this time, I had looked in the direction of the door three or four times. Sheilaji understood and said: Krishnaji is on her way. I've sent a car for her.

Sheilaji knows I almost worship Krishnaji's work. It's another matter that she keeps me in a state of terror. For my own good. For the good of a man gone hard.

The permanent expression on Nirmal's face is a smile filled with curiosity. It is the look of a mature child who wants to know and learn everything about everyone simply by listening. Often this smile has not waned even as he has listened to the useless and frightening plots of my stories. This harmless smile would provoke one to speak, and the cast of characters he had stored in his trunk would increase a little. But I have never been under the false impression that I was ever among his cast of characters. Violent political thought and ideology was not his thing—he is against violence and my work is soaked in it. I follow my characters with a loaded gun.

I said it finally: My son's name is Sukant. He's sixteen. He likes your stories but he can't understand...

—My mother says much the same thing. She was very

* From 'East Coker'.

beautiful, Swadesh. The Kayastha women of those times were very beautiful.

Nirmal wandered off into the past to sit again in the cool shadow cast by his mother. A Punjabi folk song: 'Maavaan Thandiyaan Chhaanvaan' ('In My Mother's Cool Shadow').

Nirmal: My mother said—Why can't you write stories that are easy to read like Ram (Kumar)* does? I said nothing. She always thought of Ram as a more important writer than I.

Sheilaji: And you?

Nirmal: Me too (after a short silence)—Swadesh, I was in London when Mother died. I had just left the house to catch the bus. The postman brought a telegram. I opened it. I shivered before I read it. In our psyche, a telegram is still an augury of bad news. Ram had sent it. 'Mother dead. She died without pain.' All day I sat on a park bench and thought—How can anyone die without pain?

Nirmal never talks about himself. Then lightning struck—he was telling me about his pain in an act of empathy.

Nirmal: Swadesh, in one of your long stories I was mentioned. Someone told me to read it. I understood why. He wants me to get angry with you. Do you remember?

Sheilaji said in a slightly sad tone that he once used to write long stories and talk at length...and now! I shook my head.

Gagan: The heroine is ill. The hero, who is twenty years older than her, goes to see her. He takes Nirmalji's *Ek Chitda Sukh*.

'Aashanka' ('Quandary')! I was happy to see that my memory was not entirely damaged.

Swadesh: He sees her reading this book and he thinks—this girl's life is going to be full of sorrow if she likes Nirmal Verma's books.

---

* Ram Kumar (1924–2018) was one of India's foremost abstract painters. His stories have been translated into English and are available from Writers' Workshop, Kolkata.

Nirmal: I think that was the best use that has been made of me. When we read sad books, we partake of the sadness of the characters.

Gagan: Why such a long interval between 'Sadak Aage Nahin Jaati' ('The Road Goes No Further') and 'Aashanka'? And why would one story be two different stories?

Swadesh: Actually 'Sadak Aage Nahin Jaati' was published first. It was received very well by readers and by Krishna Sobti. When she met me she looked at me suspiciously and said—Where is the first part of this story? Why haven't you written it? Frightened of your wife?

Back home, Sobti's words rang true. I went backwards and wrote 'Aashanka'.

Gagan: The description of the room is so vibrant, so alive.

Swadesh: My own room.

Gagan: And the girl, Nimmi?

Swadesh: She emerged from my soul.

When Nimmi, the girl who loved Nirmal Verma's stories to the point of madness, left, we fell silent.

Sheilaji asked: How long will we sit here?

I said: Now late nights...

Sheilaji: There have been too many late nights. Now you must turn into 'Bibi'. Talk about 'Subah ki Sair' ('The Morning Walk').*

She reminded me of many things related to the story.

Nirmal Verma won the Sahitya Akademi Award and Krishna Sobti decided to throw a party. In Ambala, I received a royal command that I was to present myself the next day. This came with the order that I should wear respectable clothes. Men swathed in shawls seem to her to be Chhayawadi poets—Romantics who, according to her, only write about trees and flowers. Other living things do not please them. She added that it was only a small party so there was no need to bring a bomb from Ambala.

---

* This refers to one of Swadesh Deepak's short stories.

I reached in the afternoon. Krishna Sobti lived on the Mall Road then. Nirmal arrived. He met everyone. He chose to sit near me though I was just an acquaintance. We talked about *Kauvve aur Kaalapaani* ('Crows and Jail') which had been given the award. I talked about 'Subah ki Sair' for a long time. A Nirmal smile flashed and he said: That would be the story you like; it's like one of yours. Suddenly one of the characters dies. But tell me, didn't you like 'Ek Din Ka Mehmaan' ('Guest for a Day')? You said nothing about it.

Swadesh: I liked it very much. But Sheilaji said I shouldn't talk about it.

Nirmal (surprised): She did? Why?

Swadesh: She said you'd be hurt.

Nirmal: How well she looks after all of us.

An unsettled silence descended upon us. Nirmal broke it with some advice: Swadesh, in your story 'Kisi Ek Pedh Ka Naam Lo' ('Name a Tree, Any Tree') you should not have sent Ajay Singh to the gallows. What a long sentence of sorrow you imposed on Maya Bakhshi. She might do anything. Girls like Maya Bakhshi can do anything.

Maya Bakhshi. In a split second, Maya Bakhshi's face united with that of the seductress, their fatal beauty becoming part of each other. Their determination to get what they wanted became one and I was sentenced to seven years for my sin. Coleridge's Life-in-Death.

On the day I returned to Delhi on the Rajdhani from Mayavini's city, I had my first shivery hallucination—a nightmare.

I was sitting by the edge of a pond. In the still water: a thin, long and wet twig. It was moving slowly, impelled forward only by the gusts of wind that urged it along from time to time. On it were perched three long-tailed African parrots. Their eyes were closed, their heads were bowed, they were lost in meditation. Now Mayavini was sitting next to me saying, 'All three parrots are dead!' She was right. She could travel to any world she wanted. The twig shook fiercely and the three parrots toppled off it into the deep water of the lake and vanished. She left too. This was my first encounter with her—three dead parrots.

TIME PRESENT

Out of habit, I wiped the sweat on my forehead with my arm. Sheilaji saw this and asked: Tired, Swadesh?

I shook my head.

She asked: What time do you go to sleep?

—Ten o'clock.

Sheilaji said to everyone: Swadesh will leave at ten. Dinner at nine-thirty. Come on, drink up.

Nirmal: Swadesh, did you feel the onset of the disease?

I didn't know of it but I received two warnings: one in English and the other in Hindi. In that big city, it was the first night (a mischievous way of saying the opening night) of *Court Martial*. The director wanted me to get there a few minutes before the beginning of the play. He didn't want the audience to know of my presence; it was to be a dramatic surprise. I was alone in the guesthouse that evening. I came out onto the verandah, one that was surrounded by a concrete jungle.

It was an upper-class area. The street outside was as desolate as the evening. The wind touched me and moved on. I lit a cigarette. I peeked behind a pillar. I saw the wind there, crouched fearfully. I may have clicked my tongue at it. The wind was embarrassed. It leapt out and went into the street to lie down. But as it went it pinched my nose sharply.

I didn't mind. 'Kyonki Hawa Padh Nahin Sakti' ('Because the Wind Cannot Read').* She's an old love of mine.

In front of me a man passed wearing a suit, even in this mild heat. He must have been going to a club. In my head, I said: British leftovers. He stopped. Turned. Came towards me. In my heart, fear said: Alcoholic. I shivered. For I do not

* Another one of Deepak's short stories.

fear snakes as much as I fear alcoholics. I looked at the floor. Any stone to hand? No, where would you find stones in a high-class area? Now he was in front of me, looking straight at me. Then he said:

Run away. Otherwise you will die. He turned. Started to walk away. Came back. Said: Don't you know English? Run away. Or you die.

He turned, walked away and disappeared. At first I was a little frightened because the wind put its mouth to both my ears and said: Why don't you run? The man said: You will die. Some people know everything. That's why. Why aren't you running? I remembered my story, 'Kya Koi Yahaan Hai?' ('Is Anybody Here?'). Then I abused myself roundly. I dismissed the wind. It got angry and went to squat behind a pillar.

I know that Nirmal is waiting for his answer: I was warned. In two languages. But I dismissed the man as an alcoholic.

Nirmal, somewhat sadly: Yes, we do that. We dismiss the bringer of bad tidings as a madman or a drunkard.

I said nothing but I did nod. Nirmal is a secret service agent of the soul. He has seen all its darkest rooms, its blackest corners. He understood that I did not want to enter into the forbidden territory of long-term memory. I did not wish to see the three drowned African parrots. They were sinister, ominous, and this had to happen to Swadesh because he is a man of machismo. This macho pride took him to a hallucinatory world for seven years. His ration card had even been made for permanent residence there. Who stopped him from staying? That Mayavini. The seductress who I had assumed to be a bad woman, for no reason. Then I had not read Katyayani's poem with the lines: *All desires are not evil.*

Nirmal understood—I do not want to discuss the person who has seduced me. She had made a simple desire known—'I want to see Mandu with you'—and I had abused her in front of everyone.

He changed the topic—Do you still go to college?

—The doctors made me quit.

—Then…your luck will change.

I wanted to answer with a line by Soumitra Mohan. I didn't. I had read the poem in the morning. I couldn't remember the title but one line had stuck: 'Bhaagya kahin thamaa hua hai' (My destiny is stuck somewhere).

How could I tell him? Why would I? The words are tough, obstinate. My appearance is different, my words are different. If the right words do make their way from my belly to my throat, they get stuck somewhere behind my clenched teeth. I, the talkative one, was alone. I, Swadesh, from whom a river of words once flowed. She killed my right arm, my right hand, with which I held my pen, with which I tied my pyjama cord. If…if…if. Dronacharya only took one thumb from Eklavya. He could continue learning the art of weaponry. This was my hand, my whole hand, my priceless hand, my pen-holding hand. But my ailing mind had limited my vision. The eye with which I saw the future was closed. At that time, I could not perhaps imagine that Mayavini would return everything to me. And then, gurgling and giggling, a flood of words would confront me with their sweet entreaty: Why do you not play with us? But I had not yet fully emerged from my macabre world: the final kingdom of the mad.

No date is fixed for a complete defeat, no time predetermined. How could you know that there was another femme fatale? She sat on the chair and announced: You will not die this time. When did I ever listen? Three attempts, three tries. No accidental death for me. All three had not killed me. Why did I not listen to Mayavini? Because I still had the strength to fight then. Because my wife Geeta turned into a fortress. I did not want to meet visitors. She would stop visitors from getting to my room. In a cowering house, cowering people. But sometimes a straw can become a Bofors gun. About five years had passed. Geeta stood by me, shoulder to shoulder, ready for war. One day, in the hospital,

I was pressing my left cheek again and again: She asked: What is it? I said: Toothache.

The woman who faced down my three attempts to go to Hell without fear, the Geeta who, unflinching, bathed me when forty per cent of my body was burned, that Geeta was suddenly defeated by a toothache. It was probably the shaky moment of her final defeat. She said: Oh Deepak, what else must I do for you? She said this because neither the moment nor the date of a final defeat is ever fixed. The door opened. I returned to Sheilaji's house from the hospital.

Krishna Sobti entered with an impressive man. Later I found out it was Shivnath. The grandness of his looks is only matched by the sweetness of his speech. Looking at him, I thought of Browning's line: 'Grow old with me, the best is yet to be.'

And since Krishna Sobti has made an entrance:

Interval

Ordinary authors enter a room, Krishna Sobti makes an entrance. As stars do. Coming in late is a way of registering one's presence—Krishna Sobti's entry into my house was ten, maybe twelve years late. Perhaps she had been waiting for me to fall ill. This evening, Sobti was not in her trademark black. Like some queen of the Mughal era, she was in clothes the colour of yellow marble. Her shoulders were not surmounted by a head; it was a rising sun. She saw me sitting next to Nirmal Verma. She answered my Namaste with a Hello. I thought she'd ask: how are you? She didn't. She knows I am her follower. What she writes, what she says, is my truth. I thought she would sit next to me. She didn't. Perhaps she did not like the fact that I was sitting near Nirmal Verma. It is also possible that she has ceased to like me. What use would a queen have for a courtier with no sword? Whose pen is now castrated? For so it has been for the last seven years. She sat far away from me, with Vikas and Soumitra. In the next three hours, she will not once ask after me nor speak to me. I was not surprised. How many have walked away from the setting sun? One more Krishna Sobti would not matter.

IN THE FUTURE

Some years after this, Krishna Sobti would write, under the nom de guerre 'Hashmat', about me and my habit of anger. Not a word about my writing. Only Krishna Sobti could mount such a premeditated and dangerous attack on a Swadesh newly returned from the morgue. Despite knowing my sorrows, my family, the sorrows of my friends, Krishna Sobti made this calculated attack. It was a shock, a real shock. And it was Mayavini who saved me. All the rights to kill me were safe in her charge.

TIME PRESENT

I don't know who said it and in what context, but we were suddenly discussing the possibility that all our religious rites and rituals were nothing more than a waste of time and money. They are dead wood. The century is near its end and still we run to Haridwar and the Ganges (by calling the Ganga 'the Ganges' we prove our modernity) for everything.

When he thinks fit, Nirmal Verma can attack with a lethal elegance.

Nirmal Verma said: Christians too have religious ceremonies woven around marriage, birth and death. Why do these not seem like a waste of time and money to us? Simply because they are white.* What is theirs is modern and whatever is part of our national consciousness is backward and old-fashioned. Because the British live in bungalows and we live in upbhavans.

I lit another cigarette. I was sitting alone, not mixing with anyone. Now that I and my words had emerged from the

* I presume that Nirmal Verma uses the term Christians as a shorthand way of speaking of the white-skinned Christians of Europe and the United States for not all Christians are white.

mirror, Soumitra could no longer say about me: A man who moves in the mirror is mad.

Nirmal kept going: Swadesh, when my father died, I took his mortal remains to Haridwar. My soul was clothed in as dense a black cloak as a father's death can weave. The pandit took me to Kankhal to offer a libation to my ancestors. There, the Ganga flows fast. I put the remains in the water. The current swirled them away. And I felt my grief wash from me with the mortal remains of my father. That day, I discovered why we call her Ganga Maiyya, Mother Ganga. We forget our sorrows in a mother's embrace.

When Nirmal was saying this, there was a sacred energy to his face.

That day, there was a similar energy to Mayavini's face. That was the day I was to be auspiciously sent off. But many years later I discovered how inauspicious my departure was to be. In that big house, a haveli really, there was a temple. After seating me in the living room, she asked for ten minutes to go to the temple. She said I should smoke a cigarette. The night before, when I had abused her, I had been smoking incessantly.

She left. But she was still there. The scent of her body was in my nostrils. To dispel it I lit a cigarette but it defeated even the pungent smell of smoke.

Why was I beginning to sense danger even as I sat there? Who did I think I was? A warrior out of the Mahabharata? One fighting on the side of Dharma whose victory was therefore guaranteed? Last night I had abused her; today I was at her home. Such pride in my masculinity. What is this Mayavini? Then again I spoke firmly to myself. A woman who is one's enemy does not bring one home for breakfast. 'Mayapot'. My own novel: *Mayapot*—Phantom Ship. Happiness is a phantom ship to which we must spend our own lives swimming when what is written for us as our fate is death by drowning. Sheilaji had angry objections to the tantric sections of *Mayapot* but I refused to delete them.

Eventually Radhakrishna published it. After that Sheilaji and I became friends. She has perfected the art of the put-down. A formula emerged. When I fight with a woman, I became fast friends with her.

Unlucky man! Will you be friends with her? Then why not use her real name? This 'seductress', this Mayavini... Why?

Because your tantra guru keeps sending danger signals from your sleeping memories. If you call these women by their real names, they will lock your soul away in their dark prisons. Once you enter, the doors close forever behind you.

Which is why she is Mayavini. And you want to befriend her. Because you want—you need a wall against which to bang your head. Where is this sound emanating from, the sound of someone teaching a parrot to recite shlokas? And why? Her familiar must be a parrot.

The seductress came out of the temple. On her face a sacred energy, but her eyes? They were eyes from another country.

She was standing by my shoulder. I only found out later that she was not my bearer of good tidings. The time for my inauspicious departure had arrived.

Then the black crows began to turn into swans. Black crows: why do they turn into swans when they lose their colour?

These crows-turned-swans still sit on filth. This is the terrible result of seeing yourself as wise. As is the case with Swadesh Deepak: a leopard with hind legs lame or even broken.

No longer can he make the killing leap. But his roar is still the leopard's. Swadesh's long scream. Wife and daughter both wake up. The son sleeps on. When you're young, you do not hear screams in the night. At this age, a lame cheetah's roar and a man's scream are the same.

Wife: A bad dream?

I: No.

Daughter: Then why did you scream?

I: I didn't. A cheetah roared.

Wife: I'll make tea.

Daughter: Have a cigarette.

The son sleeps on.

Where did you go? Gagan asks. Or was it Sheilaji? But there, I was back from my frightening dreamworld. From dreams in which I change form, change form endlessly, dreams which do not end or break or fracture until someone drops the curtain. Soumitra gave me a *Dictionary of Dreams*. But I could find no meanings to match my dreams.

He even told me how to consult it—find the dominant image of the dream. But what can I do, Soumitra? I am the dominant image of all my dreams. Once Krishna Sobti hid behind Hashmat as Arjuna hid behind Shikhandi. She cursed all Hindi writers, sparing only Ashok Vajpeyi. That was my most frightening and disgusting dream. The lame cheetah screams and the long human scream...and I am back in Sheilaji's house.

I: I fell asleep.

Gagan: You've become a recluse.

Sheilaji (affectionately): As though the women will let him!

From the life of the family, I returned to the life of desire. Now we were talking of communalism, about people killing each other over religion.

Nirmal (somewhat excited): There is a myth working here that there is no religious tolerance in India. It's a terrible lie that is being spread by our political leaders, television and newspapers. For the last hundred years people have been killing each other in Ireland over religion. America's record is no better with non-whites. In India, these riots are caused and behind them are vested interests. Hindus and Muslims study in the same schools and colleges. The police had to be stationed at the schools when integration began and Negros were admitted to all-white schools. In our country, uncountable people have achieved the highest ranks. President, Army Generals, doctors, professors—and has there ever been any protest? Have there even been protest marches about them being in such sensitive posts? No. There are many Hindus and Sikhs in Pakistan. Has any one of them achieved a similar position? No. I would say they should ban words like 'religious intolerance' from the media. India is the most tolerant country in the world.

Sheila Sandhu announced dinner. Everyone rose. Nirmal did not. So I remained seated too.

—You're not tired, Swadesh?

—After years, I'm feeling fresh. Inside and outside too.

—Good. Why did you get so angry about my story 'Sukha' ('Famine')?

In the year 'Sukha' was published, a terrible drought did happen. I felt that one should not use the sorrows of people struggling to stay alive as symbols of a spiritual drought. It is possible too that the feelings I had were the beginning of this time. We both went to get dinner and were separated. Everyone was eating as they stood. I did so too.

Vikas said: Sit down and eat.

I sat down. Vikas knows that my right arm and my right hand have only very little strength.

Soumitra said: Tonight has been Nirmal's night.

Vikas: You aren't tired?

Swadesh: Not a bit.

Vikas: Good. Sleepy?

Swadesh: Not yet.

I ate a little. Then I stopped.

Vikas said: Eat a little more.

I ate a little more. The people around me realized that Vikas was in control of me. I asked Shivnathji.

—How should I address you?

—Shivnath.

—Seems a bit cheeky.

—If you use Mister or Shriman, I will feel you're being cheeky. I'm not that old yet.

I thought I should call this graceful man by his name. How could I know then that this would be my last meeting with him, for it was also to be my last meeting with Krishna Sobti?

PLACE: IN THE CAR

Vikas and I went to drop Nirmal-Gagan to their Karol Bagh house.

Gagan: Swadeshji, I heard you were possessed. Was it a daayan?

Nirmal: Not a daayan, a chudail.

Gagan: What's the difference?

Nirmal: Where I come from, a chudail is a beautiful and mischievous girl. A chudail does not hurt you. She just causes a sweet discomfiture.

Gagan: But Swadesh will have nothing to do with beautiful and mischievous girls.

Nirmal: That's what you think. In his time, they would hide the lovely young women when Swadesh was on the prowl.

A pleasant silence in the car. Nirmal Verma, whom I had taken to be the scribe of sorrow, can also indulge in badinage. And yet his trunk is still filled with the pains of so many people. In terms of numbers, Nirmal has not written a great many books. There is no exaggeration in them but great depths. He spends from his secret treasury with great care, if not frugality.

Nirmal: Vikas, what do you do?

Vikas: I'm in the police force.

Out of habit, Vikas's answers are short and incomplete. It is his training but it is also his nature.

Nirmal: Swadesh, your characters are taking their revenge…

Gagan: Why?

Nirmal: He's inflicted so much pain…

Gagan: You do too.

Nirmal: But I don't kill them off—In each story he's taken someone's life. What kind of life must Maya Bakhshi be living? What a world of lonely sorrow he left Nimmi in 'Sadak Aage Nahin Jaati'. These characters must have got together and exacted revenge.

Maya Bakhshi's name brought Mayavini back to me—why does she stand between the two poles of revenge and belongingness? I cannot swim. So why do I think of a river all the time? Obviously not to swim in, so why this morbid obsession? Why death by drowning? It's now a recurrent dream. How can the truth of a story become the truth of a life?

PLACE: NIRMAL AND GAGAN'S HOME

A room stuffed with books. Books on the sofa too. Nirmal began to pick them up. Gagan put an illustrated book of Ram Kumar's work into my hands, one published by her. I turned the page. Now the colours in Ramji's paintings are gentle. My nerves calmed down a little. I looked at the price. Out of my reach. I gave up the idea of buying it. I thought I'd ask Nirmal why this kind of book is called a coffee-table book. I forgot. I don't know why looking at Ramji's paintings brought back a dream I have had constantly, though not in the last few days:

An old woman, giggling, constantly stroking her face, constantly turning and turning in a clearing in the jungle. She's picking up dry sticks. For a pyre?

Even with the help of *The Dictionary of Dreams* I have not been able to decode this dream. If I try to find the dominant image, other unrelated images flash through my mind: a dried-up wishing well, for instance. I decided not to ask Nirmal. No point asking Vikas, who dreams different dreams with his eyes wide open.

Is it too late to pray? Like Eliot, 'I am an old man waiting for the rain.'* If Nirmal asks, what do I say? The cause of my bodily pain, my mental sorrow is this Mayavini, this seductress who is constantly at my shoulder ever ready to bring a fresh curse down upon me.

She will not present herself to me directly because she saw *Court Martial* and abandoned all vanity and decided that she must have me come with her to Mandu. Unlucky me. As a puny prisoner of my own machismo, I replied with expletives in English, those special abuses one reserves for beautiful women. I do not remember. I only remember the essence. Was I a gigolo that she should say, 'Come to Mandu,' and I would go?

Even though I knew that Nirmal would not mock my apprehensions, I decided not to tell him. We should save some secrets. My delusion. My own delusion. Now this delusion will remain my very own for years. Many small secrets I will share with no one else. Perhaps it is my fate to live in a fractured fashion.

Gagan gave me tea. Nirmal asked: Swadesh, you are all right?

I nodded.

Nirmal: Suddenly you're completely silent and your face seems taut.

Swadesh: I can't write.

Nirmal, the writer who can dive into the sea of language and retrieve pearls, was silent for a while. I saw my pain reflected in his face. After all, he is the historian of the sorrows of man's mind; which is how *Ek Chitda Sukh* could become a constant source of inspiration and light.

---

* The lines from Eliot's 'Gerontion' are:

'Here I am, an old man in a dry month,
Being read to by a boy, waiting for rain.'

It may be a measure of Deepak's dis-ease/disease that he often misquotes his favourites. I have put them in as is, to indicate this.

Slowly he began to get lost in a state of samaadhi. He had the eyes of a dervish, a dervish who is drenched in compassion for the deep pain of another.

Nirmal: Why is it necessary to write? Can a book ever be bigger than life? Life is God's creation and nothing we create can be bigger than it, certainly none of the books we write. Every book has only one dominant colour. And life—it changes colour so often. Keats called it a chameleon. Light and darkness, joy and sorrow, laughter and tears, life is ever changing. How could a book ever be bigger than it?

Besides being a dervish, Nirmal Verma was now also a secret service agent of the soul. Language stands before him, its hands tied, his to command.

Nirmal: You and I always write tragedies. Our vision of life is tragic. How did you imagine, Swadesh, that just wanting to write would be enough? No. First you have to live with your characters for years, you must take part in their joys and personal sorrows. You will have to bleed with them, accept extensive damage to the self. You must forget your own personal sorrows first and only then will you be able to write their sorrows. You know all this. When your characters come to you with hands outstretched, your book will begin to be written and then whether it is a big book or not, it will be one that will lead you to salvation. And this long desolation will end.

Nirmal's eyes belonged to another world. He was a seer and, in my eyes, my new book began to move.

TIME: THE FUTURE

This conversation occasioned the writing of *Sabse Udaas Kavita*.* Apoorva, who must cross rivers of sorrow and joy, has some elements of me as well. Rajesh Joshi wrote a poem specially for this play. At that time, I neither knew him nor had we corresponded. It was a poem to free one of one's fear of death. It was a poem that talked of the fear of death.

* Forthcoming from Speaking Tiger in English translation.

Come, and wrap me in the threads
Of your shawl, spun of darkness.
Wipe clear from the slate of my eyes
Every scene of my life,
    O malign hag, come.

When it was done, it did not take me a second to choose a person to whom the play should be dedicated. A new book after an interval of eight years. Nirmal Verma had faith that I would begin to write again, that I would be led back from the dry desolation of my writing into the rich green fields of words. And so even though he is opposed to political violence, I dedicated a play about armed revolution to him.

TIME: PRESENT

But that night I seemed to be swimming in a river of sludge. I could not believe what Nirmal was saying.

Swadesh: But I can't live if I don't write.

Nirmal returned once again.

Nirmal: Have you read J. Krishnamurti?

I shook my head.

Nirmal: He has written that we are already dead before we take birth. Death is only the final destination to which we must spend our lives walking. Then why should we fear a destination that is already predetermined? Every story of yours ends in death. Look at life, life which passes before you in every imaginable colour.

Why does Nirmal have so much faith in my writing? This Mayavini has cursed me with the most terrible curse: Go, you will never be able to write again, not so much as a personal letter.

How could I tell Nirmal: a monochrome rainbow has no brilliance at all? But I said: How do I pass my time in a small town?

Nirmal: Do you have plants in the courtyard of the house?

I nodded.

Nirmal: Feed the birds. Watch them pecking at the birdseed. The empty spaces inside you will begin to fill up. Watch the colour of leaves change as the light falling on them changes. Go for walks. Voices will begin to accumulate in the storerooms of your mind. And those voices will then take the shape and form of words.

When Nirmal stopped speaking, a silence filled the room, a long, hopeful silence.

Nirmal's room turned into a small room inside a church.

I began to emerge from prison.

First, confession.

And then, redemption.

I got up. As I walked down the stairs, I said to Vikas Narayan.

—Nirmal spoke in the voice of the saints.

2. I Have Not Seen Mandu

Footfalls echo in the memory
Down the passage which we did not take
Towards the door we never opened
Into the rose-garden.

—T.S. Eliot
'Burnt Norton'

TIME: 1991, NOVEMBER
PLACE: I WON'T TELL YOU

Standing right in front of me she said—I have not seen Mandu.

This was the second line she spoke to me. The first was in praise of *Court Martial*. I thanked her briefly. This line 'I have not seen Mandu', did not register in my head for everything then was with reference to *Court Martial*.

Seeing me speechless, she realized I had not understood. She sought to increase my general knowledge—The palace of Rani Roopmati and Baz Bahadur is in Mandu, Madhya Pradesh.

As she spoke, by chance, I saw her teeth flashing as bright as stars in the sky. I was on full alert. I looked at her with attention for the first time. I was reminded of the heroines of the formal poets. Her head reached my shoulder. I was wearing a pullover, as one should in November; she was in a cotton sari, as one should not be in November. Up to this time, no danger signals from within. But the hand-grenade in my head shifted a little.

Who was I reminded of so strongly? And why wasn't the name coming back with the face?

I looked at her, really looked, for the first time. The sun had risen in the night. The embodied sun, in the form of a woman. A slightly hooked nose. No ornaments around her neck, no bangles on her wrists.

A renunciate? She was standing in front of me but she was not breathing. Her self-confidence made it clear she was no call girl. Besides call girls do not go to see plays, they watch films. She was certainly over thirty. About ten years younger than me.

Danger signals! Seductress! Certainly a seductress! These women never have weapons. And yet they can destroy one completely. I have experience of this although I have always managed to escape. This time too, I was certain I would be able to escape. Completely certain. Be cold and cruel with her.

Suddenly I remembered. She reminded me of my character Maya Bakhshi from 'Kisi Ek Pedh Ka Naam Lo'.

A sun walking through a room, a sun ensconced on a sofa. A terrible long sorrow for a life. I had sentenced her lover to the gallows at the moment they were to meet. Maya slumps when she hears this. She is unable to weep. What was it Nirmal had said when he heard the story—Swadesh, Maya will not spare you; she will take what is hers. I shivered—was it toothache or the auguries of an ill-starred future? Which author has the guts to confront his characters?

Mayavini came a step closer. I could smell the aroma of her body. This was no perfume. I secured my fortress. I closed the main gate. I stationed myself at a window. She was outside the fort. She said: The fort is a symbol of the love of Roopmati and Baz Bahadur. When the sun sets, one still hears them talking to each other inside it.

Another danger signal. The people of this state do not use chaste Hindi as she had. Even their English has a different lilt to it. Is she from another world? Is she here to see my play and draw me from my fastness, using the lure of her scent? To lock me up in her scented prison? Has she cast me as a parrot...one of those regular characters in the folk psyche? In our stories, the enchantress always turns a man into a parrot and locks him in her cage.

FROM THE FUTURE

February 2000: With Arun Kamal, I go to Delhi to see Satish Gujral's exhibition of paintings. Many feature a nayika with a parrot in a cage. When I asked Arun Kamal about it, he said: Swadesh, I don't know much about painting. In our folk tales and fairy tales, we always have parrots. They are never female. For the epitome of beauty is always masculine, never feminine; and a female character always wants to bring a beautiful male character into her control. And if she can't find a man then at least a symbol, the parrot in a cage, will do.

Even if Arun Kamal claimed not to know much about painting, he decoded the symbol of the parrot correctly. Was that me...a frightened man always in a state of doubt...?

Seeing me hesitate, he made an adjustment to the corner of his Himachali topi although it needed none. I thought: Should I ask why he has worn that cap for so many years? To mislead people into thinking he is from Himachal, not Bihar? In his poetry too, there is much indirection; one meets very few people in Bihar who speak and write such sweet and beautiful words. Seeing me hesitate, he asked—Did I say something wrong?

Swadesh: No, you're right. But why didn't you tell me this in 1991?

Arun was surprised: How could I, Swadesh? We just met two days ago.

Swadesh: Had you told me, it might have saved me.

Arun Kamal was saddened by this. He probably thought I was referring to some unsuccessful love affair. But no. He is a poet with depth. He would have realized that this must have had something to do with the seven-year-long exile of my soul. In the voice of a truly close friend, he said—Swadesh, you were one of the heroes of my youth. If I had met you then, how could I not have told you? But some events simply must happen. They are inevitable.

Swadesh: You would have saved me, Arun. Because you do not ridicule people. First one must believe before one can help.

Arun Kamal is a Hindi poet but an English professor too. Did he think of Shakespeare's lines:

> The lunatic, the lover, and the poet.
> Are of imagination all compact.

Arun Kamal began to walk with me on my road of sorrow. He did not take my hand, but taking it metaphorically he said: Swadesh, when you feel like it, you must tell me about that enemy. You are a playwright; I, a poet—together we will destroy it.

Together, silent, we came to Arun's room. I offered his father, now mine as well, a Namaskar. He stopped writing his diary and offered me one of his expensive cigarettes. I refused. He asked Arun: Has there been bad news? Swadeshji's face...

Arun: Not really, did someone tell you something?

Babuji: Who would tell me anything? Bad news seems inscribed on his face.

I got up. Arun got up with me. He came to the door of my room. He said: I'm taking Babuji for a walk. We'll be back in an hour. You can stay in your room. Don't worry a bit and if you get scared, say 'Bam Bam Bhole' in your heart. You are a good man, Swadeshji. Lord Shiva will manifest in your defence.

Arun left. I raged at myself. Why had I never chosen a God to defend me? When had my complete self-reliance, my assurance of my own mental powers, become a character flaw? I had never had any pride. Then why had I suddenly abused a placid, mild thirty-something woman?

Was her desire as innocent as her sentence: 'I have not seen Mandu'? In the middle of the afternoon, I began to feel fear again. I picked up the tablets lying on the table. I stopped myself. No, you bastard. You will take your tablets in the night. Not in the afternoon. The fear increased.

I cursed again and then said to the seductress:

—Please stay with me. I'm frightened.

I heard the susurration of her sari as she came into the room. In the language of silence, she said: Why do you abuse your own? You must give up these habits of anger. Go down and have a cup of tea. What is there to be afraid of?

She touched me again, smiled, her teeth flashing suddenly, and said in a teasing voice:

—What is there to fear? I'm not asking you to come to Mandu now...

THE PAST

When she said I have not seen Mandu, Kriti Verma was standing next to me. A hero of the regional cinema there. Other people too. The director and actors had not emerged from the hall where *Court Martial* was playing. I knew it would take them some time to pack up the properties. Kriti had been introduced to me a little earlier. His wife was with him and some newly-minted fans of mine. They were also a little worried since they could see no connection between Mandu and my play. The seductress realized that what she had said had not registered with me. She inserted the key and opened the lock that secured a strange place.

The palace at Mandu is a symbol of the love between Rani Roopmati and Baz Bahadur. It is possible that I got angry because she should have been praising *Court Martial* but she was talking about Mandu. The hand-grenade in my head rolled into my hand and I said:

—Then go and see Mandu.

—But I want to see Mandu with you.

I pulled the pin on the grenade and threw it at Mayavini—You bloody woman. Do you think I am a male prostitute?

Perhaps Kriti was aware that I might even raise my hand. He took my arm in a strong grip.

She took one step back. Her face paled. She caught her lip between her teeth. I realized the grenade had exploded right on her. I was happy, a petty king who takes pride in defeating another petty king and then sees himself as a conqueror of the world. Kriti said: She has said nothing insulting. As one might invite someone for a cup of tea, she invited you to Mandu.

The arrogance of my machismo turned me into a taut bow—Please, Kriti, please! Don't try to explain things: I am not known to her. How can she invite an unknown person to see Mandu with her? I know this type of women.

—But Swadeshji, you don't know her. Not at all. She is a leading doctor of this town. She loves Hindi theatre.

Now I began to feel guilty about using the hand-grenade. In those days I did not just get angry, I flew into rages. She should not have offered me disrespect in front of everyone. But she did. Because beautiful women and I have always been at war. Defeating them by some impressive method... to shame them in front of others. Low tactics—to hit below the belt. But I did not say one of those simple lines which can eliminate almost ninety per cent of the hurt sentiments in the world: I am sorry.

Far from apologizing, I did not even admit to any wrongdoing and so Mayavini put me on her hit list. By the time I found this out, it was too late.

For a delectable woman, her history is the story of her loves. At that time, I did not know this.

One should offer the supplication of love to a woman who is very beautiful. At that time, I did not know this.

Go, because she calls you. At that time, I did not know this. And so I spent seven years in solitary confinement. At that time, I did not know this. A really beautiful woman is always a rake at heart. At that time, I did not know this.

She would spin a circle around me thrice and then I would go mad. At that time, I did not know this.

She would resurrect from her ashes and her hair would be red. At that time, I did not know this.

I would become the king of the dungheap and the swamp. But at that time, I did not know this.

My state would be different from that of Hamlet's for there would be no method in my madness. But at that time, I did not know this.

The courtyard of the temple nearby was yawning. But at that time, I did not know this.

The spies of God would be set on my trail. But at that time, I did not know this.

My broad forehead would become a crystal ball telling my tragic future. But at that time, I did not know this.

I would become the old man in T.S. Eliot, for whom a boy reads a poem in the months of drought. But then I did not know this. A poem of waiting for the rains. But at that time, I did not know this.

I asked Kriti Verma to get me a taxi. I wanted to go back to the guesthouse.

Kriti said—Party to celebrate the play. Food.

—To Hell with the party. I don't want food.

Mayavini was standing right next to me. Now her face had regained its colour. She said sweetly—Sir, I can drop you at the guesthouse.

In reality she had drawn the second line of control around me by calling me 'Sir'. But at that time, I did not know this. My gaze fell upon her chest. Between two well-developed mounds, a third small mound. Is Mayavini the tribreasted one of Soumitra Mohan's poem? This was my first step into Nightmare Time.

But at that time, I did not know this.

I told the taxi driver to buy some packets of biscuits.

—How many, Sir?

—Four.

I knew I would not be able to fall asleep on a hungry stomach. In the beginnings of our marriage, I had threatened my wife with not eating in order to turn a small marital fight into a big one. She said with an understanding smile: You might as well eat. I tossed and turned up to one a.m. Then I got up. I put on the light in the kitchen. Behind me, my wife said—Get out of the way, let me warm up the food. You'll break things.

I ate there standing up. Perhaps my face was red with embarrassment. As she left the kitchen, she said: Why do men always take it out on the food? You should know this about yourself. You can't sleep on an empty stomach.

The taxi driver bought the biscuits. Outside the guesthouse, my new friend, a dog was sitting. A one-eared dog. At some point during the mating season, he must have lost his ear in an argument with the other dogs. I got out of the cab. Gave the driver a hundred. He said that with the biscuits, it came to thirty rupees. I told him to keep the change. He was startled. That's the kind of thing drunkards do.

—No, Sir. It's far too much.

—Keep it. Get your kids some sweets.

He left, somewhat confused. He did not know that Swadesh gives auto- and cab-drivers something extra in the night.

In the day, he argues every rupee of the fare with them.

I opened the door. The one-eared dog came and sat down in front of me. I pulled up a stool and sat down myself. It had not yet gone ten but the night was dark and still as if close to midnight. I put down a couple of biscuits for the dog. He didn't touch them. I ate a couple. He fell to. The taste set his tail wagging. I set the rest of the packet in front of him. A muffled sound on the floor of the verandah. It had begun to rain. In the dark, you do not see the rain, you hear it.

Now the wind was also wet. Now the wind was also cold. Suddenly I remembered the man in the evening who had warned me in two languages—Run away from here. You will die.

In the dark body of the night, he showed up again. The dog stopped eating, pressed his body against the floor.

The howl of a terrified one-eared dog.

I knew there was no one there. And yet I said to his unpresence—Go on with you. Go. No one is going to kill me. Why would the seductress of your city hurt me?

I should not have boasted of my courage in front of this absent harbinger of sorrow.

One-ear slipped behind a pillar, abandoning several uneaten biscuits.

The rain washed clear the area where the bearer of auguries had stood to deliver his ominous warnings. I cursed: Bloody bastard. Frightened off by the rain.

How could I have known then that one does not abuse the augurer, one prays to him? But then I did not even know how to pray.

Every gesture, every look, every expression of this man was inscribed upon my mind as an epitaph upon a gravestone. For a long time, those two lines in two languages made my two hands seize up. Also with fear. And after hearing them, I said nothing to anyone. When we do not understand something, we tend to dismiss it as a baseless fear or a figment of the dark side of one's imagination.

But when I told the doctors, they delivered me. The doctors of dark souls. That man's warning was now more frightening than the truth. I died a seven-year-long death.

Dr Partha Choudhury was Visiting Professor for three months at the Post-Graduate Institute of Medical Education and Research, Chandigarh. He took over my case. Dr Avneet Sharma, otherwise in-charge of my case, said he had chosen me because I was a creative person. In Bengal, creative people are given the same respect as gods. Dr Choudhury came and sat on the chair near my bed for two hours. I said nothing. He would have read my history and he would know that someone had stolen my words, left me dumb, an obstinate dumbbell. To tell the doctors anything would be to ruin my pride. A he-man. A he-man who has lost his powers. They belong to Mayavini now. Swadesh has nothing left.

Dr Partha Choudhury said as he rose—I'll come again tomorrow. He was smiling, a detective who has uncovered a clue. Geeta said—For God's sake, answer his questions. Or else he'll sit there for hours. It looks so awkward.

Things being in bad shape is fine; but Heaven forfend that things should ever be awkward. Maybe I said okay. When memories come back, they come back constantly, a dictionary spilling over. At random. Any attempt to link them up to some incident or event defeats me.

I had not been admitted to hospital yet. A graceful young woman was on the verandah of the house. She realized that I had not recognized her. She smiled and introduced herself—It's Nirupama, Swadeshji. Nirupama Dutt from *The Indian Express*.

My beloved friend Niru, and I could not recognize her.

—Niru, my memory is dead.

—That's good. It's good to forget. Memory is like a beautiful lover; she can hurt you and betray you.

Niru sat with me for a long time. She opened up a treasure-trove of memory. I tried very hard to get her to recite one of her Punjabi poems but to no avail. She opened her purse and took out a small camera and began to take pictures of me. At first I was startled and then frightened.

—Why are you taking photographs?

—To go with the piece I'm writing about you.

—Don't write about my illness.

—Why?

—Word will spread. People will come to visit. I don't want friends to see me in this condition.

—Then what will I write? It's a special assignment for *The Indian Express* so I hired a taxi from Chandigarh.

I remained silent. One does not have to persuade a good friend; they're almost a part of one.

—Okay. I have to write. I won't mention your illness. But can I ask whether beautiful women still cause you to fly into a rage? You shouldn't. What if you come up against some femme fatale?

How could I tell Niru that I had encountered such destructive beauty? That it had already taken me captive. That it had turned Swadesh Deepak, the born enemy of fiery beauty, into a bed-ridden shadow of himself?

When I came to the verandah to see Niru off, we were perhaps a little sad. I told her:

—Niru, I was in love with you once, for three days.

—Swadeshji, I too loved you once, for three days.

We said these sentences without words. Both of us understand the language of silence.

Nirupama Dutt leaves. She loves *Court Martial*.* The next day her article appears: '*The Trial* survives from Kafka to Swadesh Deepak'. Niru said what she had to, wrote what she wanted to, but said nothing about my illness. Which is why so many writers, poets and authors see her as the lady with a golden pen. Nirupama Dutt left. Now we would meet after seven years, in Delhi. She has this habit of vanishing; she reappears only when she wants to.

I am sitting in Dr Partha Choudhury's room along with some doctors studying for their MDs.

Choudhury: You may smoke.

I lit a match with my left hand. My right hand and arm are useless, bound up in an iron pipe.

Choudhury: I read some of your stories yesterday. Every story ends in tragedy. Don't you ever see sunshine in life?

Me: No. No. No.

I should not have said No three times. It's bad luck.

Choudhury: When did you go there?

Me: In 1991, I went to your land.

---

* Nirupama Dutt's translation of *Court Martial* is also forthcoming from Speaking Tiger Books.

Choudhury: Not my land, my state. What did you think of the people?

Me: Very good. Full of warmth. Except for her.

Choudhury: Her? Who? What's her name?

Me: Kaamna.

I had only to say her name and I was back in her sitting room with her. She was in a white sari, drops of water falling from her shoulder-length hair. The scent of her body was driving me mad. When she stood up, my gaze fell upon her buttocks. They were somewhat heavy.

—In a few days, I'm going to lose five kilos from my hips. Then you will come to Mandu, won't you?

She giggled and turned into a sixteen-year-old girl who revels in teasing her lovers. I went on full alert. Why was her laugh victorious? She must have defeated me. Shakespeare came back: 'So fair was never so fatal'.* What Shakespeare writes is never a lie. My fatal time had already started.

Choudhury: What was her first line to you?

Me: I have not seen Mandu.

Choudhury: That's a harmless and innocent line.

Me: No bloody sentence is harmless and innocent. When a son says after his mother has been murdered—when a great tree falls, the earth shakes—was it innocent? No. Thousands of Sikhs were killed. You are taking her side. That bloody seductress who has pushed me to the brink of madness. I am Lear on the heath. Hamlet in his darkness. I am Ophelia, moments before her death. Good night Dr Partha Choudhury, good night, everybody!†

Hearing English, two orderlies came into the room. They seized me and hustled me out.

* The Shakespeare editions I have offer Othello's line as: 'So sweet was never so fatal.'

† Deepak is riffing on Ophelia's famous last lines: 'Good night ladies, good night, sweet ladies, good night good night' which also turn up in Eliot's 'The Waste Land'.

They knew I had gone mad. Because they know one thing for sure—he who speaks English must be mad. They got me on the bed.

My elder sister, who is like a mother to me, was sitting close by. She asked: What happened, my sons?

—Saahab began to speak English again.

My sister, saddened, began to mouth a mantra. Now her lips would move soundlessly for hours. She will take me back from God. She brought me up in Shimla for many years. She is the guardian of my soul.

Last night, the susurration of cloth near the chair. I opened my eyes. She was sitting in the chair. Mayavini had got to PGI, Chandigarh. White sari, white blouse, pallu over her head, some hair visible. Now she is a sanyaasin but a discontented sanyaasin. And so an unfulfilled sanyaasin. Perhaps I spoke English.

She: Don't speak English. It doesn't become you.

I stopped speaking the language of lies.

She: You must get well soon.

I: No longer possible.

She: You will. You will, Swadeshji. Every Sunday, I make an offering at the Kali Temple.

I: A few offerings are not going to save me. I have not confessed in a small room in a church.

She: Do not wander off again. You have no idea of my powers. And you have no idea of the limitless benevolence and anger of Ma Kali. I will take you abroad for a cure. I will not let you die, Swadesh.

This was the first time she dropped the honorific -ji from my name. The curse upon me deepened.

I: I'm not going abroad for a cure. Shrikant Verma went abroad for a cure. He was Congress (I) Secretary; the party paid all his bills. But he didn't make it. I will not die in an alien land.

She: I would have to let you die first! You are mine. I have every right over you—and Lord Bhairav himself will give you medicine.

She rose and I saw the third small breast between the other two. I drew the pallu off her head and onto her shoulders. A sun blazed in the room. A small sun.

She: Close your eyes.

I did.

She: Take a deep long breath.

I did.

She: Free yourself inside. You will sleep now.

I slept. Waves in a river of sleep. Kaamna left. But had she really come? Was it her or a hallucination?

THE FUTURE

February 2000.

I met Malay in the Gomti Hospital, Delhi. For two days, I assumed Malay was from Bhopal, because he was with Rajesh Joshi. He had to tell me twice that he is from Jabalpur.

One day, early in the morning when it was still pitch dark, the two of us left the hospital in search of tea. The streets were dead asleep. Why would the chaiwalas be awake? We decided to make a round of Bengali Market.

I told Malay that I knew nothing about him.

Malay: I'm from Jabalpur. I try to write poetry. Everyone's wiped the slate clean as far as I'm concerned.

A small silence. What was there to say now?

Malay: You seem in good health. What had happened to you? In Jabalpur we heard news of your death.

I too had heard news of my own death in the Intensive Care Unit. An over-enthusiastic photographer had sneaked in and even taken a photograph of me. Swadesh tied to the bed. His nose and mouth intubated, a drip in his arm. The caption which was supposed to be 'near-dead' got turned into 'dead'. It is possible that Rajendra Yadav saw this and wrote a letter.

We were both on the footpath. No bird had yet announced the dawn. I told Malay about the augurer of the tidings who had made that terrifying prediction and then vanished. And at that moment a white cat crossed our path. I stopped.

Malay said: It's tame. It's not unlucky if a tame cat crosses your path. Or imagine what would happen in your home, you'd always be stopping and starting.

Malay: When that man warned you, was there anyone else there?

—No.

—Then no one warned you.

—But he did, twice, in two languages...

—Nothing like that happened.

—I saw him twice. I remember his clothes: coat, trousers and tie.

—When did I say you didn't see him? Of course you saw him. Your powerful imagination gave birth to him.

—He had a body as well, Malayji. He was not just a voice.

—Cutting through the darkness, your imagination invested him with a body. And your own fears put those words into his mouth.

—But there was no fear inside me.

—There was. The fear of the first show happening in that city. The fear of non-Hindi-speaking audiences. But we cannot admit our own fears. Our machismo. Our masculinity.

The tea stalls were closed. We returned to the Gomti Hospital.

Malay: Did the warning prove to be true?

—True? Completely. For seven years, I lived in a dark, bottomless abyss. My words were taken from me.

Malay: Perhaps it was some heavenly messenger descended to alert you to the coming troubles. What happened next?

How could I believe him? My machismo. My ego. How could I believe him? That fiery beauty had to be seen. How could I believe him? That enthusiastic woman, how had she accepted my abuse? How could I believe him? I had to see the marble creaminess of her breasts. How could I believe him? How could we have sat next to each other in that clear cold light? How could I believe him? Who would sit by my bedside for seven years on the same chair? Who will sing a dirge? Who would weep? How could I believe him? And how could I have thought of William Faulkner:

Between grief and nothing, I will take grief.*

Malay: What happened next?

The cassette inside me stopped, the film show stopped. Mayavini is a personal secret, a part of my soul that can never be shared.

The mistress of wounding beauty never dreams. This is the secret of her allure. I am well aware of this truth. On the day that I enter her dream, all the playthings of her glass house will disappear. That will be when I will no longer be able to see the yellow upper slopes of her breasts.

She is two-breasted or tri-breasted.

I should not have looked so long. For beauty takes your eyes and looking too long only increases the desire to acquire.

I had forgotten this sage advice I had received from my badly-behaved elders as I sat in her room, bathing in the scent of her body.

THE PAST

Even two Calmpose did not help me sleep in her city. I berated myself: Stop getting angry. Get rid of this anger at beautiful women. Control your words. You're a writer, not a goon. I did not even have her phone number. Apologize before you leave. You and apologize! That would be something. A leopard never changes his spots.

Out of habit, I got up before dawn. I washed my face. The name of the play I was going to write flashed upon me: *Kaal Kothri* ('Death Cell'). A long ray of light entered the world. The characters took on bodies and the mise-en-scène became clear too. The play's last scene, the monologue, wrote itself. It was an attack, anger, then contentment and finally, liberation. Theatre people. Glittering lives on the stage. Lives

---

* *The Wild Palms/If I Forget Thee, Jerusalem* by William Faulkner.

lived on credit otherwise. With great pride, I thought: I'll write this in ten days. How could I have known that it would take me ten years to write it, that I would find myself in my death cell? I stopped to wonder why this new play seemed to be working between the two poles of rage and remorse. Perhaps because of her. I understood nothing. I slammed the tumbler from the table on the floor. It did not break. It was made of copper. There were particular reasons for my anger. My writing has never had any external inspiration. Certainly never a woman. I know that a woman will first absorb you and then diminish you. Again you're attacking her? After all, I'm an upside-down man. Ma said I was born upside-down. So what were these transient regrets? What was this forgiveness about? Apologize to whom? It is in the leopard's nature to attack.

I read two more pages, deleted some words. One falls in love with the words in a play. This worthless love can be fatal for the actor and for the director. Ranjit Kapoor told me this. The first production of *Court Martial* in Delhi was directed by Ranjit Kapoor. He pointed out: Swadeshji, you use words with economy. When someone makes a long speech and is given a short answer, the strength of the play increases. If both characters give long speeches, it becomes an elocution competition. When Vikas Narayan gives a long speech, Captain Kapoor says: So what?

Ranjit took off his glasses and wiped the lenses: Without using abuse, how do you make your language so trenchant and insulting?

How could I respond to that? I did not think it right or even necessary to explain that my very being is ferocious. I draw people to myself and then I destroy them with a single small sentence. Such as: Do you think I am a male prostitute?

Ranjit's advice: If you want to lessen the rage in your plays and in your life, make friends with women.

Now how could I explain to Ranjit that I could scarcely befriend those for whom I have had a hatred since the time I was born?

To distract yourself when in a state of mental tension, it is important to do something. I started to shave. But the characters beyond the monologue in *Kaal Kothri* began to surround me.

Give us our lives. I cut my cheek. Blood in the foam. I put a pinch of powder on the cut and then started after the other cheek. The raving and ranting woman in the play said: Write down my name. I wrote it down. I cut the other cheek. And laughed—a middle-aged cowboy bitten on the cheeks by a girl in her teens.

In this guesthouse, they only give you morning tea. I told the servitor on the very first day: Bring four cups. He put the cups on the stool. I told him to sit down. He did so, but a little anxiously. He was afraid I might make some out-of-the-way requests. I offered him a cigarette. He took one and put it in his pocket and lit a beedi. I asked him:

—Do they do black magic in your city?

—Yes, Saahab, the women here take possession of you.

I changed the subject.

—Can you change the sheets?

—Right away, Saahab.

One by one, I drank all four cups. He came back. He changed the sheets. The room looked brighter.

—Did anyone work black magic on you?

—Yes, Saahab, yes, it's been twenty years since I came here from Bihar and I've never been home once.

As he left, I slipped him a tenner. Now he will bring me tea after my bath as well.

I filled a bucket with cold water. I do not take showers. As I began to pour water on my head, I stopped. Half-naked, I came back into the room, lit a cigarette. Why are there clear signals coming from the alert sections of my soul?

That extraordinarily beautiful woman is waiting for you.

Do not let that make you happy. Yesterday you abused her, today she waits for you. And so for whom are you all ready and bathed and dressed at seven in the morning?

If theatre people go late, they come late too.

When she opened the taxi door, she stooped a little—

The upper slopes of her breasts were yellow.

Would her entire body have the tint of real pearls?

Waves rise and fall within me. Some eclipse me.

At this point, I am conducting both sides of the conversation. When authors come to drama via fiction, their depth is great and their grasp is sure.

(*Speaking for her*)—I should not have told you to come to Mandu with me.

—Sometimes what we say and what we want can be very different.

—Why do you get so angry?

—You had me mesmerized and a molehill turned into a mountain.

Cut. End of conversation. I was speaking just one side of the dialogue.

I wrapped myself in a towel, sat down. The wind was coming in at the window and nipping me, I thought, and I wanted my temperature to reach zero degrees or below.

May those raging words die stillborn. My back to the door. He brought tea. My dear friend Rajendra Kaul once said:

—Your back is so smooth, like an Irish woman's.

Kaul is a CBI officer. He must have visited Ireland.

—Why Irish?

—Look at British women's backs. They all seem to have skin disease. Half their lives they spend sun-bathing. But Irish women! Listen, my fine writer. Do not let a beautiful woman see your back. She will wind herself around you and bite you too.

He put the tea on the stool. I asked—Do you have children?

—No, Sir. Just those I left behind in Bihar. The one here is barren.

—Showed her to a doctor?

—No, Saahab. I prefer her this way. She's always wanting it. And what demands. An ever-youthful woman.

I made general sounds of agreement. This man probably knows all the heroines of the Kama Sutra. Since I was silent, he left.

Bisected and divided by the barred skylight, the light came in.

Now it is just born. By afternoon, it will be a criminal.

Dry your feet. Slip on the polished shoes. My obsession. He came to take the empty cups. He took away the shoes to polish them.

A line from the wireless began to be taped inside my head.

—Get ready quickly. You have to go.

Was I like W.B. Yeats—between hatred and desire?

A primal happiness was taking birth inside me. The kind a leopard feels when its prey is within reach, its stomach pressed to the earth, its body gliding silently forward, every ounce of strength now concentrated in its limbs...and then the fatal leap. Leopards always survey the sky with their necks at a particular angle. The all-victorious: William Blake's animal—'Tiger burning bright. In the forest of the night.'*

A tiny doubt manifested itself. Who is the hunter? Who is the hunted? I scolded myself. Where had this question come from?

I am the hunter. A successful hunter. Let someone try to defeat me. I did not know that I was locked in a duel with Mayavini, the internal seductress.

She has unimaginable powers at her command. Omens of the terrible cold war to come began to present themselves. Faiz Ahmad Faiz's warning sounded:

Jung thehri hai; khel nahin, ae dil†
Dushman-e-jaan hain sabhi, saare ke saare qaatil.

---

* In most versions, this is 'Tiger, tiger, burning bright / In the forests of the night;' or 'Tyger, tyger...'

† The version more commonly in circulation reads: *Jung thehri hai, koi khel nahin, ae dil...*

(War has been announced, o my heart! This is no game
Everyone's an enemy, everyone a murderer.)

Then it happened. I would forget my own address. Each morning would dawn, soaked in blood. For seven years. Even my own people began to doubt me. Everything about me was a lie. How could I tell them that a huntress had turned me into her prey and for the next seven years had sentenced me to a living death? My pride would not allow it, my pride which is the size of a mountain. I will become a prisoner of war, but one with no protection from the Geneva Convention. I could not register a complaint with the Human Rights people. Some punishments must be suffered in silence.

There she was. Her kameez was completely white, the clothes of a supplicant. The moment of truth was upon us. A confrontation of the mighty. Had the force of my desire brought her here? At first, I was happy. Such an easy victory. When Julius Caesar conquered England, he wrote to his wife—I came, I saw, I conquered.* Was Mayavini a masochist, her masochism only fed by every attack upon her?

Someone appeared in the doorway, blocking the light. A driver in uniform, his cap in hand. He greeted me and said, Sir, Didi has come to fetch you.

—Who Didi?

—The person you met after the play last night.

He turned to descend the stairs. I shivered a little. He could kill me in a moment, suffocating me. He was not just a driver. A bodyguard too. I got down the stairs. She got out of the car. A white sari. Her shoulder-length hair wet.

I spoke first. A very good morning.

I thought she seemed to be a little shy. It's the kind of greeting you'd offer a mistress or a lover after a night of love. Never a wife.

I looked her over carefully. Her body was like that of a

* Julius Caesar, says Plutarch, wrote this to the senate after a victory in Asia Minor.

barren woman, firm and tight. Every bit was in the right place. It was only later that she told me she had two daughters. Her hips were a bit heavy. Should I tell her?

I warned myself: Such personal secrets are not shared with strangers. On her wrist, a thick red string. On her little finger a straw ring. We got into her long foreign car. The driver raised the glass that cut him off from us.

She half-turned to me and said:

—Oh God, Swadeshji, you're even fairer than I am. Where did you get this colour?

I was silent. A small laugh shook her. For the first time, I smelled the fragrance of her body. When she laughed, she looked years younger. Her face was rejuvenated. Her teeth were like stars; a wind blew swirling like a whirlpool. For the wind has no image of its own. So why a name? Because the wind cannot read. I remembered one of my own stories. Such a happy person. Perhaps I won't have to apologize for the abuse last night. Suddenly I discovered a frightening truth. With a woman who laughs so beautifully, it would be impossible to keep things within the bounds of friendship. But love was not on my agenda. How could I love this woman who on our first meeting had said in front of everyone:

—I have not seen Mandu. I want to see it with you.

I have always wanted relationships on my own terms. I am a man, after all.

—You say very little, Swadeshji.

—I like to listen.

—You didn't ask how come I'm so fair while my features are so sharp.

I looked at her.

—My grandfather was from your Punjab. He migrated here. He raised a business empire. Hard-working folk.

—Nothing like that. Look at me. My work is to smoke forty to fifty cigarettes a day.

—Tell me something. You are Krishna Sobti's friend?

—Krishna Sobti is nobody's friend.

—You must have met her?

—How? Krishna Sobti lives in Pakistan.

She was shocked by this.

I explained—Read what she has written again. That very Pakistan where every feudal lord is called a Shah and his praises are sung. If the king is happy, the kingdom will naturally be happy. In every hand a flute, that's become the story of everyone's life—everyone's *Zindaginama*. It's a story of prosperity. Then tappe. Folk songs. Hindi readers stricken by terror. Paeans of praise. When someone asked Agyeya for his opinion he said—When *Zindaginama* is published in Hindi, I will read it. Locale: Pakistan. Language: almost Punjabi. Then how can Krishna Sobti possibly live in Delhi? She tells Nirmal Verma to watch the swine that wander around the house. But as for her, she does not watch the people who wander around her home.

—You don't like her?

—I neither like nor dislike her.

—The critics call her a great writer.

—That's a conspiracy of critics. When they call a writer great, they're writing an obituary. For after that no sensible thought can happen about the great writer's work.

A middle-aged woman came in with a tea tray.

—Didi, shall I serve?

—No. I'll manage. You can go.

She looked at me, adjusted her pallu over her head, and casting a conspiratorial smile in my direction, departed.

—Not for me.

—Why not?

—I need to smoke when I drink tea.

—Then smoke.

—There are all kinds of gods here.

—A little smoke doesn't matter to the gods. Yes, they do grant my wishes. Last night I prayed that you would come to my house and here you are. Despite all that anger. No one has ever scolded me, let alone abusing me the way you did. Not even my husband.

—Your husband must be very ugly.

—Very ugly. But very rich. But how did you know?

I lit a cigarette. The first drag was bliss.

—Swadeshji, you look very good smoking a cigarette. Right out of a Hollywood film. Slim, trim, tough and cruel also.

I liked that. But I also became alert. Was this the first tunnel full of landmines laid out for me?

—You must never have fallen ill, right?

—Once. Only once.

—What happened?

—Brain haemorrhage. But Rajendra Yadav refused to believe it.

—He's a writer, not a doctor. What happened?

THE PRESENT

I was in Lucknow at Amritlal Nagarji's house. We were discussing why Hindi authors are always so serious. They have no sense of humour. Nagarji said—Swadesh, you should do your basic reading. I can't remember the exact chapter but it is written in the Constitution—Hindiwalas cannot laugh. It's always as if their mothers have just died. They whine, they whimper, they hesitate and they grow thin with worry at the state of the nation.

His son, Sharad asked me:

—Swadeshji, did you never think of going to Bombay? The films...

Nagarji interrupted him—Sharad, what disaster would you wish on him? Do not offer such advice. The women there will eat him alive.

Nagarji was now speaking out of context.

—One man who knows how to chat and how to laugh out loud is Rajendra Yadav. Have you met him?

—Yes. I know him well.

—No one knows Rajendra Yadav well.

I got up to leave.

Although I insisted that he shouldn't bother, Nagarji came to see me out. In the courtyard he said:

—Swadesh, beauty can often be dangerous. And with you it's not anger, it's rage. In a confrontation, you will be destroyed. Be careful. Be watchful.

I had no idea then that he had already foretold my dark future. I do not know what made me stoop to touch his feet. Perhaps I'd only ever done that for my parents. Nagarji stopped me.

—What caste are you, Swadesh?

—Brahmin.

—Brahmins do not touch the feet of others. So saying he returned inside.

Cut

I was returning after teaching in college. I had a foot up on a chair to undo my laces. I fell down. Blood gushed from my mouth. They called in the most successful and the most idiotic doctor from the next city.

He gave me a shot and then literally ran for it, shouting over his shoulder:

—Brain haemorrhage. Admit him to hospital.

He ran because he was afraid I would die on him and that would ruin his reputation. My friends from the armed forces got me admitted to the Army Hospital. I recovered in four days. The Commanding Officer Harminder Singh said—Nothing happened. Because you are a perfectly healthy man.

Around the next month perhaps, I was with Rajendra Yadav in Delhi. I told him about my brain haemorrhage.

Immediately, he said,

—You're lying, Deepak.

—Why? I was upset.

—Because you're Punjabi and Punjabis cannot suffer from brain haemorrhage. Because Punjabis do not have brains.

THE PRESENT

—He's an interesting person, is Rajendra Yadav, and a good friend too.

—Everything one says about Rajendra Yadav should be in the past tense. His relationships, his affairs keep changing rapidly. But I like him for these very shenanigans. He knows the art of badinage.

—Oh dear, your tea has gone cold. I'll make you a fresh cup. Be right back.

She went into the kitchen, leaving her scent behind her. I ran my eyes over the books. Almost all were on religious subjects. Generally on Jain thought. I took one off the iron shelf, one that was bigger than the rest. On the title page, in English—*The Black Tantra*. Underneath wild genie women were doing things to a man that were beyond the scope of my imagination. The man was defenceless and appeared half-dead. But his face showed an untamed happiness. I put the book back. She returned with the tea. I took a gulp.

—You make good tea.

I stopped looking at her. If you look at beautiful women for too long, your eyes get addicted. You can't stop looking.

—Do you believe in God?

—No. I've never gone into a place of worship.

Now her eyes were filled with compassion for me.

—You will begin to believe very soon.

This was her final statement.

—Show me your hand.

—Why?

But I extended my hand. Now there was a colourful thick string around her fingers. Just like the one around her wrist.

—This string...

—Not a string, a talisman. Your protection.

I let her tie it. I do not argue about foolish things. She kept hold of my hand.

—So soft, so fair!

—Men are supposed to offer praise, not women.

—I'm trying to remind you of that!

For the first time we laughed together. The room blossomed with the scent of it. The window pancs clicked and clinked.

She looked in that direction, as if surprised.

—It's the wind. It wants to come in.

—Why?

—The wind loves to listen to the conversation a stunningly beautiful woman and a man might have.

She still had hold of my hand.

—The wind loves to listen to sweet words but you don't. How sweetly I asked you to come to Mandu with me. And you abused me—you bloody woman.

—In the class to which you belong, affairs are possible; love is not. And in matters of the heart, we do not walk with care. Got that, Kaamnaji? Which is why I said N-O, NO, with such emphasis.

—You know my name is not Kaamna.

—I do. But I always rename my friends. It makes two friends out of one.

—You are strange, really strange, Swadesh.

She was no longer suffixing my name with -ji.

—Tell me, when you are writing, how do you feel? Tired?

—When I write I'm impotent. Impo.

—Then I'll never let you write.

—I know.

She laughed out loud, laughed with all of her body. The earrings danced on her cheeks. She laughed so much that the religious books in the room frowned at her.

—Some breakfast...

—Call for it. Annapurna will fetch it.

—No I'm going to make it myself. It's been years since I cooked breakfast for anyone.

She went to the kitchen door. I stopped her—Wait. She turned to me. I could see her cheeks flaming.

—Have you read Marlowe's *Dr Faustus*?

She shook her head.

—Helen, later called Helen of Troy, elopes with Paris, the Prince of Troy. It was taken as a national insult by the Greeks. Thousands of ships with soldiers attacked Troy. This gave birth to the myth of the femme fatale. In our own literature we have the example of Draupadi. Do you know what Marlowe wrote about the fatal beauty of Helen?

'Was this the face that launched a thousand ships
and burned the topless towers of Ilium?'

For a while she was quiet. She came towards me. Her clothes began to change. Her own clothes began to vanish. In their place a chiton appeared. She grew by a few inches. She had changed from a woman into a dream.

She moved into her dreamtime. On her face, a frank pride; in her eyes, taboos.

—Please, make me Helen of Troy.

I did not tell her she was already Helen of Troy.

—So that you also can launch a thousand ships.

THE PRESENT

I said this and touched her bright arm as she went into the kitchen. When she was in the kitchen, she took on the form of Helen of Troy. My soul was sent on a seven-year-long vacation and armed soldiers were loaded onto warships and sent after me. I lost all context. From the hole in my soul first all my loved ones left, followed by the Sobtis and Yadavs. A leatherworker bound me in hide and laid me down on a cot.

Now I was a vegetable without thoughts. In a vacuum, there is no ego and no rage. Words began to abandon me. I was admitted to lower kindergarten. C-A-T—Cat. R-A-M—Ram. The teacher refused to teach me bigger words. Those would take seven years.

My days of brokenness had begun. I had no gods or goddesses to whom I could pray. Despair slammed shut the window behind which the courieres of good news would stand. I would read a book and finish it by evening. But the next day I could read it again. In the night I would forget it all—the story and the characters. I read Flaubert's *Madame Bovary* twenty times. I turned into a woman. Madame Bovary and I became one.

Once I actually thought of sending a mercy appeal to the President. I didn't. Because he did not seem wise enough to be able to write on water.

Some old buffer came home and offered advice—Why don't you cry?

That is the end.

My mind kept asking me to bid goodbye. But to whom? Now how would Piyush Dahiya be able to do an issue based on Swadesh Deepak? Can you see me, Helen of Troy? Or is it too late? In the heat of summer, I felt the winter of Siberia creep up on me.

Accept your sins. Like the hero of *The Scarlet Letter*.

First salvation. Then death.

Then you will be able to hear the music of the dawn. An earthquake came; an earthquake went. I knew nothing of it. For, one by one, my senses had begun to die.

My daughter Parul did not want to study in the college in which I had once taught. My colleagues would stop her and ask how I was.

—Arre, nothing has happened to Professor Deepak. He's having a good time. All day he lies in bed with a book in his hand. He is a lucky man.

This was when I discovered an ugly truth: that the educated could be vicious and cruel while the domestic help—the milkman or the postman—would stop a while just to inquire after my health.

Tired of this ostracism, my daughter left for Delhi. I began to be terrified—Geeta might be the next to go. My dreams became frightening. I was even scared of drowning in a bucket of water. And so I stopped bathing.

For God's sake, sit by me, I'm frightened.

In this huge expanse, I fight alone.

No one comes, no harbinger with a message of joy.

My soul began to weep incessantly.

For my time had not yet come.

THE PRESENT

When I am with Vikas Narayan Rai, Mayavini does not show up. After all, there are two commandos with me.

This time I'm in a guesthouse. Friends drop by in the evening.

Soumitra Mohan comes early in the morning. He knows I should not be left alone too long. I began to travel backwards, on a journey into the past.

I see him but do not greet him. He understands.

—Had she come?

I nodded.

—Did she say anything?

I nodded.

—What did she say?

—Swadesh, why did you open the cage and free my mynah?

Soumitra and I looked at the chair on which Mayavini sat and talked about me freeing her mynah from its cage.

3. How Many Murders Have You Committed?

Hippolytus:	Do you see my plight, Queen, stricken as I am?
Artemis:	I see, but my eyes are not permitted to shed tears.

—Euripides*

I had been released from hospital. I have to visit PGI, Chandigarh once a week to consult Dr Pratap Sharan. He is one of the most learned men of his discipline; from Patna, he speaks so softly that you might imagine it is Agyeya you are sitting next to. A source of unlimited support. The carnivorous butterfly still visits my room but not every day. When she comes after a few days, she says:

—Good girls keep their promises.

She said: *Aap bahut sharaarati ho gaye hain.* (You've become very mischievous.)

I: If you're going to call me mischievous, perhaps you should use 'tum' instead of 'aap'.

She would come to the hospital when my elder sister was dozing and the doctors were on lunch break. At those times the difference between darkness and death would be a single step. Now she would begin to feel regret, for her punishment had far exceeded my crime.

—I cannot stop.

—Why?

—Because I cannot.

That day she left, giving me no encouragement. I had become a mixed metaphor. I am still afraid of crying. When they release me from the hospital, I will go with her on a picnic. To the Sunderbans.

---

* Presumably from *Hippolytus*, but I have not been able to find the exact reference or the translator's name.

It was the beginning of my illness. I had stopped reading the newspapers. In the morning, I would sit in the verandah. Geeta put a cup of tea on the table. She picked up the newspaper from the gate. She walked towards the kitchen. And stopped.

—Why don't you read the papers?

—I don't understand them.

—After twenty-five years of being a professor of English, he doesn't understand the papers. Nonsense. Please try at least.

In order to try, I picked up the paper. On the front page was a photograph of a political leader. Slowly his tongue began to extrude and he turned into a lizard. I took off my coloured pyjamas and began to turn into a Lukman Ali* and vanish. But I did not have my disciple with me. To whom could I tell my ghost stories?

Languages were slipping out of my head. Telepathy was with me still. I could talk to people who live in distant cities at will. But to speak to people close at hand, you need language. Once I asked Piyush Dahiya in Udaipur:

—How is God doing these days?

After a pause, he said:

—How are you doing these days?

Now I will not talk to Piyush. He can sniff out the truth. Now whom can I ask whether God will allow a bargain to be driven? What if I bury my corpse deep, full fathoms five? Now everyone speaks to me in an abstruse language. Nothing is the matter with you. Listen to bhajans. Take a deep breath and chant Om in your heart. Drink four glasses of water first thing in the morning. What easy remedies people have.

The sparrows come visiting, hopping between the

---

* This is the title of a long narrative poem by Soumitra Mohan. Some parts of it have been translated into English by Samartha Vashishtha and Shailendra Shail and published on www.asymptote.com

garden plants. The brown 'seven sisters'* come too, always demanding their share of food. On the wind, the sound of their nibbling. A huge bird dives like a fighter plane. Its wings do not move. It comes to rest on the highest branch. Like a tyrannical king, it looks around.

The sparrows and the 'seven sisters' fly off, shrilling insistent warnings.

THE CREMATORIUM BIRD

I remembered what my mother said. A frightening bird like that means someone will die.

I was very happy. Who could it be but me? My death wish was dominant—I would try three times. But this crematorium bird would save me. For itself.

Where do I want to go?

I want to go in another direction. Perhaps there is no other direction. My body is evidence of my regret. But these days Mayavini speaks in French.

She does not know Hindi nor does she speak it.

Coleridge sits by me to tell me news of myself.

> Weave a circle around him thrice.
> And close your eyes with holy dread.
>
> ('Kubla Khan')

When, as a child, I was in pain, my mother would advise: 'Be strong, Kaka.'

How much longer must your Kaka be strong? He has been bedridden for a year.

MORE ON THE CREMATORIUM BIRD

My refusal to bathe causes daily disputes.

—Why won't you bathe?

---

* This refers to the Jungle Babbler (*Turdoides striata*), a brown bird that travels in a flock of five to ten but by local legend, in groups of seven.

—What if I drown in the bucket?

—Why won't you change your clothes?

—If these tear, what will I wear?

—There are ten sets of kurta-pyjamas in your cupboard. But you won't change. You want people to think I don't give you clothes to wear.

Swadesh silent. His son Sukant, sitting next to him, silent. He is in the eighth standard. Incensed, Geeta grabs the edge of the kurta. One jerk and she will tear it off me.

Sukant: Mummy, behave yourself.

She walks off inside, her steps hurried.

Sukant asks: What is wrong with you?

It's been a year and he does not know what's wrong. He went off for tuitions. My family has stopped sitting with me. My food is placed before me. I eat it.

I lose weight rapidly. I was always lean. My clothes loosen. They hang on me.

I suddenly thought of Mirza.* Mirza, who wandered the streets and lanes in memory of Saahibaan. His wife and children would curse him. No one fears a disarmed warrior. Mirza, ruler of the dead.

My misfortune is that I cannot take the name of my Saahibaan, nor even that of her city. People would mock me. Sorrow introduced me to her and then sealed our friendship. And I was convicted. Moments of happiness and gentleness vanished. I stopped writing. The wind would never again be cold for me, nor wet; it had turned to fire. I remembered the one-eared dog. It was in his city that I met her. When I am awake, I begin to doze. When I try to sleep, I find myself awake. Is she always at full strength? She is.

For extraordinarily beautiful women do not dream. Thus sorrow does not so much as touch them. Thus every mother's son is driven mad.

---

* *Mirza Sahiban* is one of the most popular of tragic romances in the Punjab.

Sukant returns from tuitions in the night. I am surprised that he comes to see me. Normally he avoids me.

—The Deputy Inspector-General's daughter is in my tuition class.

I look at him.

—I told her yesterday that you don't bathe. She talked to her father.

What will he say now?

—Her father said the police arrest anyone who doesn't bathe.

If a DIG said it, it must be true. The senior officers know the law.

I stood up—I will bathe.

—Bathe in the morning.

—No. I want to bathe now.

My wife took out a clean pair of kurta-pyjamas—Should I bathe you? How will you soap your back?

—Do you think I can't take a bloody bath myself?

She was shocked. Where had my anger returned from? Is he recovering...? As I bathed, I thought: What great laws our police have! If you don't bathe, they arrest you.

I am alone up to two p.m. Geeta is at work, Sukant at school. It is winter now.

Solitude has its own pale beauty, its own peculiar happiness. From the wooden cupboard, I take out an old photo album. I am shocked to see that I am smiling in every photograph. Who took those smiles from me? Where have they gone, those days when I was happy? Now time is like the summer sun: merciless. I have nothing to do with the sweep of seasons. They do not register, neither in my mind nor in my body. On frigid winter mornings, I sit outside in a banian. I begin to become a sanyaasi. Or a mental cripple. She has cast her spell over my heart and turned it into a stone. Nonstop pills. Some of my loved ones say—Your eyes are those of a saint. Your eyes are the eyes of a drunk. Things begin to move from their places. I will not go to the mountains.

That year, in her city, in her house, near her, she said:

—Swadeshji, we have guesthouses in Manali, Dharamshala, Mussoorie, Nainital. Let me know when you want to write and I'll phone the manager.

—I do not like the mountains.

Her eyes fill with surprise. Writers are supposed to like mountains.

—Mountains are stupid. Dumb and static. What can one say to a mountain?

—Call me to you when you're there. Then you'll like them.

—And everyone will know why we're there.

She began to laugh and kept on laughing. I noticed for the first time that her eyes get smaller when she laughs. The religious texts in her room grow angry with her. She stops laughing. The stream dries up. She takes a breath and says:

—I thought of that phrase: '*Aapke moonh mein ghee-shakkar*' (Your words are sweet as honey stored).

A borrowed happiness and a borrowed address cannot last long.

I returned home in a flash.

A heart upon which a spell has been cast turns to stone.

Then the order of things is disrupted. And Robert Browning's words come back—*I want this woman.*

Sorrow became my friend.

I have no idea why I started seeing, in a half-doze, a dog baying at the moon.

I want to read Nirmal Verma's *Ek Chitda Sukh* again.

Now the wind does not blow here.

Mayavini said: You have defeated age. You are forty-five. You look thirty.

I should not have been happy at that. If you challenge age you turn into a picture of Dorian Gray.

Every mother's son will be driven mad at the sight of you. My body is now a witness to my remorse, my regrets.

My body understands no mantras.

I want to go in another direction.

The wind is beginning to turn cold.

After many days, I went to college. I stayed in Kaamna's city for thirteen days.

I wear British clothes: a double-breasted blazer, a red polka-dotted tie, steel-grey trousers. I am a follower of the fashions of the 1930s and 1940s. Today I must introduce my class to Robert Lowell: American poet, thrice institutionalized in mental homes.

When I get to the classroom, my MA students are delighted to see me.

I always give them five minutes to chat. Then they fall silent.

They asked about the metropolis in which the play was performed.

They enjoy the story of my friendship with the one-eared dog.

Nimmi, somewhat forward, asks—Sir, did someone fall in love with you?

—Yes. Someone did fall in love with my image.

I had no idea that after saying a couple of things about Lowell, I began to talk about Shaw's *Saint Joan*.

Someone reminded me: I think we are doing Lowell and not Shaw.

I was completely silent. The class was looking at me with amazement and fear. What has happened to Deepak Sir? He generally can talk for hours without notes, and today? The somewhat-forward Nimmi said: Sir, take rest today. We will do Lowell tomorrow.

I left college. I sat on the bridge on Mall Road. The roads of the cantonment are generally empty. If I go home early, questions will be asked.

I lit a cigarette. I did not understand what tomorrow meant. The word 'tomorrow' began to expand, to turn into months and then years. The fear inside me took hold and said—Perhaps your tomorrow is very long. A line came back from some poet: *Tomorrow and tomorrow and tomorrow.**

Reason spoke—So what if you forgot what you wanted to say today? Take your notes to class tomorrow. You're human. Human beings forget. Why are you sitting on this bridge like some unsuccessful lover?

At that time, how could I have known one should not trust logic?

At that time, how could I have known two plus two equalling four is no answer?

At that time, how could I have known that my today would fill me with such revulsion that tomorrow would die?

At that time, how could I have known that dreams would be meaningless and frightening too?

At that time, how could I have known that I was the hero of Kafka's *Metamorphosis* who has started turning into a cockroach?

At that time, how could I have known that my own folk would look at me distrustfully—nothing has happened to him, he's pretending to be ill.

Vikas Narayan would not doubt, would not question.

My wife would say to Dr Avneet Sharma—Nothing is wrong with him. He doesn't want to work. Dr Avneet would explain nothing to her.

At that time, how could I have known that history was coming to a silent end?

The chest of the moon is frigid.

The mantras of the body are at an end. Reason is drowning.

I want to say: Murder that bird.

---

* Shakespeare in *Macbeth*.

Now you will not be able to change a dirge into a celebratory song.

I was turning from day to night.

THE PAST

Afternoon. Asleep. No one at home. So why was I feeling the wind's waves so strongly? As if someone else was in the room. On the chair by my bed. I opened my eyes. Mayavini was sitting there. Her first time in my room. The same white sari. Her head covered by her pallu. She was singing a dirge, a lament, in the style of Punjabi women. Today I could not smell her body. The room was still. Peaceful. The echoes of her weeping were also stilled. Is she my master poem then?

—When did you get here?

—When you saw me.

The door was closed. How did she get in? The python inside me began to read my horoscope.

—The door is closed. How did you get in?

—Closed doors don't stop me. I go where I want.

—You must be tired. Would you like a cup…

—My body is still in the city where we met. At this point, my disembodied self is with you.

My heart began to pound. I had begun to walk towards the dark and bottomless cave.

—Why did you stop answering my letters?

—There was nothing to say.

—There was. Lots to say. But you decided to deny me. You like me. But you deny it. Your male arrogance.

—It's late. Death is knocking at my door.

I reached for her hand. Nothing there. She was disembodied. I was terrified. The room was terrified. She was looking at me. Her eyes were filled with compassion.

—My Swadesh. My poor Swadesh. Your name will be synonymous with suffering. And I can do nothing about it.

—Are you a demoness?

—I am Mayavini. The internal seductress.

The birds have stopped calling since she has arrived. They come at this time generally to drink water from the clay pots. Some even bathe. Other birds protest—My turn, my turn. They are terrified so they haven't come.

—What are you reading these days?

—Dr Hardev Bahry's dictionary.

Mayavini is never surprised. Today her third breast is not there.

—Why so sad?

—The wolf has no daughter so I am sad.

She sprang up. No susurration of the sari. Her feet were dusty. Had she walked all the way?

—I'll open the door.

—If I can come through a closed door, I can leave through one. I'll write.

—Don't. I tear up your letters without reading them.

—Why? Read them at least. They could be good.

—No good letters come now. The moon has measles.

—Do you want to sleep?

—Yes, I want to sleep.

—Then close your eyes.

I closed my eyes. She put her hand on my forehead. I did not feel her touch. The birds started chirruping. So she has gone. The wolf is sad. He doesn't have a daughter. Am I going into slumber? Yes. Slumber...

From behind the screen door, Geeta calls—Here's your tea.

Now she does not enter the room.

I went to the door.

—Why so pale? Something frightened you? Did someone visit?

I shook my head.

—Who would come to see you anyway?

And with that wounding arrow à la Kavi Bihari,* she went away.

Recently, Gyan Chaturvedi came from Bhopal to see me. A dear friend. Geeta complained to him that now no one comes. Earlier, every evening was a full house.

—Bhabhiji, no one comes to worship a broken idol. Now everyone knows that Swadeshji is not going to be much use to them. You'll have to get used to it.

Saying that last line, Gyan looked sad. And actually, he is one of the most mischievous of men, and authors among us.

In the evening Geeta came with Sukant into the room.

—Explain this poem to him. Since you've spared yourself everything else.

I looked at Sukant. He said: It's Robert Frost's 'Stopping by Woods on a Snowy Evening'.

This is a very popular poem in India. When Pandit Nehru died, the last line—*And miles to go before I sleep*—was found on his blotting paper.

I've taught it at the MA level. I read it again. I could not understand it at all. A false poem about false self-confidence. A poem does not only have to be good. The question is—does the poem go anywhere?

Sukant said—I didn't get it. Angrily, he jumped up.

—I'll never come to you for help.

One more bridge down.

He went into the next room and complained to his mother. She marched in, fulminating.

---

* This is a reference to the 17th-century Hindi poet Kavi Bihari 'Satasai' who wrote of himself:
Satsaiyaa ke dohre jyun naavak ke teer
Dekhan mein chhote lage ghaav kare ghambir.
(The couplets of Satasai are like the arrows of a hunter / They look small but cut deep.)

—You've been a professor of English for twenty-five years and you can't explain a poem to your own son. You are shaming me. Nothing is wrong with you. You've just got into the habit of lolling about and eating at your wife's expense. What kind of man are you, no shame at all.

She was going from middle-class to low-class in her language and she was not even aware of it.

Some of my father's fire-hot feudal blood was still in my veins but it has cooled. Had she said something of this kind earlier, murder would...

The wolf is sad. He has no daughter.

When a man is impotent, when he is unemployed, when he is ill, all the old quarrels, real or imagined, resurface. And they take over; their fangs are revealed. Geeta's nails had grown long indeed.

Once I thought I would say—I earned for twenty-six years. But then I remembered my mother's advice: *Ek chup, sau sukh* (One moment of silence, a hundred moments of happiness).

Late in the evening, my son called: Come and watch TV.

Dr Avneet Sharma's advice was that I should watch TV. And now I am frightened of Sukant too. The DIG's daughter studies with him. What if he complains? If the police can arrest you for not bathing, perhaps they can arrest you for not watching TV.

A serial was on. I had forgotten the storyline, the names of the actors, everything. I had to ask Geeta and Sukant.

What is this actress' name?

Why is she crying?

Where are her children? It's nighttime, they can't be in school.

When she cries, why do the leaves fall from the trees?

Sukant: Keep quiet. She isn't married. Her lover has betrayed her.

Geeta: Sukant, don't tell him anything. He won't understand. He's going mad.

She got up and went to the kitchen.

Sukant: Don't you want to watch the serial? It's your favourite.

Geeta: No. I can't breathe in this man's presence.

The house had turned into a convent-run school. I got up.

Sukant (angry): Sit down. Watch TV.

Deepak: I'll just go to my room for a bit. I'll return.

Sukant: But why?

Deepak: The wolf is cold; he has no daughter.

Sukant paled. I went to my room. The rain came down. It was not the monsoon. Today the wind was with her and together they roared like the vanguard of an army. The skylight thundered with the sound of bullets.

The electricity failed. Sukant came to the door of my room—Don't sit alone in the darkness. Come to the family room. We've lit candles there.

Now he feels sorry for me. Why did he say 'We've lit candles there' in Hindi? Perhaps he doesn't know enough English. He's only in the eighth standard.

The TV is off. I'm pleased. I don't have to ask; I don't have to be scolded.

I asked Sukant: Why do people fear the rain?

Sukant (annoyed): How do I know?

I: Why do people greet the rain with black umbrellas?

Sukant: Don't speak such tough Hindi with me.

I was silent. Startled. How did Hindi become 'tough' to someone born in a Hindi author's home?

Geeta was standing in the doorway, listening. Now she leapt in.

Geeta: Sukant, get the scooter out.

Sukant: Why?

Geeta: I'll leave your father on the Grand Trunk Road.

Sukant: Why?

Geeta: So he can jump in front of some truck or bus. It won't become a police case. He'll be free. And we'll be free too.

Sukant (screams): Both of you are mad. You will drive me crazy. How am I supposed to study? I'll fail. Oh my God. Why did I take birth in this cursed home?

He went to his room. For a long time, he cried loudly. I did not try to quieten him. He is very close to me. I am his hero, his role model. When your role model begins to break before your eyes, it is natural to cry.

Sukant fell asleep weeping.

Teenagers go to sleep while crying. They also cry while sleeping.

When she advised me to kill myself by jumping in front of a bus or truck on GT Road, a minor negative of my halcyon days became a positive.

A thin nineteen-year-old girl. A girl who does what she wants and bears the consequences.

That girl began to like me.

Not because I was a writer. But because of my anger. And she could never bear sycophants.

She did not fight her family for this. She simply looked at them with her big eyes. They read all that she had to say in her eyes. Do what you want then. I like Deepak. That's it. We got married.

When days of sorrow turn into years of sorrow, so much dies.

In my kind of illness, good wishes and blessings die.

The opposition becomes strong. The votes increase. Power slips away.

I am transformed. I am ruptured.

The mantras of my body and my soul died.

I want to read *Lolita* again.

Up to this day, I have seen neither Dharamvir Bharati nor Kamleshwar.

Sheila Sandhu sends me loving reproof. Swadesh, be a man.

Nirmal must be angry. He has not written a letter for years.

Why do all the people who love me seem angry with me?

Why don't I die?

Dr Avneet Sharma explained—This disease lengthens your life. There is little strain on body and mind.

Inside, the many echoes of silence die.

Krishna Sobti advised from Delhi—Try to write, Swadesh. Perhaps the evil spirit will be defeated. Victory was always supposed to be yours.

I sit at my writing table. My brain burns with delirium. I want to perform the final funereal rites for this stranger, this person who was once Swadesh. He should be buried.

The bird flies after the dwarf.

Mayavini says—Kill that bird. Destroy it.

What do I do? Now when she is present, there is no sun. Why did I always trust my spring?

Has the silent era of my history arrived?

Why don't you kill yourself by jumping in front of a bus or truck?

PGI, Chandigarh. Dr Avneet Sharma's room.

Sukant is with me today. Geeta doesn't have much leave left. Perhaps she is saving it for the bad days to come.

Avneet offers me excessive respect. He had read my stories as a student in Jammu Medical College. It was his love of literature that made him opt for psychiatry as a specialization. He likes to investigate the dark corners of the lives of others; he likes to plumb their secret depths.

Avneet: How are you? And don't say, 'I'm fine.'

He hates it when I say that.

Avneet: Your wife didn't come with you this time?

Sukant: She couldn't get leave.

Avneet (mischievous): Couldn't or didn't?

I: She does not speak politely to me.

Avneet: Say it straight. She abuses you. She tells you you should die.

I bowed my head.

Avneet: She could even kill you. Be ready. There is no acceptance of this disease in our country. No social sanction. When they see someone in rags and in filth on the street, first the children and then the adults pick up stones to throw at them. And we become barbarians. Total barbarians.

My head remained bowed.

Avneet: You need the patience of a mountain to deal with this disease. It's normal for a wife to abuse you, even to beat you. You are fighting the disease. She is fighting the social stigma and the disease. Nothing extraordinary about what's happening with you.

I am always surprised at how elegantly the doctors of this department express themselves in Hindi even when they are from states like Punjab, Kerala and Tamil Nadu. Have they all been taught by Dr Namwar Singh?

Sukant: He doesn't shave. He doesn't bathe. He has stopped eating.

Avneet: In his imagination, he is internally dead. And a dead man neither shaves nor eats. This happens. Don't be afraid.

I bowed my head.

Avneet: Do you want to say something else, Swadeshji?

I shook my head.

Avneet: That's okay. You must be tired.

I got up.

Avneet: My advice? Get yourself admitted to the hospital.

Swadesh: For how long?

Avneet: At least three months.

Swadesh: I can't remain in hospital for three bloody months.

We came out of the room.

Sukant: You should not use words like 'bloody' for the doctor.

Swadesh: I used it for the hospital. When did you get the

notion that you know more English than I do?

Sukant and I go to the bus stand. I am in a hurry to get back to my room. Mayavini is to visit me in the afternoon.

As soon as we got home, Geeta asked Sukant:

—What did the doctor say?

—Nothing. He wants to admit him for three months.

—What did he say?

—He doesn't want to be admitted.

—And why would he? He's living the easy life here. And what would this swinger-winger do there?

She has new words and phrases to use against me these days. Her linguistic reach goes from Hindi and English to French and Latin. She must have a secret dictionary of her own.

She was turning from a woman into a tunnel filled with landmines.

Where do I get the patience of a mountain from?

Where did my days of self-confidence go, those days when my neck was stiff with pride?

Why can I no longer take hold of the sun as if it were a ball?

Is there any difference between a dervish and a mental cripple?

Who stole my spring?

There is no method in this madness.*

I had decided to die. The end.

I got up in the morning. I need to look at the newspapers now to figure out what day it is. I don't read them though. Sunday. Holiday. A day of suffering for me. Everyone at home. All day, they will nag me. All day, they will advise me. In their eyes, a familiar contempt; on their lips words that feel like sticks and stones that might break my bones. They only wait for my death.

I thought of the Hollywood films I had seen, the romantic

---

* This is a reference to *Hamlet*.

novels I had read. The heroine puts a heating rod into the water. She puts her hand in. She dies. What an easy way out.

She heard me moving about in the bathroom.

—What are you up to so early in the morning?

—Going to bathe.

—Why so early? Do you have an appointment?

—I just feel like it.

I spoke harshly. The decision to die robs one of fear.

—Go on then. Why go on bhaan-bhaan about it?

Having deployed another phrase from her secret dictionary, she departed. I closed the door.

The heating rod in the bucket. The switch on. I look in the mirror. I am unshaved. An uncouth thought. The suicides I have seen never have beards nor are they properly shaved. I hadn't shaved yet.

I lit what I thought was the last cigarette of my life.

A wisp of steam from the bucket. I thrust both my hands into the water.

Nothing happened. Not so much as a mild jerk.

Is the switch on?

Madman! The water is heating. The switch must be on.

Who is playing hide-and-seek with me?

Has Krishna cursed me to be Ashwatthama?*

Will I be denied entry into Eliot's rose-garden?

I have been deleted from my own existence. I am raw meat. I become God.

I am my own ghost. Someone else sleeps in my bed.

Now the echo of each word I speak swallows the next word.

I am the prisoner of my own bones.

She is my banner. I am her flagpole.

Now she will not reveal her name nor will she ask mine.

Her name is certainly not Mayavini.

---

* Ashwatthama is cursed with immortality by Lord Krishna in the Mahabharata.

Why did I give her my key when I was with her, in her city, in her home?

Now only the unreal come to meet me.

When I sit out on the verandah, a bird comes to beg.

Why does the body remain absent? When I met Ebrahim Alkazi the first time, he said:

Suffering is your destiny. Don't try to escape it. The door is closed...

FROM THE PAST

I got home from Delhi in the afternoon. I dropped my shoulder bag.

Geeta: Don't unpack. You got a telegram from Alkazi Saahab. He's called you to meet him tomorrow. At noon.

I: I just got back. How am I...

Geeta: That's your decision but for what it's worth, I think you should go.

I: Okay.

Usha Ganguly wrote from Calcutta that her group Rangbhoomi was going to take *Court Martial* to Delhi. Alkazi had gone to see it. He liked your play and my direction. Our good luck.

At that time I had written the first draft of *Jalta Hua Rath* ('The Burning Chariot'). I had never met Alkazi nor had I seen any of his work. He sent me his Triveni Art Gallery address.

Not that he wanted to do it. I knew enough to know that he had taken sanyaas from theatre.

At eleven a.m. I got to the Lalit Kala Akademi with Soumitra. He was working there at the time. Soumitra is never surprised. So he never asks anything. You can tell him what you want when you want to. If I were to say I've married again, he'd say—Well done, let's discuss this at home.

I told him why I'd returned within a day.

—Well done. It will do the play some good to meet Alkazi. I'll walk you to Triveni.

—I'll go. I know the address.

—It's one thing to know the address and another to know the way. We'll have lunch together.

—I could get late.

—No. Alkazi never gives anyone more than fifteen minutes.

Soumitra left me outside Triveni. Alkazi greeted me enthusiastically. First he took the bag off my shoulder and put it on the table.

—Relax. It's safe. Sometimes we carry the whole home with us.

I was silent.

—First, let's have lunch. It will get crowded in Triveni. Don't mind my asking. Can we converse in English? I know Hindi, but not very well.

—We can. I teach English literature to post-graduate classes.

—That's it. That's the reason you have quoted English classics in *Jalta Hua Rath*. It's apt. Very apt. These are a meaningful part of the theme and structure of your play.

As I ate, I spilled my daal and veggies on my shirt.

—Don't you ever come out of your creative world? We should be trained to lock one world and enter another.* Both must be separated.

I ate more rice, dripped more daal.

—Do you have a daughter?

I was startled. I nodded.

—Swadesh, you are lucky. Share things with your daughter. A daughter never makes fun of her father.

—She is small as yet.

—No, a daughter is never small. She is a second mother.

In his room, he took out the *Jalta Hua Rath* file. On every page, notes and pencil marks. He read a little then:

—The central character is Baba. An intellectual and a mad man. Who is he?

* The Hindi original says 'word' but I have taken this to be a transliteration error.

—Baba is me.

—I thought so. I just wanted to confirm it. Madness in the great makes them great. This is a political play. You've named names and attributed misdeeds. Zail Singh, Indira Gandhi, Rajiv and others. Aren't you afraid?

—I am never afraid of anyone.

Alkazi's eyes dimmed. He was a little sad.

—You should always be afraid of someone. It keeps your mind intact.

Was he predicting my future?

—Do you know why I called you here? I wanted to see who can write a tragedy as great as Shakespeare's *King Lear.*

—No, Sir. *Lear* is the greatest.

—No, Swadesh. *Lear* is the tragedy of a king. *Jalta Hua Rath* is the tragedy of a country.

I wanted to smoke a cigarette. I twitched in my chair.

—Let's go out, Swadesh.

Outside, under a tree, I asked—Can I have a cigarette?

He answered with a touch of mischief—That's why I brought you out here.

People, coming and going from Triveni, greet him. I liked it that he introduced me to none of them. He must have known that entry into my world is forbidden.

—Swadesh, you are a very well-dressed person. I like it. People of your tribe dress like beggars and talk like beggars.

—Credit Geeta. She keeps me like this.

—Good lady. But a poor woman. Doesn't know the dangers of keeping a husband well-dressed. Okay. Let's go in. You have smoked three cigarettes.

We came in and sat down. He flipped the pages of the script.

Alkazi: In a play, the gestures are as important as the words. These replace words in a more powerful manner. Look at this instance. The police want to clear the area of beggars and beat them up. The little beggar-girl's finger gets crushed under a boot. When Baba asks if it hurts, Durga tells the story—how she ran, fell and how the policeman ground his foot on her hand. Cross it out. She must not speak at all.

I asked with my eyes what I should do.

Alkazi: She will raise her hand. The blood drips from it. Then a long scream. She will give a long cry of pain.

That was when his wife came in. She said—Satyajit Ray is dead. Doordarshan is here. To interview you.

Alkazi (in a stern voice): Tell them to wait. I am talking to Swadesh. Oh, this is Swadesh Deepak. You read his *Jalta Hua Rath*, no?

Wife: I was really disturbed. A terrifying play.

Alkazi: Let's go for a drive, Swadesh.

The car moved along the roads around Bengali Market.

Alkazi: When you write a cruel play like this, do you ever think of the effect it would have on the audience? And have you thought of anyone to play Baba? You can name film people too.

I: Pankaj Kapur.

Alkazi: I thought you'd say Naseer.

I: Naseeruddin Shah sees himself as larger than the characters in a play.

Alkazi: You're right. But it's sad. Okay, Swadesh. When we begin, you'll have to stay with me for a month. We will look after you.

I: I'll be here, Sir.

Alkazi: Please don't call me Sir. May I ask you something? We've been together for a day. You haven't said anything of your own accord. Why are you so tense?

Swadesh: She has put her signature on my soul.

Alkazi: (startled, rising a little out of his chair): Who has done what?

Swadesh: She has put her autograph on my soul.

Alkazi asked nothing further. He understood. His eyes were compassionate. He came to see me out.

Alkazi: Do you believe in God, Swadesh?

I: No, Sir.

Alkazi: Even so, may God bless you.

I returned there. Now I would only meet him after seven years. God did not bless me.

THE FUTURE

Lunch at Sheila Sandhu's. Krishna Sobti was also present. When I told them that Alkazi would do *Jalta Hua Rath*, they congratulated me lovingly. Sheilaji asked suddenly:

—How many collections of stories do you have?

—Four or five.

—What kind of author are you? You don't even know how many.

Sobti said: He has many other beautiful things to remember.

Sheila: We should do your *Collected Stories*. It'll take three volumes at least. What do you think, Krishnaji?

Sobti: Rajkamal should have done this years ago. Swadesh is different from all the rest.

Sheila: So that's fixed. Swadesh, a short introduction…

I: I won't write it. I can't write about my own stories.

Sheila: Don't then. Tell Dr Namwar Singh. He will.

I: Never mind knowing him, I've never even seen the man.

Sheila: I don't believe it. You're joking.

I: I try not to concern myself with those who write obituaries for Hindi literature. I do not go, uninvited, to seek blessings from anyone. How would I have seen him?

Sheila: You are a strange man. There is a touch of madness in you.

Sobti: He is certainly strange. So he's a hero with the girls. The most beautiful Hindi writer.

Sheila: Don't get swollen-headed, Swadesh. She means your face, not your writing. After all, she's Hashmat too, remember. With a surgeon's knife. Get the stories in order, we'll publish them next month.

Sobti: Deepak is the blue-eyed boy of Rajkamal and Sheilaji.

When Sobti said this there was nothing in her voice, no cheer and no enthusiasm. There was a faint trace of complaint though.

In the evening, I shared the news of my *Collected* with Soumitra. He was silent for a while. Then he said:

—Sheilaji shouldn't have said that in front of Sobti.

—Why? It's not as if Sobti is my enemy.

—In every author's imagination, there are some enemies. It takes time for a book to come out from Rajkamal. Your books take a month and they're out. *Court Martial* took ten days, I think. Which is why Sobti called you Sheilaji's blue-eyed boy. Now your *Collected Stories* will not be published.

—Why not? You are wrong.

—Because Krishna Sobti is your senior, as an author. She probably feels her collected works should come out before yours. Swadesh, senior authors have a beggarly pride in themselves.

Soumitra was right. After a few months, some of Sobti's incomplete books were put together and brought out—*Sobti Ki Sohbat* ('In Sobti's Company'). My *Collected* has not yet been published.

That word-tantrik Soumitra Mohan was right. The beggarly pride of writers...

On the bus to Ambala, she took the empty seat next to mine. I thought to ask if she'd bought a ticket. She understood—Don't worry, I can come and go without tickets. My body isn't here.

Was this the beginning of my nightmare time?

Why is the moon in such a rage these days?

Such a woman cannot possibly be a woman. Inside me the desire to forget was being born.

I was entering her fortress. Such a well-scrubbed and freshly-bathed jailor.

She smiled and became my supernatural dream.

A frenzied play is about to begin.

Now I was beginning to fear her.

I saw clearly that she got out of a running bus. Perhaps she did not care for the buses of Haryana Roadways. If a woman, however beautiful, comes too often to meet you, you cease to like it. Perhaps I am like Narcissus—someone who is enchanted by himself. Must stop her from coming.

My heart was now orphaned.

Words refused to descend onto paper. Words refused to associate with the spoken words I heard. I began to resent visits from friends and family. My world shrank and became the size of me. My deep friendship with the wind ended. From a man I was turning into a monad. The days of my terror had begun.

My mind began to absent itself.

That night for the first time I screamed out loud.

Geeta ran into my room. She put on the light. I woke up.

—Why did you scream? A bad dream?

—I didn't scream. Why would I scream?

—Sleeping men don't hear their own screams. Did something scare you?

—You know nothing frightens me.

—For once stop playing the tough guy. Your pen doesn't write with ink. It writes with blood. Real blood. Read any of your stories. Someone always dies.

Was Geeta right? Mannu Bhandari* once asked me—Swadeshji, why do you follow your characters with a loaded gun?

Geeta: Why is your face pale? Alkazi Saahab will direct *Jalta Hua Rath*. You should be happy.

I: Please don't cross-examine me.

Geeta: Close your eyes, I'll stroke your hair. You'll fall asleep.

---

* Prominent Hindi author of novels like *Aapka Bunty* and *Mahabhoj*.

When someone strokes my hair, it's as if an air-conditioner turns itself on inside me, slowly lowering my mental temperature. She has the healing touch in her fingers.

FROM THE FUTURE

I got out of PGI, Chandigarh in five months. I became an outpatient. I had to see the doctor every week. Now Pratap Sharan is my doctor. He has the eyes of a seeker. Dr Avneet Sharma has become a Reader at the Ludhiana Medical College.

Dr Pratap Sharan: How are you?

I: Fine.

Sharan: You always say the same thing. How's your wife?

I: She's well. She takes good care of me. I've gained five kilos.

Sharan: I told you she would. She's a great woman. She does not know her own worth. We take people for granted. She stood like a rock by you. Generally, we see that educated women leave their husbands in cases like this.

I: How long do I have to keep coming? I feel well now.

Sharan: One never fully recovers. You'll have to be on medication for the rest of your life. So please keep coming. I enjoy speaking to you. Have you started doing any serious reading?

I: Yes. To test myself, I started Krishna Baldev Vaid's *Kaala Collage* ('The Black Collage'). And I understood it. So I feel fine now.

Sharan: Vaid is a difficult writer. I haven't read him.

I: He is the Henry Miller of Hindi. He doesn't talk to me. He's the writer of meaningless lives.

Sharan: Now you can come back in a fortnight.

That made me happy. The further away your next appointment, the better your doctor thinks you are. As I rose, I complained—No writing is happening.

Dr Sharan understands what it means for a writer not to be writing. He said—Swadeshji, you know that writing does not happen just because we want to write. Your interior world lies in ruins. When some people finally come to settle there, they will begin to write for you. But it will take time.

I left his room.

On the bench against the wall, a healthy young man. In white khadi. A well-trimmed beard but his hands, his hands were cuffed! Two armed police officers as escorts. He looked at me. In his eyes, I saw the desiccation of an endless desert. One of the officers said: Saahab, please sit with Tejvir for a while. Talk to him.

I sat down.

Police officer 2: Tejvir is the best prisoner in our jail at Ambala. He's always laughing and smiling. MA Pass. The jailor talks to him in English.

Police officer 1: He's serving a life sentence. He's committed two murders. No one knows what happened. Now he will not speak nor sing nor take part in games. Sir, talk to Tejvir for a while. Perhaps he'll find some consolation in that. First, he was being treated at the Government Hospital. But the Civil Surgeon has sent him to PGI, Chandigarh.

Police officer 2: Saahab, Tejvir is the best prisoner in Ambala Jail.

I took Tejvir's cuffed hands in mine.

—Why did you kill them, Tejvir?

—Killing them was my dharma, Sir. If I had not, my younger brother would have had to.

—Are you not afraid of the sentence?

—When one kills to maintain the order of justice, one's strength increases. Guru Maharaj himself places the sword in one's hands.

—Do you read?

—I do. But romantic novels do not appeal to me. I read religious texts. The Gita, the Gurbani, the Mahabharata and the Ramayana. These days I am reading Swami Vivekananda's works. Saahab, what do you do?

—I was a college professor.

Tejvir bowed to touch my feet. He touched his head to my feet. I explained that one should never touch anyone's feet.

—A guru is God embodied, Sir. It was through the benevolence of such that a farmer's son got his master's degree. Sir, if you don't mind my asking, what is it like to be with a woman? I have never been with one.

—Tejvir, a woman can bring momentary happiness, it is true, but she can also bring one an aeon of unhappiness. She is the destructive element in God's creation. First her fatal beauty binds one and then she destroys one. Shakespeare wrote—So fair was never so fatal. Think of Draupadi, think of her fangs.

Tejvir: Sir, will I get better?

I: You certainly will. The doctors here are better than those in Delhi.

Tejvir: How long did it take you to recover?

I: Seven years.

Tejvir paled, and in a terrified voice, he asked:

—How many murders have you committed?

I thought of all the characters I had killed in all my novels, plays and stories.

In a powerful voice, I said to Tejvir:

—I have killed sixty people.

Tejvir jumped away from me. The police officer touched my shoulder.

—Sir, best to leave now.

On the bus home, I thought I could make a good long story out of Tejvir. That reminded me of Nimmi. Beautiful, stupid Nimmi. She took my long story, 'Kisi Ek Pedh Ka Naam Lo', which is really almost a novella and came back the next day with the complaint—This is a very long story.

—You should have torn up some pages and read the rest.

She got angry—Why do you always mock me? You must think me stupid.

I touched her nose and said—Yes, and fat-nosed too.

—Where fat? Why are you after my poor cute nose?

—Should I go after the other bits too?

—Oh shut up! Get a phone. Next month I go to America. My marriage has been fixed with someone there.

—From my side, you can go to Hell.

—Now you're angry. Okay, I won't go. But will you accept me? Do you have the courage? No. In fact, you are a coward.

—What gift should I give you for your wedding?

She ran her hand over her long hair. The window was ajar. Autumn leapt into the room and settled on her face. She began to cry without sound. I did not try to calm her. After a while, she said:

—I will wash my face and go. I will never come here.

After she had washed her face, she looked like a schoolgirl.

—I'll write to you when you go to America. Will you reply?

—No.

—Will you call me?

—No. I will kill your memory, inch by inch. Do you know you are fated to suffer? As soon as I leave, the time of your sorrow will begin.

She left with no farewells. I stopped writing long stories.

I have not been able to write Tejvir's story.

I felt as if everyone on the bus was staring at me.

Had I not emerged from that cave yet?

Those whose brain cells begin to die never totally leave the cave. Dementia becomes their constant companion.

They go on no internal journeys.

When your insides are a desert, when words are unfamiliar, writing stops.

The second curse.

THE PAST AGAIN

'Life is a tale told by an idiot.' Shakespeare had not seen me. How could he have known this to be true? My history has a swollen stomach. I have become grotesque.

My pills are now my point of view. I do not feel much hunger. I feel no hunger at all. A canister has been tied to my tail.

Such a woman cannot be a woman at all.

The lines from my palms have been erased.

I cannot find the portal of her fort.

My heart is orphaned. I am a refugee in my own home. I am her slave, hostage to her desire.

'That is no country for old men.'—W.B. Yeats.

My time has been castrated.

My family's anxieties for me have turned to anger.

They want me dead.

I am waiting for Godot.

Languages have begun to turn away from me.

The doctors have almost been defeated.

Now sadhus and tantriks will take their place.

Outside the gate, the sound of a motorcycle stopping. It's Billy. First my student, then a colleague and a sincere and responsible friend. Geeta makes a list of the medicines and leaves it on the table. Billy gets them. He comes three times a day. He also controls me a little.

He came into my room, touched my feet, looked at me attentively.

—Any orders?

I pointed at the paper on the table.

—Read the paper today?

I nodded.

—What were the main headlines?

—A bald sadhu drowned in the Ganga.

—Really? That wasn't in my newspaper.

—Such items appear only in my newspaper.

He said a long o-o-okay and sat down on a chair by me.

—Sirji, come on, be brave. Your wife is scared, your children terrified. Parul is unhappy in college. The teachers talk to her in a sarcastic manner. I have to restrain myself from beating up my own colleagues.

Billy is a fearless fellow. He might even beat anyone up.

—You've exhausted every day of every kind of leave you had. Now you are without pay.

—Any other bad news?

—The doctors refuse to give you medical certificates. After all, it has been three years.

—Get one from Sunny.

We call Dr Neeraj Kalra 'Sunny'. My elder sister's son-in-law. He has great respect for me.

—I went yesterday. He gave me three months' medical. That's the last certificate he will give you. Then he says you have to be admitted to PGI, Chandigarh.

—I will not go to any bloody hospital.

—What will they think? How will you manage?

—I'll find a way. There's always a way out.

Billy took off his glasses and looked at me carefully.

—What way out is there other than PGI, Chandigarh? I hope you're not thinking of doing anything stupid. No good will come of that. You'll only be sending your wife to police stations and courtrooms. I'm off. It's time for class. You're going to have to suffer. Shave. You don't even listen to your wife.

I shaved. My hands shook. I cut myself in two or three places. Breakfast or a nap? I took a nap. But only my body slept. Something was leaking from the holes in my memory. I could not remember anything good that had happened. Terrifying memories were sitting on my doorstep, all day, ever-ready to enter the room.

The door opened. I knew it was her. The room filled with light. She opened the door with such force it seemed it would never close again. She always brings the spring with her.

From the window, a piece of yellow sky leapt into the room.

She sat down. Rays of light spread over her legs.

—I saw *Court Martial* again yesterday. Fantastic. The audience really connected.

—Where did you see it?

—Same place. My city. Where you had come. And where you abused me.

—We should forget about those abuses.

A small smile played on her lips. She pushed the hair back from her forehead.

—That's one thing I want to remember. That was the first time a man abused me. Your face was a burning sun. I liked that, Swadesh.

—I'm going to die. What then?

—I will have to let you die. And I will have you at any cost.

—Then why give me this terrible disease? If all my brain cells are destroyed, what will be left for you?

—I will get you. When you were completely healthy, you would not talk at all. Now I will keep you all for myself. I will cure you. I have many diverse powers.

—Do you never feel like weeping at my state?

—My eyes are not permitted to shed tears.

A weak anger began to fill me.

—On the one hand you say you like me. On the other, you take this dreadful revenge. You are total darkness. You have probably eaten the flesh of human corpses from their pyres. Soon you'll feast on my flesh as well. You play hide-and-seek with a dying man. You will never get me. Never. Never. Never.

—You're angry again.

Her voice was sad. Her eyes were sad.

—I wanted to possess every inch of you. My dream man. I have been waiting for ages.

—Now your nightmare man. My bones stick out of my body. Will you have me?

—But I wanted control of your soul. I wanted to possess your bright and powerful soul.

Her head bent and was almost touching her chest. Those who master the spirit can also be defeated. I suddenly thought she was more helpless than I.

—You poor helpless seductress. Give me your hand.

She proffered her hand. I could not hold it. The sun returned to her face. But her eyes were a desert.

I was on a bed of disgust.

Around her the crackle of dead leaves.

I was taking samaadhi in a mausoleum.

Suddenly I was beginning to like her. Death warrant.

I knew she was preparing to leave.

I said—May I ask you something?

She was surprised but pleased too.

—Send me to another country. I do not want to live among my own.

—Then you will forget how to speak.

—I am sick of dead words.

—Right, I'll send you.

—When?

—Very soon. You need a passport, a visa. You are not disembodied as I am. Tell me, when you return from abroad, will you visit me once?

—Why only once? I will come and stay with you.

—No, I can't catch the storm. Before you go, you will want to meet friends: Sheila Sandhu, Sobti, Nirmal Verma, Soumitra. Should I inform them? And yes, we'll have to increase your height by two inches. You look white. Taller, you'll look like a foreigner.

—No, I don't want to meet the friends of my bright days.

—I cannot come to meet you abroad. Okay, I'm going to kiss your forehead.

She bent down and kissed my head. She left without closing the door. And a bit of blue sky left with her.

Vikas Narayan Rai came over. As he sat down, I said:

—I want to die.

—In your state, anyone would want to die.

Vikas never talks nonsense nor does he deliver himself of lectures. I was glad that he acknowledged my sorrow. He will do something. He is, after all, high up in the police force.

—Vikas, do your gunmen obey your orders?

—Yes.

—Then order one of them to shoot me. He should kill me.

Vikas lit my Charminar cigarette. He looked at me. Expressionless eyes.

—He will. And will hang for it. A life sentence for me. Would that be right?

My hope to free myself from my body failed. If Vikas can't do it, no one can. Now only Mayavini can do something. I began to prepare to go abroad. Vikas understood I was planning something.

—Deepakji, dying is almost impossible. Why not try to live instead?

—What do I do staying alive? My mind is impotent. My body impotent too.

—You will write. You will write another play like *Court Martial*. Your pen will fill with more dynamite.

—The dogs howl at night. My lament. Sheilaji does not call. I do not have a telephone. Enlist me in the army. Nirmal is annoyed. I feel so hungry. No hunger at all. She will send me abroad. I will learn French. Or I will study under Kishori Amonkar. Then 'Ud Jaa Re Kaaga'* ('Fly Away, Crow').

—Sleep for a while. You've talked a lot. You must be tired.

—I'll sleep. What will you do?

—I'll read something.

I slept for fifteen minutes. Vikas with a book in his hand. Geeta back from work. Vikas and she greeted each other. Their conversation runs all the way to Namastes to each other. She sat down near me and looked at my face. Something there made her sad.

---

* This refers to the bhajan by Meerabai which may have been sparked off by a memory of Kishori Amonkar, noted exponent of the Jaipur gharana, singing it.

—Why is your face so pale? Don't be afraid. I won't let anything happen to you.

—Yes. You are my Durga. My protecting goddess.

—Vikasji, he speaks a lot of English these days.

—Let him. We understand English.

—I have hit the nail on the head.

When I met Krishna Sobti the first time, she said—Swadesh Saahab, you look like a commando. Sharp eyes. Always searching. A body ready to attack.

Krishnaji is a badshah of language. In a few phrases she sums up a person.

Vikas: You remember some things perfectly. Your memory is strong.

I: I remember things in bits and pieces. I am a Greek phoenix. Was it my dead body you saw in the Ganges?

Geeta put her hand to her head.

Geeta: Vikas, Deepak was a very handsome man. Look at him now. He's lost fifteen kilos.

I: I am king of the dead and the mad.

Geeta and Vikas went outside. They were talking about me. They came back.

Vikas: You should listen to the doctors. Get yourself admitted to PGI, Chandigarh. I am there for you. Don't worry about anything.

I: No, I'm going abroad.

Geeta: Where? How? Where's your passport?

I: She will get one made.

Geeta: Who she?

I: My Mayavini. She'll come with me. She'll look after me.

Geeta: Who is this bloody Mayavini?

I: She is my bloody Mayavini!

Her face was filled with terror. She said 'Oh my God' and she left.

Vikas: I'll have dinner and leave.

I: I don't want to eat.

Vikas: At least eat with me.

I: I will.

Vikas: Have you got my telephone number in your diary?

—Yes, but how can I call you? I don't have a phone.

—Don't worry. Just tell the police station here. They will do the rest.

—Don't come and see me, Vikas. I don't like talking.

—I will keep coming. We'll sit quietly.

I slept until late in the night. This was the first time Mayavini visited me in the night. She kept holding my hand and looking at me.

—That day I was in your city. You took me home. You told me to stand at the door. You returned with a spoonful of salt. You made me lick it. Why?

—I was protecting you from the evil eye, Swadesh.

—Didn't work. Look at me.

—I am that unfortunate soul who laid a curse on you herself.

She signalled me to bring my forehead close to hers. She bent over and kissed me. With no contact.

—Go. Come tomorrow. Abroad. Preparations. You'll come. Abroad.

She was all skin and bone. Total sand. A real woman in every sense of the word.

—I do not have the power to come to you abroad. When you return, I'll come.

—It will be late then. It may be very late.

—Do not scare me. It is never very late for me. I will take you with me and I will make you into the shining Swadesh you once were. All the best.

—I do not accept good wishes. Go. Go, my Mayavini. Go in peace.

She left. Geeta was outside the door.

—Dinner.

—I don't want to eat.

—Suit yourself!

My innermost circle began to abandon me, one by one. September. The heat sucked the life out of you. The sorrows on the threshold looked into the room. I sat down. A messenger from God. Leave these foreign lands and go home. Ma used to say—Kaka, God loves you very much. He will never give you sorrow.

How much Mother knew! That bloody sadist God.

Something moving outside. A soul perhaps. It's running away. Scared off. Ageless.

Immortal. Two-faced. I hurt someone. No. I got angry. And then a seven-year-long spell in a fearsome Hell. The theory of karma. A conspiracy of the rich. The beautiful weapon of the ruling class.

Robert Browning—'God is in His heaven, all is right with the world.'*

Swadesh Deepak—'God's not in his heaven, nothing is right with the world.'

Sleep came. Late. Like a mischievous lover who comes late and then insists on leaving early. Ghalib Saahab asked—*Neend kyon raat bhar nahin aati?* (Why does sleep not come all night?)

The twins who do the housework came. They were in the verandah. To their Namaste, I replied:

Jibajajib, jibajajib. Tantarara tantara tantarara.

The elder one went out. She asked—Saahab, tea?

—Jibajajib. Tantarara. Tantarara.

She went in. Both ran away. Saahab's gone mad.

—Jibajajibjib. Tantarara. Jibatantara jib.

My teeth hurt with the repetitions. My cheeks hurt. My throat went dry.

Tea. Make some tea. A warm shawl. Light both stoves. It cooked quickly. I took a glassful and sat on a chair. The

* From 'Pippa Passes'. Browning's lines read: God's in His heaven— / All's right with the world.

shawl was on fire. My pyjama was on fire. My kurta is burning. No pain. Let it burn. A train came slowly onto the verandah. The guard got out. An English guard. I asked:

—Where does this train go?

—Ask in Hindi. I am British. So I know no English.

—Where does the train go?

—Nowhere.

—May I get on?

—Where do you want to go?

—Nowhere.

—Then get on.

I got on. The guard waved the red flag. The train picked up speed. It was an electric train.

4. A Blind Man in the Dark

A man who moves in a painting is a madman.

—Soumitra Mohan

I have often seen myself moving in pictures. But at that time I had no idea, no idea at all, that this meant I was going mad. Soumitra did not tell me. He must have done this out of respect for our friendship.

And Geeta does not like to talk about disgusting things.

Details of the next five days courtesy my two sisters and my brother. I spent those days in the Intensive Care Unit. The doctors told Geeta clearly: He will not survive. Death can come any day. My heart was an orphan. She smiled and became my divine apparition. During those five days I heard sound—sound without words.

I was at peace. When the undesirable is inevitable, the mind is at peace.

Truth is never merciful. We never get to choose our fates.

My younger sister would call loudly—Veerji,* it's me, Savita, your younger sister. Look at me. Recognize me.

Kanta would say—Son, it's me Kanta. Try. Recognize me.

—Look, it's your younger brother Billu from Jaipur. You remember? He hero-worships you.

I closed my eyes. Why were these people making so much noise? Why were they tormenting me? In all that shouting, I discerned no words.

Why had the English guard put me off the train? Had the death warrant been issued?

---

* 'Veerji' is the honorific younger siblings use for an elder brother.

When she looked at me and smiled, I was paralysed. Poor thing. Now she prays at the Kali Temple. Where is it written that every prayer must be answered?

And for the likes of me!

A procession of doctors—from the Burns Unit, the Neurology Department, heart specialists, psychiatrists—all came and went from the ICU. I was their shared patient. The cardiologists were perplexed. They could not get an ECG because my chest was burned.

Everyone asks me to recognize them.

I am in my chosen Heaven. My eyes see but no recognition dawns.

My ears hear but no words are deciphered.

My arms, my chest, all bandaged courtesy the Burns Department.

No pain. No groans. No moans.

The doctors' greatest worry: No reactions. Is he brain-dead?

My little sister tries again.

Geeta: Why are you disturbing him? Let Deepak rest in peace.

Savita: Bhabhi, we lost our father. Now Veerji here is our father. How can I let him be peaceful? I have to try. Maybe he will recognize me. Maybe he'll see. Bring Sukant here.

Geeta: Sukant is a child. This will upset him.

Elder sister: No it won't. Children are tougher than you think.

Geeta is silent. She has been outvoted.

Billu: You wait here. I'll go to Ambala and fetch him.

The doctors asked Geeta to step out of the ICU.

When she came back, her face was set in stone. In her eyes, the look that comes from trying to harden one's heart to accept bad news.

Elder sister: Geeta, Deepak is constantly looking at you. I think he wants to ask you something.

Geeta: I know what it is. Let me tell him myself.

She sat down on the stool by the bed. She turned my head to her face. I could see Durga in her. In difficult times every wife becomes Durga.

She took my left hand in hers and pressed it: Are you afraid?

She looked into my eyes and saw no fear.

—The news is bad today. The doctors say you will not survive. No hope. There is no hope at all.

She went out quickly. Mayavini, sitting in a corner of the room, got up and sat by me on the bed. She wiped my mouth with her sari pallu: So much dirt. This shining face has turned so pale. I will fill it again with colour.

I felt that I was not in the naked light. There was no distress in my breathing. Who was standing, face pressed against the window panes? The winter was constantly naked.

—Now I won't take you to Mandu. How about London? Oxford? I'll show you the graves of Shelly, Keats and Eliot. Do you know what Eliot's epitaph is? 'Please pray for me'. I hear no one prays for him now.

—Perhaps you didn't know, Swadeshji, but you were my dream man. A man lost to me for centuries. Now I must have you. You cannot die. The doctors are wrong. I will not let you die.

I could not speak. I could not understand. But my Mayavini understood everything.

She was bent over me. A breast, as shapely as any in Khajuraho, touched my cheek. An intoxicating fragrance.

Without speaking, I said in Yeats's words: 'But one man loved the pilgrim soul in you.'

My elder sister Kanta told me: Geeta sat by your side for five days and nights in the ICU. We tried to get her to sleep.

One of us would sit by you, we said, but no, she wouldn't move. To tell the truth, Kaka, I never thought this slip of a girl would have such strength in her. God Himself gives us strength in times of grief. I knew then that she would not let you die.

Now I must tell Rajendra Yadav that he must keep his promise and get Geeta a Mahavir Chakra. He had come to Ambala. I introduced him to Geeta.

Rajendra Yadav: You've been married to Deepak for twenty-five years.

Geeta (startled): Not yet. Why?

Yadav: Let me know when you get there. I will recommend you for a Mahavir Chakra.

Geeta: But why?

Yadav: That's the least you should get for living with scum.

Geeta was shocked. She did not know Rajendra Yadav and his sense of humour. Like Bernard Shaw. I have heard him guffawing in the worst of times.

When I was ill, it was advised that we keep the news from my mother. I was always her favourite. I had only to squeak a little for her to begin to weep copiously. She would insist her husband fetch the doctor. He would not. But the eyes of the feudal fellow would fill with distaste for this illiterate woman. He preferred Mirza Ghalib to most living persons. He lived a royal life; he died a regal death. No sympathy-seeker, he. To his daughter sitting by his side: Betiji, I'm off.

And truly it was his last moment.

Billu said: Dr Chari, the head of the Burns Unit, would come twice a day. Everyone was scared of him. Despite the fact that he never shouts at anyone and never raises his voice. And yet the room would fall silent. He's one of the top four burns surgeons of the world.

He picked up my right arm and shook it. The middle of it had begun to stiffen. He told the doctor with him: Tie it to an aluminium rod otherwise he will lose the use of his right arm forever.

Elder sister: If you tie his arm up, how will he eat?

Dr Chari: For some weeks, he will neither eat nor do anything else. The rod won't bother him. He's almost brain-dead, which is why he feels no pain. He doesn't cry out. I think we will save him by the grace of God. Pray. Just pray.

Billu told me that all new entrants to the ICU would have blood drawn or injections given. Only they couldn't find a vein to inject me. So a rubber stent was put into my leg and injections were given through that.

I had not yet said a word. The doctors had asked to be told as soon as I spoke.

I tried to run out of the room. I was tied down with straps.

There was no day for me and no night. I was outside time. The clock and I were no longer in step. All seasons were the same for all the clocks had stopped. I was begging to get outside of myself too. I was becoming a dervish with only one cry on my lips: Ya Allah, Ya Allah.

This was the beginning of my good days. When you are sure you have no hope of being saved, it's good news. I had no fear.

THE FUTURE

Yaadein maazi azaab hai, ya Rab
Chheen le haafza mera Rab.
*Nahin chheenta yaad-daasht.**
(Memories of the past torment me, O Lord.
Take from me the ability to remember, my God.
But He does not take away memory).

I could not make it to the first show of *Court Martial* performed in Bombay by Nadira Babbar's Ekjute troupe. I was preparing then to 'go abroad'. She heard I was ill. I got out of hospital. When Nadira came to Ambala, I asked: So how did it go?

---

* This sher is by Akhtar Ansari (1909–1988).

—Swadeshji, *Court Martial* is one play that makes the director redundant. All the actors have to do is say their lines properly and the play works. We've done fifty shows. Rakesh Parmar was the director but people insist on crediting me.

After two minutes, Nadira did not let me feel we were meeting for the first time. She had the gift of instant intimacy and won each one of us over.

—Geetaji, you told me on the phone that Swadeshji was ill. And here he is in the pink of health, fit as a fiddle. Listen, you've got to let your husband off the leash from time to time. But I don't suppose you will.

—Why would you say so?

—It would be difficult to be parted, even for a few days, from such a handsome man.

Geeta had roses in her cheeks. I had seen her blush after years. Nadira asked my daughter Parul: And you?

—I'm a journalist with *The Indian Express*.

—Then I can't talk with you. I'm terrified of your tribe.

Nadira: Written a new play?

I: I'm revising *Kaal Kothri*. I'd done the first draft before my illness...

Nadira: Don't talk about your illness. God has given us the ability to forget. Forget about it. And send me *Kaal Kothri*. Every week, there's a play reading at Prithvi Theatre.

At that time a well-placed railway official came with two of his followers. No friends of mine, they come when they sniff out an attractive woman. They see women and their tails begin to wag, their tongues loll and they begin to drool. I introduced them.

Singh: Oh, you're Raj Babbar's wife.

Nadira: No, Raj Saahab may be my husband but I have my own identity.

The word 'identity' scared Singh. He had probably not heard such a word. The courtiers tried to save things.

Courtiers: Singh Saahab is Divisional Manager, Commerce. A high post.

Nadira: I know. Raj Saahab's father was also in railways.

Nadira smiled. I realized that she was going to pull the pin and cause an explosion. In English, they call this 'deflating' someone.

Singh (surprised): Really? What did he do?

Nadira: He changed the pin couplings. One of the smallest jobs in the railways.

Singh Saahab suddenly remembered he had some urgent work. He rose and would not stay despite our urging. The followers did what they did best. They followed.

Nadira: Some men live in their trousers.

The family left us alone for a while.

Nadira: You seem a bit frightened. I had heard of your temper. That you had slapped a truly beautiful woman in front of a dozen friends.

I: I didn't hit her. I was about to.

Nadira: Theatre people will add their own two bits. As you fought your disease, you must fight this fear. I don't say your fear is baseless. But the Swadesh of *Court Martial* can fight anyone. Ekjute is going to celebrate a festival. You have to come to Bombay. *Court Martial* completes seventy shows. And you haven't seen a single one.

I: Bombay I can manage; Calcutta is out.

Nadira: When did I say Calcutta? Your favourite director Usha Ganguly will definitely come.

Suddenly I had travelled back several years in time. Usha had seen Mayavini; perhaps she even knew her a little. Usha said: She is so beautiful, so attractive that you can scarcely believe that she's a woman. She's a miracle. The embodiment of a miracle.

To hear the word 'miracle' in the mouth of a Communist frightened me again.

IN THE PAST AGAIN

Why would I fear a death warrant issued by doctors? The President himself came to tell me—I have commuted your death sentence. But there will be some months of token imprisonment. You are not a good man. You hurl curses at beautiful women.

The Burns Unit increased the number of injections. They feared that the burned areas would rot. Dr Naidu was now in charge of those bits of me. He changed my dressings himself.

Even though he knew I understood nothing, he would talk to me.

—Writer Saahab, when you get well, write in my language. I speak Hindi but I can't read it well.

—What long books you guys write! Here I can't manage a letter.

—Don't worry, Deepak Saahab, the scars won't show. I'll operate. We'll do a skin graft. You will be a handsome man again. Even if you don't feel pain, scream a bit. Your doctors, your family would like that. They won't be so frightened. Why have you become like Bhishma Pitamah on his bed of arrows?

When Dr Naidu comes into the room, he brings hope with him.

I got a little tired of his optimism. After such torment, I had got to the doors of death. And Dr Naidu would not allow me to open them.

The corpses of dead relationships surround me.

I am no longer an independent human being. I am a toy in everyone's hands.

Why has the light become so terrifying? What ended my friendship with the wind?

Nirmal Verma's birds are dead, their place usurped by crows.

Why do I feel such anger at Krishna Sobti's *Mitro Marjani*?* All the time, everywhere, skirts raised.

---

* Translated into English as *To Hell With You, Mitro* (Katha, 2007) by Gita Rajan and Raji Narasimhan, Krishna Sobti's novel tells the story of Sumitravanti, a woman with a savage tongue and great sexual desires, and the impact she has on a middle-class household.

When anyone falls sick, the small-fry Hindi authors are delighted.

Every breath is a struggle.

Your fiery beauty, the slant of your wrists; a leitmotif.

Why do I remember this? This is not life. These are rumours. Before all the rest, the journalists of *Jansatta* found me in the ICU. The newspaper had a Chandigarh edition then. He asked my sisters, keeping vigil outside, about me. He came in to confirm what they had said; he asked me a question. When he told the duty nurse he was a journalist, she got angry.

—Journalists are not allowed here. It's against rule.

He said to the attractive nurse: Behenji, everyone is always angry with us. Everything in this country is against rule. It's not just PGI that has rights over Swadesh Deepak. Everyone in the Hindi sphere has a claim to him. You probably don't know that he's our young generation's favourite writer. He wrote *Court Martial*.

He kept the nurse talking while he took two or three pictures with his pocket camera. By the time the nurse found out, he had made good his escape. He probably knew it was against the law to take photographs of a patient like me. He could have been arrested.

The next day, the news item was printed. No one who saw the photograph could have recognized me. The mouth tubes and oxygen mask obscured my face. My eyes were visible but they were fixed, staring. The caption read: 'Swadesh Deepak, close to death'. By some technical fault the 'close to' got separated from 'death' and when the news item got to other centres, I was dead.

I only found out later that my death had been announced.

FROM THE FUTURE

Summer. The electricity fails. I am in the verandah, Geeta in the kitchen at the other end of the verandah. An unknown, well-built young man comes in. After greeting me with a Namaste, he says: I have come from Sirsa.

From his pronunciation, it is clear that he is from Haryana.

—I've come to meet Swadesh Deepak Sir.

—And so you have. I am Swadesh Deepak.

He looked at me amazed. Frightened, he asked:

—Are you really Swadesh Deepak?

The mercury shot up. I forced it down again. I'm afraid of my own anger now.

—Yes, I really am Swadesh Deepak.

He put both hands to his face. He began to cry audibly. I was worried and startled. I had not even said anything. Geeta beckoned me into the kitchen.

—Why is that man crying?

—No idea.

—You must have said something.

—He just got here. How could I have managed that?

—Well, calm him down.

—I don't know how.

—I know that. I know it at my own cost. You only get angry when you see someone crying. You have no pity for anyone.

Out of habit, she fires this barb as she leaves the kitchen, carrying a glass of water. It did not sting; it did not penetrate. I am protected by Karna's kavach.*

Geeta put her hand on his shoulder. He got up, touched her feet and drank the water.

—Behenji, I've come from Sirsa. My name is Amrit. Our group has decided to stage Sir's play *Court Martial*. We went to the college there to ask for donations. The English professor told us that Swadesh Deepak was dead, that the news had appeared a few months ago. Our president is a retired colonel. We had a condolence meeting. Many

* Karna in the Mahabharata has magical armour to protect him against all foes. He is only eventually defeated after being tricked out of it.

people came to offer their memories. After some days, his photograph appeared in *The Indian Express*: the news that Sir's play *Kaal Kothri* is to be staged at Chandigarh's Tagore Theatre. Colonel Saahab issued orders: 'Amrit, go to Ambala. Find out for yourself. The newspapers these days are useless. They'll print anything. Sometimes dead, sometimes alive!'

When Amrit invited me to Sirsa, Geeta declined on my behalf.

—Behenji, I'll take him there by taxi.

—No. The doctors forbid it.

—Why?

—He is neither dead nor alive.

Amrit shot up and left. Perhaps he feared some more terrifying news.

I went back to my two worlds: the dead and the living.

Geeta: How much people love you. Write something. It's been years.

I: The hope of writing is what has kept me alive.

Geeta: Then go for some time. Or you'll spend the evening fighting with everyone.

I closed my eyes. I was asleep immediately. And back in the ICU.

FROM THE PAST

Mayavini in the middle of the night.

With her, the entire jungle. She knows I love trees. I was hibernating. She ordered the birds on the trees to sing. They began to chat; I woke up. She smiled. I became a poem.

—Do you remember when you were at my place I suggested an idea for a play?

—Did you? Remind me.

Now we were in the drawing room of her house. She was sitting on the sofa next to me. Her shapely thigh was pressed against mine; primal desires began to turn in their sleep inside me. I wanted to push her sari aside and see if her thighs were as bright and shining as her face.

—The subject of the play dates back to the time of the Mahabharata.

—I am not part of the Mahabharata industry.

—First hear me out. Dronacharya asks Eklavya for his thumb. How could a Dalit boy surpass his upper-caste student Arjuna in the art of archery? And he asks for the thumb because this is the digit used to pull the string of the bow.

—Go on.

—Have you ever noticed how in national and international competitions these days the string is pulled with the middle finger?

—So what?

—Perhaps Dronacharya had a moment of regret. Perhaps he had taught Eklavya to draw the string with his middle finger.

I lit a cigarette. She was looking at me, waiting for an answer. I enjoy telling women bitter things as much as I enjoy leaving them. It is an essential part of my strategy.

—It would make a good theme for the stage. The kind the Head of a Department of Hindi might write. Everyone gets better, and in the end, a family photograph. The audience no longer wants such plays. Because they're fed up of these lies dressed as ideals. In the form of tales of kings and queens. The play will be meaningful when Eklavya cuts off Dronacharya's fingers for even asking for such an unjust and inhuman guru-dakshina.

—How can the play go on after that?

—Of course it can. Everyone gets together with Eklavya and revolts.

—So write it from that angle.

—It cannot be written. When a man becomes a part of the system, a courtier or a worker for the king, he loses all sense of sin and repentance. These are the signs of bright souls, not of servants. Dronacharya can have only one regret—not asking for Eklavya's life.

She took out a cigarette from my case and gave it to me.

—Smoke it, you're ranting. What a lot of things you know about.

—Nothing like that. It's just that you live in a naïve world.

—So write a play about me then.

—It would take ten Swadeshes.

She took both my hands in hers.

—For me one Swadesh is a feast. You should stay here a few months in every year.

—Where? And how would I earn?

—We will have a bad time. One can't spend too much time with a male prostitute; it palls.

—You are impossible. Are there any words other than 'No' in your dictionary?

—Many words. Words full of heat. And they are telling me that it is entirely unnecessary for us to live together to be friends.

She opened her eyes wide and looked at me. The blood had risen into her face. In words rich with hubris, she said: I want to possess you, Swadesh Deepak.

Using my full name was an insult. My mouth was full of ash. How could this woman be a friend when she wanted to acquire me and on her own terms?

—I am sorry for you. Really sorry. Never try to win a man by threats. Just pamper him a little and the fool will be yours.

—I don't know how to pamper. She seemed helpless.

—Never use your beauty as a weapon. Weapons do not frighten me.

—No one frightens you.

—Not true. I am very scared of my wife.

She smiled. Outside the windows: tension. The religious books shifted and shook.

—Perhaps I haven't told you but both my daughters are very ordinary to look at, rather ugly. They resemble their father.

—They'll be difficult to marry off.

—Marriages aren't decided on beauty but on bank balances. I wasn't saying that. I wish I had a son like you. Strong and violent.

—That would destroy you.

—But I want to be destroyed, Swadesh. I cannot live this safe, schedule-driven life. The moment I saw you I wanted to be destroyed by you.

To answer this, I used Shakespeare—'If every day were Sunday'.*

She was still looking at me with eyes wide open. On the tip of her nose, drops of perspiration. Her body poised to attack—a female man-eater. She said, and though I remember her sitting in front of me, her voice seemed to come from some distant desert, dry as sand and just as desolate:

—Swadeshji, is your dictionary composed entirely of words of refusal?

I enjoyed seeing girls heaving with rage. In truth, it is because rage leaves them helpless. A sweet word. One sweet touch and they bloom like sunflowers.

But I, I am five-foot-eight-inches of ego. But I, I am a man who delights in his own strength. I wanted to twine my body with hers. But pride got in the way and I was cursed. She could be a good friend, not a lover. I do not like women who want to buy me flats. But I did not know the volcanic nature of their love.

She cursed me. A seven-year-long curse. When I think about it today too, I decide in my favour. She had no moral or even immoral right to punish me for seven years. To kill my brain cells. To take my pen from me. To turn me from a man into a cockroach. But no one can stop a female man-eater. The Man-Eating Tigress of Kolkata. Now she had become Sylvia Plath:

* This might refer to: 'If all the year were playing holidays / To sport would be as tedious as to work.' *King Henry IV*, Part 1.

Out of the ash
I rise with my red hair
And I eat men like air.

('Lady Lazarus')

I thought I'd explain it to her. I had done no wrong. I had saved her from myself. Her forehead would have been branded with a Scarlet A; she would have become Hester Prynne.* But female man-eaters cannot understand logic and systems.

The man-eating tigress had decided to attack and kiss. But then I did not know of this frightening decree: that when a beautiful woman destroys one, one's entire body, every inch of it, is filled with pleasure.

But then I did not know that my sun was in her hands.

But then I did not know that I would be reduced to begging for death, day and night. But she would hold my life's strings firmly in her hands.

But then I did not know that she was Mayavini, possessor of different and strange powers.

By the time I found out, it was too late. My weapons had been taken from me.

I turned from Deepak into dementia.

I told some bits of the story of her annoyance to my friend, retired Colonel Shichokand. I complained:

—I neither teased nor touched her and yet she was so furious.

The Colonel smokes more than I do. He lit a fresh cigarette.

—You bloody idiot. Who made you a writer? That was precisely the reason she was angry: that you neither touched

* The heroine of Nathaniel Hawthorne's *The Scarlet Letter* (1850), accused of adultery and branded with an 'A'.

her nor teased her. A beautiful woman has divine right to be touched, to be loved. You scorned her to prove your bravery. You should have joined the army for such bloody brave misdeeds.

—Now what do I do?

—Nothing for you to do now. She will do it all. To Hell with your macho image.

He lit another cigarette and said, more in sadness than in anger: Now suffer in silence. A real man must suffer silently.

Afterwards, when I was in hospital for five months, Colonel Shichokand never came to see me even once.

I could not share this secret with anyone, not even Vikas Rai. My ego. My pride. He-man Swadesh terrorized by a woman? This was my mistake, for she was no ordinary beautiful woman but Mayavini. Tennyson came to mind:

> The mirror crack'd from side to side
> The curse is come upon me...
>
> ('The Lady of Shalott')

I began to fade into a photograph in a book.

I forgot how to cry. I began to shrink, like a winter day.

Evil spirits wear white clothes. She comes.

I began to be afraid to speak. I grew afraid to leave my room. Perhaps she was imaginary but even so she was not unreal.

This woman could be in two places at once: with me and somewhere else entirely.

The nails being hammered into me developed rust. Why are the nails rusted?

An extremely beautiful woman is the mistress of merciless powers.

And so the sun fled.

I do not understand the tactics of flight. So I found myself in the ICU.

The drunken guards of the king were sleeping.*

I was in the state of samaadhi and torture at the same time. My younger sister told me that a pretty and fair nurse came into the ICU. I was a mess: my hair had grown unchecked for a month. My beard was half white. I had not bathed for weeks. It is possible I was stinking. She looked at me and said, with her nose screwed up: What an ugly fellow. Disgusting.

What could Savita say? Hospitals make cowards of us all.

The nurse could not find a vein to inject me so she kept puncturing me here and there.

Younger sister: Sister, take it easy. How many times will you poke him?

Nurse: He doesn't feel a thing. He feels no pain. And where is he going to survive?

Younger sister: It hurts me to watch you hurt him. He's my elder brother.

The nurse looked at me with deep contempt and said—Who knows who used their influence and shoved this corpse into the ICU?

Mumbling and muttering to herself, she left the room. She was angry at not finding a vein. My mrityu-nritya, my death-play continued: I could not move, I could not speak. When would my time come? I was remembering myself. My illness. People listening to me with respect in their eyes. But now words had been silenced. I could hear nobody, never mind how much rice a tantrik threw into the river, never mind how many cows were fed with fresh green grass. Now I would not return. I was disgusting. I had become a stink.

THE FUTURE

He came in clothes made of khadi. A Nehru jacket. No Gandhi cap, however. Nehru had obviously abandoned Gandhi.

---

* This may be a reference to *Macbeth*.

The man: Swadeshji, I've come to take your blessings. I want to read you some poems. Vishnu Prabhakar* is my mother's brother. You must know him.

I did not tell him that I had neither seen his uncle nor had I read his work. His face was suffused with patriotic fervour. It was as if a Dalda dabba were hanging from it.

I: Please do not read any patriotic poems to me.

He: You surprise me. How did you know that I was going to read patriotic poems to you?

I: If your uncle is Vishnu Prabhakar, it follows that your poems are going to be patriotic. I do not want to listen to them. I find them vulgar.

He: Just one. A small one. Barely ten pages. I will not leave without your blessings.

I gave in. Patriots talk a lot.

I: If you must, but read quietly.

He: But you have to roar a patriotic poem. Listen and it will infuse a current of life into you.

Nothing inside me felt infused.

To Delhi. The Sahitya Akademi. The man on the bench outside the room looked at me with questioning eyes. I told him I wanted to meet Shaani.† He shot to his feet, all agog now. He looked me up and down.

He: Meet Giridhar Rathi.

I: Why? I want to meet Shaani.

He looked scared. Actually I had abandoned my anger in the hospital. He must have thought me a poet or a madman.

* Vishnu Prabhakar (1912–2009) was a noted Hindi writer whose works had elements of patriotism and social upliftment.

† This refers to Gulsher Khan Shaani (1933–1995) who, among many other things, edited the *Samkaleen Bharatiya Sahitya* ('Contemporary Indian Literature'), a magazine published by the Sahitya Akademi, from where he retired in 1991.

He: Shaani Saahab has passed away.

I was silent. Shaani and I had a livid friendship. I knew his name Shaani meant anger. Or so he had said.

I: No one told me.

He: Few people know. He was not a political leader. He was a writer.

I went into Shaani's room. A gentle bearded fellow was there. On his face, a poem. He came out from behind his desk to hug me.

Rathi: I was sure you would get well, Swadeshji. When your entire oeuvre is full of violence, you must be strong. You can defeat anyone.

I: How did you know about my illness? No one was told.

Rathi: For five years, even Soumitra Mohan did not know you were ill. He thought you had gone underground as is your habit. One of my poet friends went to Chandigarh. Pramod Kaunswal of *Jansatta* told him about you. He went to see you at the hospital with Kaunswal.

I: I didn't know.

Rathi: How could you? You didn't recognize anyone, nor were you speaking. You were on some other planet.

I: I haven't read any of your poems for a while.

Rathi: I haven't written any for a while. I've begun to ask myself some questions about the value of writing.

Giridhar opened a drawer and said: I'll give you a cigarette.

I thought I'd say I only smoke my own brand. I didn't. Giridhar pushed a Charminar packet across the table. I was shocked. According to my knowledge, this was the second writer to smoke Charminar. I was the first.

—What are you writing?

—Nothing right now. I have not forgotten those days. I still feel scared sometimes.

—Do not try to forget. Have you ever thought of writing about that time? Many creative people have battled with this disease. No one has written about it. Vincent van Gogh had a similar problem. Someone else wrote about it—*Lust for Life*.* Shelley's own compatriots called him sad, mad and bad Shelley.† He did not write about his experiences. Robert Lowell was in mental hospitals, admitted three times. He wrote nothing. Sylvia Plath killed herself. Here Niralaji‡ also suffered from the problem. He would have spells of normalcy. He didn't write about it either.

I: It's tough, very tough.

Giridhar: But then you only write about what's tough. You've never taken refuge in a school or an -ism.

I: I don't want to write about my illness.

Giridhar: When did I say you should describe your illness? You have to say what it feels like to be crushed by a mountain.

I: I don't remember the events in any order.

Giridhar: Forget about time and the sequence of events. Liberate yourself from past-present-future. Write it down as it comes back. Genre, style, forget about these things. If you want, write a poem; put in dialogue as if it's a play—a fractured prose for a fractured autobiography. And then we will have the first book that is like us.

I: I was in the Intensive Care Unit for days. I have no memory of that time.

Giridhar played with his beard. He smiled.

Giridhar: Actually, we make excuses for not writing. Look at me. Up to now, just one collection of poetry. While you were in the ICU, your relatives were probably with you. They will tell you about those days.

I: I'll have to ask my doctor about this.

---

* Irving Stone's novel *Lust for Life* (1934) is based on the life of Vincent van Gogh.

† 'Mad, bad and dangerous to know' was a phrase Lady Caroline Lamb used to describe Lord Byron.

‡ Suryakant Tripathi 'Nirala' (1896–1961), a near-legendary figure of modern Hindi letters.

Giridhar: Oh, we should always ask our doctors.

I got up. Giridhar came to the door with me. He said—Swadeshji, do not write just because I urge you to. I know you will have to relive those days to write about them. Write only when Swadesh Deepak tells you to write.

We parted ways.

I am angry with Giridhar Rathi. Why encourage me to write?

THE PAST

When the senior doctors came on their rounds, my elder sister asked:

—Why doesn't Deepak recognize anyone?

—Some brain cells are dead. When we do a tomography—that's a coloured x-ray of the brain—we'll know for sure.

—But after so many medicines...

—Behenji, there is no cure in the whole wide world for his condition. The brain has billions of cells. Sometimes, the living cells take over the work of the dead cells. And if that happens, then his ability to recognize people will return. We can pray only.

My sister sponged my face with a wet towel. She was saddened by the state of my face.

—No one would recognize Deepak. Who knows who has cast the evil eye upon him!

She began to pray silently, and would continue to do so until evening. When the world denies one consolation, one turns straight to God. My elder sister had no idea of the merciless powers of a woman. When a beautiful woman comes to a boil, she becomes remorseless.

It takes my sister three changes on the bus to get to the hospital. She is tired. Age and this exertion take their toll. She begins to doze off.

Someone sits down on the empty chair. A dwarf woman with hair longer than her body. Sandalwood paste on her forehead.

I did not recognize her at all. She smiles. It is my Mayavini.

—Swadeshji! Look at the results of what I did to you. I have become a dwarf.

—No, it isn't your body; it's what's inside that has shrunk. Our height is determined by our self-perception.

—I live in a wilderness now.

—The jungle grows inside us.

As she speaks, tears fill her eyes.

—Kaamna, I don't think you could like me now. I may even repulse you. Or frighten you.

—You ought to try to think beyond the body. It was your violent soul that I loved.

—My soul is a beggar now. My eyes beg for help. You should not have taken everything from me.

—What I have taken, I will return. I will take you abroad for plastic surgery.

—No, I want to die in my own country.

—I must revolt you.

—No, now I like you very much. I recognize you. I talk to you. Only the fortunate find themselves with such beautiful enemies.

Hearing this, she began to grow in size again. The dwarf vanished. Mayavini returned.

—Now go to sleep. You're tired. I'll come again.

—How do you know I'm tired?

—I know everything, Swadeshji.

When she touched my head, calmness descended. With her little finger, she wiped some of the sandalwood paste off her forehead and put it on mine. I turned fragrant.

That night I spent swimming in a river turned black. I slept without break. When she comes, does she take some sorrow with her? The sorrows she herself gave me? The sorrows that I have not yet revealed to anyone? Any listener would dismiss them as figments of my imagination or deride me for my weakness. It is a mystery why family members and friends are always sure the mentally ill person is lying.

Nothing is actually wrong with him. He is lying on the bed only to evoke sympathy. Often Geeta, tired and angry, would say—Nothing is the matter with you. You are shamming. You don't want to work. I felt scared to say: I have worked for twenty-six years. I held my peace. I knew that in her quiver she still had plenty of poisoned arrows.

Dr Pratap Sharan said in a sad voice: In our country, cancer has found acceptance; even AIDS is now acceptable, but the mentally ill are not. They have those short films on TV in which Shabana Azmi will explain that AIDS is not contagious, that AIDS patients need love, not hatred. Up to now no organization has ever made a film on the mentally ill. Shabana Azmi has never said that psychiatric patients need love, not hate. Which is why psychiatrists have to fight not just the disease but the attitudes of society and the family too. Your wife is educated, sensitive, and yet one day she might beat you physically. I don't know why this disease makes other people cruel. In America, one out of every three people goes to see a mental health specialist.

Dr Pratap Sharan stopped, smiled, said:

—I've been talking too much today.

While I was in the ICU, my family was mined for pieces of my history. My file began to bulge. They asked Geeta: Any involvement with other women?

Geeta: No, never. Deepak has never been involved even with me. His only involvement has been with writing. He has fans in plenty. No friends. I have a strong feeling he doesn't like women.

This, the most common of all reasons for my kind of illness, proved misleading.

—Any feeling of failure as a writer?

—No, not at all. The play *Court Martial* was at the height of its success. When Ranjit Kapoor presented it in Delhi,

Deepak was praised to the skies. When Usha Ganguly did it in Calcutta, an important critic wrote in the *Telegraph* that 'after *Court Martial,* Tagore has become irrelevant'. Deepak was happy, really happy. For the first time in his life he was getting so much appreciation and praise.

Both were silent. The doctor understood that my history was not going to yield to easy formulae that could be put down in a file.

Geeta: This started after he came back from Calcutta. He stopped talking, stopped eating, stopped meeting people. Deepak, always so dapper, suddenly stopped changing his clothes. He lost all interest in himself.

—Something happened in Calcutta?

—How do I know? I wasn't with him. Moreover, he never shares his inner life.

The doctor understood that Madam was irritated. He left, but he would be back the next day to scratch around a little more.

When Dr Naidu came, Kanta asked:

—Will Deepak's arm always be tied up like that?

—No Mataji, we'll operate and he will recover. When the flesh burns, it melts and pulls the joint together. It's called a contracture.

—What a terrible thing to happen to my brother. He had a body like gold.

—Nothing bad has happened, Mataji. He was burned beneath the neck. With his clothes on, nothing will be visible. What if his lips had burned? Or his nose? If his eyes had burned, what would he have done? God has been kind to him.

—When you change the bandages, why does he feel no pain? He doesn't make so much as an 'uff'.

Dr Naidu smiled. Out of habit, he teased:

—He must feel the pain but your brother is a real man. He will never show pain. Like Bhishma Pitamah in the Mahabharata, he will take his rest on a bed of arrows.

Kanta could not help smiling. What a happy heart Dr Naidu had.

The neurosurgeon came. He spent a long time looking at me. The Burns Unit doctor raised the sheet to let him look at the burned area. The psychiatrist gave him my file, still quite slim, which he read.

—So, he's a creative person. Nothing for us to do right now. Some vital parts have been burned. We can't perform any of the important tests. I'll come again in a month. He must speak. There's a danger he may spend the rest of his life as a vegetable.

He left. Whoever comes, talks about danger. Perhaps my sun has come to the hospital and stopped its ascent into the sky.

The horsemen unsheathed their spears. I could see them. They will hunt me down. Their bodies were in attack mode. They would follow the king's orders at all costs. They were hunters to the death. I felt no fear at all. I had been waiting for them for seven years. Yeats is one of my favourites. Sometimes he sits by me and reads me a poem.

> An aged man is but a paltry thing
> A tattered coat upon a stick, unless
> Soul clap its hands and sing...
>
> ('Sailing to Byzantium')

My coat was in rags; why should I hold it together? I will cast it off. I tried three times but it would not be cast off.

The second time: I got up at midnight. I took out a new blade. I took a big tin and I went into the big room. No one sleeps there. I put three pillows behind my head and reclined on the couch. I lit what I thought would be my last cigarette. I was calm. Free of fear. I put the tin on the side of the couch. I did not want the blood to fall on the floor. I am a cleanly person.

I cut deep into both my wrists. Thin fountains of blood spurted. The blood began to run into the tin. Eyes closed. A last thought: how happy Geeta will be that I have not soiled the bedcovers. I do not know when I lost consciousness. Or when the flow of blood stopped.

The light was on. Something woke Geeta up. She came running into the big room. She saw the tin nearly full of blood. She called Parul. My eyes opened. I was only half dead. Geeta's face was drained of blood but Parul's face showed no expression. She has great self-confidence and the ability to think fast and come to correct decisions. Don't let him sleep, Mama. Keep him talking. I will bring Sunny Uncle.

Sunny Uncle is really Dr Kalra. He is like a God to the poor. My elder sister's son-in-law.

The scooter started. Parul feels no fear about driving five kilometres in the dead of night. She does not once suggest we send her younger brother Sukant with her though she knows that at this time drunkards rule the roads.

Geeta brought tea. Gingerly, she pushed the glass into my hands. I could not hold it. She brought it to my mouth. I shook my head.

—Cigarette.

She put one to her mouth, lit it, put it to my lips. I took a long drag. Geeta smiled. I smiled too. A faded photograph of the early days of our romance appeared. Then, these stupid gestures had meant so much. When in love, we turn from bodies into fragrances. She said:

—Why do you get after yourself? I will not let you die. If you had succeeded, do you know what would have happened next? The police would be in the house, the news would be in the papers. How would I show my face in public? How would I live in this city? And where would I go if I had to leave? You sold the house in Delhi. How would I raise Parul and Sukant? You are not your own enemy, you are your children's enemy, my enemy.

—My name has been erased from the nameplate.

Tomorrow evidence will be given about me. I have become a black statement.

—How brave you used to be. What a tough man you were.

Geeta was sad.

—I am waiting for the postman. I didn't even go into that room.

Geeta changed the subject.

—Another cigarette?

—Yes.

—Now no day is free of fear of her. She lives in another city but stays with me.

—Who are you talking about?

I had not introduced Geeta and Mayavini.

—If the moon were to smile, it would resemble her face.

—Who is she?

—I want to go to Russia. I have to meet Mayakovsky. My address has changed. Tell everyone a black address. Now no one sits on the bench of memory. The stones do not talk to me.

—Shut up. Do you even know what you're saying? Pull yourself together.

—All my tomorrows are dead. Every day a pale-faced girl brings me sherbet.

—You did not fear a soul. Now what has happened to you?

—A black body is inside me. I am terrified. I can hear the cannonade of horse's hooves. They are coming for me. I want to cry. I can't cry.

—Think about me, think about your children.

—I want to write poetry. When you cannot escape, you write poetry, but even so you do not escape.

—You writers are so cruel. You think of nothing but writing.

—She wrote to ask, why are your photographs so bad?

Sheila Sandhu had said in Delhi:

—Swadesh, you writers are really cruel.

THE PAST: WITH SHEILA SANDHU

I went to meet Sheilaji at Rajkamal Prakashan. She saw me from her glass cabin and got up. She took my hand, brought me in.

—When did you get here?

—Just now.

—How long are you staying?

—As long as you say I should.

—Why this lover-like talk with me? You should have tried it thirty years ago.

—I'm always late. Had I been born twenty years earlier…

—Have you seen Krishnaji already?

—No, I came straight here.

—Deepak, there's something about you. Which is why Krishnaji likes you so much.

—Yes, as soon as she sees me she greets me. In a loud voice she'll say—Here comes the well-born bastard. She's the only Hindi writer who uses bad language becomingly. It must be of her that Ghalib Saahab said: *Gaaliyaan khaake bhi bemaza na hua* (Even her abuse did not make me unhappy). She has a strong sense of humour. Like the British, she can make fun of herself.

We had tea. Mohan Gupta came in. Even after leaving Rajkamal, he was aggrieved that my manuscripts bypassed him and went straight to Sheilaji. This bothered him. He felt that if I were forced to send them through the proper channels, this would teach me, as it had taught other authors, his importance in the scheme of things. Now my books get published in a month. Mohan Gupta is a good man but not a good friend. He doesn't even know what he has said. And he cannot drive a car well. Once I did travel with him. As soon as the key is in the ignition, he turns into Nadia Hunterwali.*

* This is a reference to 'Fearless Nadia' (1908–1996) as she was called. Born Mary Evans in Australia, she came to India with a circus and became the queen of B-grade movies. She was rechristened Nadia by Homi Wadia, the director of the stunt films in which she excelled, and whom she later married.

He never drives on his side of the road. And he shouts at other people, admonishing them to drive with manners. It is not without danger to be his friend.

—You're right, Swadesh. Krishnaji knows how to make every word count. Remember how I took you to lunch at the Shri Ram Centre?

—Yes, she was not in her national dress, black, that day.

—Yes, I was quite shocked too. I remember asking: How come you're in a salwar-kameez and a shawl? Krishnaji smiled. Twenty years dropped off her. I could see that she had the eye of the fish in her sights and she was going to let loose an arrow.*

—I thought: I am having lunch with Swadesh. Might as well wear 'womanly' clothes so I should look like his mother. In black, who knows what people might think? For whatever his claims at writing, the scoundrel is a handsome man.

The arrow found its mark. It was winter but the warmth in her words brought us all close to each other.

Back from the Shri Ram Centre.

Sheilaji—Have you received a letter from *her*?

I nodded. Sheilaji does not use Kaamna's name.

—Did you reply?

—Every third letter.

—Are you a friend or an accountant? Why do you let her upset you?

—Ranjit Kapoor told me why. When the first show of *Court Martial* was held in Calcutta, he happened to be there. He didn't only see the play, he also heard about the storm I caused. I told you that Ranjit Kapoor got me to write *Kaal Kothri* in twenty days. The rehearsals were on at Shri Ram Centre, I told Ranjit my problems.

—I have become addicted to writing long speeches in my plays.

---

* A reference to the performance of Arjun at the swayamwara of Draupadi, who shot an arrow into the eye of a revolving metal fish while observing its reflection in a pool beneath.

—Bhai Saahab, every artist has some addiction or the other. Look at me: I'm addicted to marriage.

The peon brought in the post. A letter from Mayavini. She asked if she could come to Delhi to see the rehearsal and the new play. I was shaken.

—Is this a letter from that woman you attacked?

I nodded.

Ranjit: The problem with small-town people is that they do not know how to flirt. They have no idea what a flirtation is. You turn friendships into tragedies. When I first went to Bombay, if a woman so much as smiled at me, I thought it was an invitation to share her bed. Let her come to Delhi if she wants to. How is it a problem for you?

How could I tell Ranjit that to say yes would be to admit the defeat of my pride, my ego, my machismo? In those days I was a feudal sort of man, who wanted everything on his own terms. Which is why Rajendra Yadav is completely right when he thinks of me, calls me scum.

Ranjit's strength lies in his capacity for clarity.

—Bhai Saahab, now write a comedy. *Baal Bhagwan* ('The Child God'), *Court Martial*, now *Kaal Kothri*. Enough tragedies. One day you might become a tragedy yourself.

Ranjit Kapoor did not know that he was making a forecast of my bleak future.

From Ranjit, I returned to Sheila Sandhu.

Sheilaji: Deepak, you get angry easily. Do you remember how we first met and immediately got into a fight? You got angry and picked up your manuscript and rose to your feet, thunder rumbling, lightning flashing.

Deepak: My fights with beautiful, wise women always turn into friendships.

Sheilaji: Lunch? Home or hotel?

Deepak: Home.

Sheilaji: I know why. So you can take a two-hour siesta afterwards. Such is my fate.

Sheilaji smiled. I smiled too and that ugly scene faded.

PLACE: SHEILA SANDHU'S HOUSE
TIME: AFTERNOON

Sheilaji's home is sad and silent these days. Everyone keeps to their rooms. Hardev Sandhu did not come into the hall either.

On their doorstep sits a Greek tragedy. It can enter at any moment. More terrifying than a tragedy is waiting for its consequences. We all know this. One can only pray.

Sheilaji: Deepak, Krishnaji called. A strange call. I was shocked.

Such an old friend, such a beloved friend. I have no idea how she could talk like that. Deepak, God save me from my friends. I can deal with my enemies myself. You know there's been a case about an Amrita Pritam title.* They asked me to give evidence. I said it would be difficult. You know how we're beleaguered by adversity right now.

I was silent.

Sheilaji: She got angry. She said I think Amrita Pritam is a better writer than she, and so I do not want to give evidence. I said I thought all the authors who are published by Rajkamal are fine writers. How could I tell her the case has improved the sales of her book?

I was silent.

Sheilaji: Then came a letter, ripe with rage. It suggested she was thinking of withdrawing her books from Rajkamal. Deepak, your tribe writes about human relationships, you write about the warm honesty of friendship, but really, you writers are very cruel.

I: Inside Krishna Sobti there is an obstinate child. If you pay her no heed, that child takes offence.

---

* This refers to a court case that began when, in 1981, Amrita Pritam published a book called *Hardatt Ka Zindaginama*. Krishna Sobti's novel *Zindaginama* had been published in 1979 and she claimed that the use of the word 'Zindaginama' in Pritam's title amounted to plagiarism. The case polarized the Hindi sphere and lasted for twenty-five years before being decided in favour of Pritam.

Sheilaji: But children are never cruel.
That was when Sheila Sandhu said authors are cruel.
Now Geeta says the same thing. Are they right?

PLACE: PGI, CHANDIGARH
TIME: SEPTEMBER 1995

Manzoor Ahtesham does not write letters. Perhaps he has found out that I do not even open letters. I just tear them up. He is wise. A diviner. When I read his letters, they brought to mind the letters of Keats. Jehangir Sabavala writes one letter every year. I have not replied to four of his letters but they still come.

Soumitra Mohan does not write letters nor does he write poems. Mayavini does not write letters. She comes herself. I don't know who told me that Atal Bihari Vajpayee wants to see *Court Martial*. Someone has stolen my rainbow and whisked it off to Calcutta. She doesn't get angry; she gets even. What she likes, she destroys. Why doesn't Nirmal Verma like my writing? Because of its violence? Isn't everything violent? Have I turned beggarly? Someone asking for sympathy in spare change. Lies. Complete lies. I have not allowed anyone to find out about my fractured life. Yes. W.B. Yeats knows everything. He sits by me. He reads me poems. When will Deepak speak? A shared worry. The doctors offer no encouragement. Do not fear, eat up your nice fruit, chant the name of God, do not take the name of Marx.

I am a man
More sinned against than sinning.

(Shakespeare, *King Lear*)

I did not abuse her deliberately. I was born with a bad temper. Who will write my story—Jagdishchandra or Rajendra Yadav? Not Rajendra, he's a rascal. He'll smack his lips over it. He will introduce women into my tale.

By some chance, I am alive. But why didn't I get my

chance? If *Court Martial* is a good play, why did it augur my downfall? Now I will write nothing. Delirium means delirium.

I have been exiled. My name has been cut off the voters' list.

Flowers always dry quietly.

Why doesn't Swadesh Deepak speak? But I am happy. Words are betrayers.

Today the pretty, fair nurse is on duty. She looked at me and said:

—He stinks. Sponge him.

Savita (angrily): Remove all the tubes you've stuck into his body. Forget sponging him, we'll give him a bath.

Nurse: Speak politely, Bibi.

Savita: You learn politeness first. You've called him ugly; now you're calling him dirty. Are you looking to marry him? This is my brother lying here. If he could hear and understand you, he'd chop you up. That's a tiger lying on the bed there. Do you know what's it like to see a brother reduced to this? Perhaps you do not have a brother.

The nurse was a little startled by this. Those who came with patients did not speak in this manner. Were they some minister's...?

—I was telling you for your brother's good.

—My brother's good is in God's hand, Sister.

It was now time for all the beautiful women to take their revenge on me. At ten, the doctor came on his rounds. He looked at the chart. He looked at me. He went out and began to talk to the others. My younger sister overheard their conversation. She came in and asked the elder one:

—What is a vegetable? They were saying Veerji could become a vegetable.

—I think a vegetable is something you eat, like greens.

Billu's gone out. We'll ask him when he gets back.

When he returned, they asked.

—When a man turns into a lump of meat, they say he's a vegetable.

Elder sister: Oh God, have mercy on poor Deepak.

But God had no intention of showing mercy. All three began praying silently. Who will look after him if he's a vegetable? As it is poor Geeta has been caring for him for years. Who knows how long he will live. Their family problems began to increase in size. Their children's futures began to look bleaker than ever. They had no time at all for me. Their prayers turned inauspicious. But who could actually begin to say this? The younger one said:

—May God protect him from this. How much more suffering is in store?

The elder: You're right, Savita. I'm now seventy. I have pain in my joints. I would have taken him in but how will I deal with a bed-ridden man? You know how I have a platoon of relatives always coming and going. What do I tell them? That he's mad? It's not a question of space. The house is big enough but I'm afraid of what people will say.

As your home gets bigger, your heart grows smaller. What people will say seemed to be more important than a patient's life. The inauspicious prayers began to take the form of words.

The younger: Take him, oh Lord. End his pain.

The elder proceeded to put the stamp of morality on these prayers.

—Which is why death is referred to as release in our dharma. When He sees so much pain, He calls you to Him and releases you.

It was decided to include Geeta in the inauspicious prayerfest. Now everyone began to think of their own release. Long ago, Rajendra Yadav had said something that came back now.

—Swadesh, you're still mentally an adolescent when it

comes to human relationships. The demands of the middle-class make us cruel, which is why the unity of the family is breaking down. The retired father, the sick mother, they all become enemies in the home. Only in your story 'Maatam' ('Mourning') have you escaped your romantic notion about families: when the daughter who laments the passing of her father in the day seeks the pleasure of sex in her husband's arms at night. But of course, Hindi is still a language of mothers and sisters. Abuse is all you will get. Anyway, let's talk of something else. Any liaisons lately?

—Nothing these days.

—Liar; tell me, when you write, do you put in page numbers?

—Yes.

—Which is why your stories end so suddenly. If you put page numbers in, you think this is getting too long, who knows how many issues the publisher will spread it over. The long story is your forte. Do not put page numbers in and do not consult your clock.

I should have asked Rajendra for advice about Mayavini but I already knew what he would say. He is a stern critic of my pride.

—Pandit, just go and meet her. Or call her to you. Why are you such a coward when it comes to women? If she's so beautiful, introduce us. These Hindi women fatigue my eyes.

Now my family goes out of the ICU. The fear of the first days has evaporated. When someone has tubes stuck into every conceivable part of his body, he's not going to die all of a sudden, they think.

She came into the room. My eyes opened. Her clothes were bright and colourful. The weather changed in my room.

—You're looking like a bride. I even want to touch your yellow blouse.

—If I'm a bride, we should get married.

—You are a naughty nymph.

—This is my tragedy. In our national psyche, only men

are allowed to flirt and tease. If a woman tries, she is branded a slut. All I said was let's go to Mandu. And you turned into a loaded gun.

—The clothes of my soul are filthy.

—I will wash them clean.

I kept looking at her. She was an ember from a fired-up bong. The weather kept up its little game.

—Why did you give me such a terrifying sentence? My body gone, my mind gone. Just because I got angry.

—I did not get angry at your expletives. Remember I took you home the very next day. You kept saying No to me, as if I were Saratbabu's Chandramukhi, a woman who pleasures men. My powers began to hiss inside me.

—If I get well, I will come to you.

—Now you will not come nor will I call you. You cannot commit to anyone. We will meet after ten years. And that too for only five minutes.

—You even love according to a time-table. I want to be with you.

—These words now lie between us as a curse. You do not want to be with anybody. You can only be happy in your Narcissus's world.

The windowpanes clinked. It was evening. The birds were silent. Keats said in my ear—'And no birds sing.'

The same look. The same brightness. The same slightly heavy hips. I could not lose her again. The four corners screamed. I began to burn up in that cold room. Was it exile again? Or fire? She is a perfect woman. Perfection is terrible. Betrayer. It will be repeated again. Endless dense darkness. Eliot explained this: In my end is my beginning. The image becomes a metaphor. Language becomes grammar. How do I welcome life? A pitiable guest.

She put her hand on my head and asked. You are angry inside, aren't you?

I shook my head.

—Do you know why I have these bright colours on?

I kept looking at her.

—To hear your voice. Don't let your first word be a cussword.

She became playful.

—But I want to be with you. You can bring back life to my crippled world.

—Okay, I will keep coming back like this. On one condition—when you get well, I must be the heroine of your first play.

—Done.

—What name will you give me?

Her eyes were filled with tears, all of a sudden.

—Swadesh, my Swadesh, my bloody Swadesh. What do I do? How do I keep constant watch over you? Who will save you? When you are well, how many more battles will you fight? Oh God, you pitiless God.

She came in tears, she left in tears. My river dried up.

The fifth day: the sun is off to bed. Something happened in my brain. I shook my head. The crying increased. Billu put his hand on my forehead. I jerked my head strongly. He said:

—Didi, I think Veerji's time has come. Offer a prayer.

All three begin to pray.

They were deluded, of course. My time had not come. Actually, Dr Hardev Bahry* had opened his dictionary in my head. The words were taking their places, their numbers increasing. I was confused. Dr Bahry was not just a great scholar, it would seem, he was also the kind of man who would understand the pain of others and share their sorrows. He shut his dictionary—I'll come tomorrow. Fear not. It's just that you do not have the habit of looking after words and bringing them up properly.

The first word crept to my lips. I opened my mouth. The

* In most places, the name is transliterated as Dr Hardev Bahri. I have used Swadesh Deepak's spelling for the author of at least thirteen dictionaries including the *Rajpal Concise Hindi–English Dictionary*.

word was born. My younger sister's ears are sharp. She heard even this whispered word. She was delighted.

—Didi, Billu, Veerji is speaking.

All three came to stand by me. Kanta asked:

—What do you want, son?

—Cigarette.

Savita ran off to call the doctor. Didi began to weep.

The doctor came in. A familiar face. He asked:

—What do you want, Mr Deepak?

—Cigarette.

The doctor told my brother: Get him a cigarette.

My brother smokes. He lit one and put it to my lips. I took it in my left hand and took a long, deep drag. This signalled my return to the world to which I was accustomed.

—Do you recognize me? You've been my patient for five years.

The words strained and struggled, then leapt out.

—Dr Avneet Sharma. Why didn't you come earlier?

—I was on holiday. At home in Jammu. Deepakji, two years ago, I told you: get admitted to hospital. You refused to listen. Now look at the state in which you got to hospital. But don't worry. We won't let anything happen to you.

Younger sister: When will he start eating? He's had nothing for five days.

Avneet: Don't rush things. Everything will take time. This is a long battle; it will take four or five months more. Don't keep pushing him to talk; it'll tire him.

He bade me good night and left.

Younger sister: I thought he'd say his wife's name or ask for Parul or Sukant. Instead he asks for a cigarette.

Elder sister: Have we ever understood this brother of ours? And this could hurt people's feelings. Don't tell anyone. Come on, let's stretch out. Sitting here for five days has meant my legs are all caught up.

I dozed. On the chair, a man pushed the white hair back from his face. He placed a pair of golden spectacles on his nose. It was Yeats.

—Congratulations, Swadesh. You spoke!

I got a shock. I tried to pull myself up in my bed. I failed. I was held down by restraints.

—Sir, you spoke Hindi?

Yeats's smile became gentler.

—I made friends with your poet Nirala in Heaven. He gets very angry if one does not memorize one's lessons. But he is interesting. Next time, I will be reborn here. And write poems in Hindi.

—The seductress could not kill me.

—A seductress never kills outright because she loves you too. She kills by inches. Do you remember my love for Maud Gonne?* The whole of Ireland knew of it. But not she. God made them so. You love her and you hate her. The eternal Helen of Troy. For you to launch a thousand ships.

—What can I do, Sir?

—Nothing, Swadesh. Now that you've started speaking, the real test begins. People are vulgar. They will ask vulgar questions. Be silent. Be calm. Forge another personality. Yes, we can be many beings.

—What can I do? I cannot even write.

—Dream. When I was defeated by my seductress I wrote:

I being poor have my dreams only.†

Yeats rose. He said:

—Swadesh, I won't be coming back.

—Why? Did you take offence at something I said?

—No. My visa has expired.

I was terribly sad.

—Niralaji is trying his best. Perhaps I will get an extension. They're afraid of Nirala over there as well.

Yeats left. I was not afraid.

With Nirala on your side, how can you fear?

---

* Maud Gonne (1866–1953): Irish revolutionary, suffragette, actor and activist for Home Rule; Yeats's muse.

† The Yeats line from 'Aedh Wishes for the Cloths of Heaven' is: 'But I, being poor, have only my dreams;'.

5. 'Do I Know You?'

> If I can live without pain, it would not be a life of happiness. I would be in search of another pain and I would not have to go very far, for it would be standing on the threshold of my room, ready to fill any empty space in the room.
>
> —Nirmal Verma

I was shifted to the ward.

This is where the jungle begins.

Fear did not follow me; it walked by my side.

This was where I began my turning and turning on the same spot, movement without direction.

It was an extraordinary time—neither death nor life.

The rains came and black umbrellas were unfurled in welcome. It was not life-giving rain.

The clothes of my soul were soiled.

The sunlight of her city scorched me for seven years. The same look. The same imposing appearance.

I made a decision: I will never fight with another woman.

I would not seek one out even if she were a doctor for my soul.

On the day I was shifted to the ward, the man in the next bed, Sikandar, a young Sikh with a shaved head, burbled happily.

—Baabyo has come with bananas for me.

Baabyo is the sweetest term of address in Punjabi.

My bed was surrounded by doctors. Nurses lined the walls.

I was now Ted Hughes's jaguar.

A glucose drip was set up. Two injections were administered. I was completely barricaded in. The nurse gave my sister four tablets.

They were to be given after an hour.

—You've tied our Deepak down. How will he turn over?

Avneet Sharma: For four or five months, he'll have to sleep like that. He will get used to it.

As soon as the doctors and nurses left, the visitors who had come for the other patients surrounded my bed.

—Gosh, he's so badly burned.

—Good God, how many tubes and things.

—The doctors were saying he's not out of danger.

—His wife hasn't come.

—Maybe she's left him. Who'd want to stay with a sick man?

Sardar Harnam Singh, Sikandar's father, snarled at them:

—Go on with you. Your mum's not getting married here.

My elder sister looked at him with grateful eyes.

—What does he do?

—He's a college professor.

—Some golden woman* must have cast her spell on him.

—He didn't even look at other women.

—What of that? A golden woman can look at him. But he will get well. On his forehead, a pure spirit sits. It's only that he's been cut to pieces, like Mirza the warrior.

—May God listen to your words.

—Prabhuji listens to everyone. If you need help with getting medicines or anything just let me know. With Professor Saahab's blessings, my son may recover his health.

How strong the rope of hope is! It lasts until the last breath. The others who had been admitted with me had begun to die. I was left to suffer. The mentally ill are always supposed to have supernatural powers. We can feel a bestial rage when someone expresses pity. This nameless horror had destroyed the temple of my soul. Now no one comes

* The golden woman or the 'sohni aurat' is one of the many women who haunt the imagination of the people of the Himalayas and its foothills. In one version, she appears in the night and to set eyes on her is to be blinded forever by her golden beauty. In another version, she blinds you to the charms of other women.

here. I will stay with Mayavini whatever the cost. She is my liberation.

I began to dream of her, of the fragrance of her body. I sat in her scented room.

Someone was coming. I could hear the sound of light footsteps.

I hid my dream immediately.

Kaamna had come. She sat down on the chair. I opened my eyes. After a long time, a familiar smile. In her gold-framed spectacles, she was delectably sexy.

—You're almost well, Swadeshji. I told you I wouldn't let anything happen to you.

—I survived. But this is a time that may drive me mad.

—Nothing will happen. You are very strong. You will defeat time. Right, I didn't tell you. I've been reading Vikram Seth's *A Suitable Boy*. Such a tome. About fourteen hundred pages? It's like a tourist guide to different cities.

—What fat books you read. How do you find time to visit your patients?

—I can do everything. I'm a doctor from Harvard. A child specialist.

—If you're a child specialist, how will you cure me?

She became naughty again, a mischievous sixteen-year-old.

—Hasn't anyone told you that you're still a child?

I touched her wrist. It was cold. The coldness inside me began to melt.

She was saddened, a lighthouse gone dark.

—You have disarmed me. I mean to have you, whatever it takes. But my horses begin to pant with all that galloping.

—May I recite Sylvia Plath to you?

Love is a shadow
How you lie and cry after it.
Listen: these are its hooves; it has gone off, like a horse.

('Elm')

—Swadeshji, you have hidden your springtime in your jhola. You used to laugh once. And it suited you. Perhaps you don't remember. Give up the idea of oblivion. The lines of fate in your hands will rewrite themselves.

—Kaamna, I'm a prisoner of time. My heart is orphaned. Can you hide me somewhere?

—When I offered, you took offence. My powers are also being taken from me. Well, let them be taken. Then I would no longer be able to do the revolting things I have done to you. I am also being punished. Believe me, I was a good woman once.

In her voice was the sigh of falling leaves. For the truth never has any mercy.

—Kaamna, listen to me for the last time. You can never make me ill. I blamed you because of my diseased obduracy. If you ever talk like that, I will not spare you.

A small mischievous smile on her lips.

—That's what I wanted. That you should get angry.

—At that time my ego was as large and senseless as a mountain. Perhaps I was even a sadist. And please stop adding 'ji'. Or the formal 'aap'.

—I'll drop the 'ji' and keep the 'aap'. May I say something? Don't give up the ego entirely. You'll become ordinary. I don't like ordinary men. I still remember your savagery with pleasure.

She became a bearer of light. The corpses inside me began to stir to life.

But it was a weak happiness. Were she to go, it would go with her. I was still afraid to move or speak. She was still a dream, unreal.

—Kaamna, the horsemen pursue me. I can see them. They are hunting me down.

She put a hand on my brow.

—Swadesh. It's only I who am after you. I am in front of you as well. You've talked too much. Close your eyes. Long breath now. We'll sleep all night. No one else should come to you in your dreams. I have bought all the rights.

And I slept all night.

Years afterward, I could still see Alkazi in my dreams. His shining face would appear to me. I was frightened. Memory was returning. Were my days of amnesia ending? If so, then one by one, the sorrows seated on my threshold would enter the house; if so, had the time to recite the last shlokas been delayed? Would dark springtime return and deprive me of words again?

Where are all the colours? What happened to the scents? Now all that I had was the bitter stink of a hospital room. What had Geeta said so proudly with all her brothers and sisters around?

—Our marriage has lasted twenty-two years and through all that time, he's never had so much as a cold. Come rain or shine or storm, he's off for his five-kilometre walk. More of a health addict than a writer.

At that time, we did not know that misfortune, in a different guise, was hovering around us. Misfortune does not like arrogance at all. Out of the millions of her nets and snares, she chooses one and throws it over you. And she does not even tell you your crime.

Then my heart was orphaned. The characters in my interior dark room abandoned me. I was empty. I was lost. My family and close friends were sure that I was inventing excuses not to write. Nothing had happened to me. The mentally ill are always seen as liars.

That was when I learned of the merciless powers of a woman. She who cures had made me ill. Slowly everything began to become obscure. Everything became inaccessible. It seemed to be my fate that I should live with deceit and insomnia and that even simple things should become messy. Far from being able to write, I could not even think. She had my kavach hidden away. Beautiful women are terrible plunderers. They loot everything, bit by bit.

I laid my head upon her thigh. My bones tore through my flesh. Now I was truly Mirza, badshah of the dead. But I had no Sahibaan. Who would make offerings for me at the tombs of pirs and fakirs? I had no options left. I fell asleep again.

In the morning, the nurse removed the feeding tube. Sikandar's father wiped my mouth with a wet cloth.

The tea trolley came onto the verandah. He bought three glasses. He offered me one. I refused. He coaxed.

—Two sips at least, Professor Saahab, or The Giver of All Things will be unhappy.

He saw that my arms were tied down. He poured a spoonful of tea into my mouth; my lips and tongue warmed up.

—That's good?

I nodded.

—So drink some more. This is the grace of the true God.

After drinking half a glass, I refused any more.

I asked Harnam Singh—Why does the goat eat grass?

He looked at me, startled. I asked the Shimlawala in front of me. Mr Shimla was always lying in bed, fully dressed in a coat, pant, shirt and tie.

—Don't know. I'm an accounts officer. Ask something about accounts. You are a stupid professor.

Sikandar chirped—Me, I know, I know.

—Tell me?

—Baabyo, the goat ate grass because there was no chicken to eat.

The nurse came in. She looked frightened. She pushed my hair back with a comb. She straightened the sheet. She said:

—Dr Chari of the Burns Unit is coming. Speak properly to him. He's short-tempered.

Dr Chari entered, a junior doctor behind him. He was so tall he had to bend down to speak to you. His face reminded me of Nirad Chaudhuri's.

—How are you, Mr Deepak?

So Dr Chari of Kerala also speaks Hindi. I nodded to indicate I was fine.

—Don't you want to speak to me? Tell me in words.

—I'm fine.

Avneet Sharma says—He never complains. He feels no pain.

—He will. From tomorrow, he'll be in the Burns Unit.

He looked at the nurse—Get his hair cut. And a shave. Today.

—Yes, Sir.

He made a note on his pad. Then to Dr Naidu—Show me the burns.

Dr Naidu uncovered my right arm, lifting the sheet. The arm was crooked.

Dr Chari grabbed it and yanked. The arm remained crooked.

—Contracture. He may lose the use of his right arm. Cut away the dead skin.

—How will we get him to the Burns Unit? No skin is left.

Now Dr Chari said with a touch of firmness.

—Then you must come here.

—Yes, Sir.

The burns doctor, the psychiatrist and the cardiac specialist were all trying their best. Whoever asked them questions got no answers. My belief in words had vanished.

Yes, when Kanta gets there in the morning after changing three buses, I do reply to her greeting. Sikandar sees her and shouts—Eight o'clock. Bhainji has come. She's brought bananas for me.

Kanta puts four bananas down near him. She peels one and holds it close to my mouth. I keep my mouth firmly shut. Sikandar peels his and eats it in a single gulp.

—Sikandar is a good boy. Now, feed your elder brother a banana.

Sikandar thought about that, peeled a banana and proffered it.

Sikandar: Bossman, eat it or Bhainji will cry.

I shook my head. Sikandar was enraged.

—Not eating? Don't. I won't eat either. You die. I die.

He swept the bananas off the bed. Then he covered his face and began to cry. Something moved inside me. I touched him with my left arm and said:

—One banana, only one.

Sikandar peeled a banana and fed me with his own hands. The fully-dressed Mr Shimla shouted:

—Sikandar Zindabad.

All the others in the room picked it up: Sikandar Zindabad.

Sikandar looked at his father:

—Bapu, your Sikandar is a smart one. He's well now. Completely well. See. He fed the Bossman a banana.

His father stroked his head.

—My lion-heart, with the Professorji's blessings, you will recover too. Serve him well.

Kanta: Bhai Saahab, where can we find a barber? We've got to get his hair cut.

Harnam Singh: It has to be cut before ten a.m. Dr Chari will be angry. I'll fetch him.

Kanta: Please don't trouble.

Harnam Singh: Let me earn some merit, Behenji. If I serve a teacher, my son will recover. You're a wise woman. You must have heard the saying: *Guru, Gobind dou khade, Kake laagoo paay.**

A short barber entered the room. He was naughtiness personified. His hair, I saw, hung down to his shoulders. His beard surged up to his nose.

Barber: Sir, that will cost a hundred.

---

* This is from a Kabir doha. I offer a rather inadequate gloss. 'If both my guru and God were to appear before me, whose feet should I touch first?' the seeker asks. The answer: 'The guru's, for how else would you have recognized God?'

Harnam: Hey, twenty-five is the rate we fixed.

Barber: That's the hair of five men. My scissors and clippers will be worn down to half.

Harnam looked at my sister. She nodded. The barber slipped another pillow under my head.

Barber: Baabyo, please don't move, not a twitch. Lie there as if you're at attention. Okay. Dilip-cut or Amitabh? I think a Dilip-cut would suit you. The Devdas look.

Kanta: Cut his hair very short.

Barber: Why so angry, Madam? Would I do myself out of business by cutting his hair short? Send for tea. I might even need lunch before I'm done here.

He wrapped me in a white cloth. He began to hop around the bed. The sound of my locks falling on the cloth. My head felt lighter. The scissors worked on.

Sikandar: Don't make the Bossman bald. I won't give you bananas.

The barber put his finger to his lips. Perhaps the hair in the middle of my head was not a pleasing sight. The scissors worked on.

Barber: A bucket of hot water. An empty bucket and a big towel. The star is ready for his shot.

First he clipped my beard with his scissors. Then he soaped me up. And asked:

—Shall I give you Prithviraj Kapoor's moustache out of *Mughal-e-Azam*?

That would frighten everyone off. No one would dare give me an injection.

I shook my head.

Barber: You've taken a vow of silence? How about a moustache like Shatrughan's?

Sikandar: Don't trouble the Bossman or I'll tear a hole in you.

He shaved me, walking all around the bed. Then he washed my head and dried it.

—Behenji, a nice new kurta.

Kanta tried but the kurta wouldn't go on. My right arm was held stiff with rods. The barber cut the kurta in two places and made it a woman's gown and then slipped it over my head. He brought me into a half-sitting position with the help of a pillow.

—What a handsome man. May the Guru spare him.

Kanta tried to give him a hundred rupee note.

—Give me twenty-five, Behenji.

—You said hundred.

—Can I cheat the sorrowing? No, no. When Bhai Saahab gets well, I shall expect laddoos.

My body felt light. My eyes drifted shut.

Now I began to talk to myself. Was this long darkness a preparation for the future?

How did my grammar go so wrong?

But I am grateful. At least she does not come armed.

Was no option left to me?

Why had my rainforest dried up?

Yes! Now a jungle had sprung up.

Your smile has found a home in me. Your scent haunts my dreams.

Today the clothes are new. The sadness is old.

Rajendra Yadav would have said: I want to lie entwined with you. But my pride, my low pride!

Kanta touched my shoulder and said: Dr Chari is coming.

My monologue ended.

He came in and stopped at the door; the fifteen to twenty doctors who came with him also stopped.

Dr Chari: Where is my patient, Swadesh Deepak?

He smiled. The doctors with him smiled too. Everyone sitting in the room smiled too.

Dr Chari: You look a new man. When you clean the outside of the body, the interior is also cleansed. You haven't greeted me yet.

Deepak: Namaste, Doctor Saahab. Why would you say my insides have been cleansed? I can smell burning corpses.

Dr Chari: Fire always purifies. I was told you're a writer. Give me your books. I'll read them.

Deepak: But I write in Hindi.

Dr Chari: Please do not insult my intelligence. I did Hindi up to the matriculation in Kerala. So give me any two of your books. But I warn you I won't return them. The other doctors will also read them.

He lifted the torn kurta. He looked at my burned chest. With a gloved hand, he touched the rotten flesh. He ordered Dr Naidu—Clean that chest today. Bandage it. Change the dressing every alternate day. It can pose a danger.

—Yes, Sir. If Mr Deepak can be released from restraint...

Dr Chari: Dr Avneet! Is he a violent patient?

Dr Avneet: No, Sir.

Dr Chari: Can you release him? He must come to the Burns Department. It will be difficult to bring all the instruments here.

Dr Avneet: Yes, Sir!

Dr Chari: Mr Deepak! Bend your right arm.

Deepak: This bloody pipe tied to the arm stops every movement.

Dr Chari: This 'bloody pipe' in your arm will save it from becoming useless forever.

He turned to leave, and stopped by the long-nosed nurse.

Dr Chari: Sister, your name?

Nurse: Kuldeep, Sir.

Dr Chari: Sister Kuldeep. No patient is ever ugly and disgusting.

Nurse: Yes, Sir.

The nurse went red. She looked at me with venomous eyes. I realized I had made another enemy. We take revenge on the weak when we are shamed by someone strong. I remembered my days of success, how insignificant women like this one had shuddered and shivered in front of me.

My ropes were untied. A bedsheet was thrown over my upper half. Dr Naidu welcomed me with a smile.

—Our author has arrived. Our sentinel is here.

He moved the sheet aside and explained.

—I am going to cut the dead skin. You won't feel anything. But do not look at the direction I'm cutting in. It may damage your heart.

Behind my back, I would hear the scissors at work.

—Your back was saved; it's only burned in two places.

My neck and chest took a long time. I grew tired. I moved.

—Let's take a break. Go sit outside. I'll see some other patients.

A seven- or eight-year-old Sikh boy. Acid burns on both legs. On his privates too. My own wounds seemed minor.

Kañta: Did it hurt, Kaka?

I shook my head

Kanta: Use words or you'll forget how to speak.

—What do I say? What do I tell you? Words have become enemies. They punish me.

I wanted to catch butterflies

Constant glimpses into another world.

You haunt my dreams in scented clothes.

All time is displaced.

Everything was a dream; everything was also reality.

Dr Naidu called me in again. Now he sat to work on my right arm. He kept nipping off bits of burnt flesh with a small pair of scissors.

The joint became visible. The burnt flesh became a knot. I tried to bend my arm. It would not move. I fell into a reverie. My elder sister asked: Doctor Saahab, will Deepak's arm never move again?

—Of course it will, Mataji. We will operate. And graft some skin. We'll make it new again.

—Will it take long?

—Oh, burns take a long time to heal. The new skin forms slowly. Four or five months, at least.

—How much pain will God inflict on Deepak!

—God never inflicts pain! On the contrary, he saved your brother. What if that filmstar face had burned?

Dr Naidu bandaged my right arm. I was happy when he didn't stick the tube in before covering it up.

He hadn't forgotten. He stuck it in the arm and wrapped it over.

—This pipe gives me a lot of grief. It's torture.

—Right. But it's what will bring that arm back to normal. Dr Chari's orders. You don't know him. I do. He's a volcano.

Dr Naidu looked at my bandaged torso and smiled—You've become Spiderman.

Kanta: Why have you bandaged up half his body?

Doctor: The air, Mataji, the very air. Germs have a great friendship with the air. Now you must come every alternate day.

We came back to the ward. The patients and their relatives were staring, owl-eyed, at us. Sikandar spoke up—They've wrapped Bossman up in a whole bolt of cloth. He's going to feel so hot.

—Yes, son. You get a cooler for him from home.

—Great idea.

Sikandar was happy. He began to eat a banana. Without anyone asking, people tell you their tales of woe. And others listen with attention and sympathy. The room was like a family.

A patient with curly hair shook his head constantly. His father, sitting by him, told us his story:

—My son was always watching TV. And so his head began to shake. He's an engineer in Delhi.

Sikandar: No, Masterji. He must have started shaking his head while watching TV. Nothing wrong with him. Take him home.

Masterji's tale of woe was left incomplete.

Kanta: Tired, Kaka?

I nodded.

Kanta: Have some milk and then sleep.

—To Hell with milk.

Kanta: Don't drink if you don't want. But why speak in English?

My eyes began to close. I was returning to my rainforest.

Maybe I fell asleep. Maybe I dozed. Out of habit, I began to talk to myself.

—Now there is to be no hearing of my case.

—I must prepare for a dark future.

—I am grateful. At least Mayavini does not come armed.

—Now I will have to spend the rest of my life in the rainforest; no option left.

—All I did was to let anger govern me. And for that a lifetime sentence.

—The doctor said: Mental patients live longer lives. They have no stress.

When Julius Caesar conquered England without much of a fight, he sent his wife a three-word letter. *Veni, vidi, vici.* (I came, I saw, I conquered.) Was she my Julius Caesar?

W.B. Yeats: 'It must go further still; that the soul must become its own betrayer, its own deliverer, the one activity, the mirror turn lamp.'

My sister touched my shoulder. I came out of my rainforest.

—Food's here. Eat something.

—No. I've decided to starve to death.

—Then I won't eat either.

—Don't.

—I won't come to the hospital from tomorrow.

—Don't come.

Sardar Harnam Singh must have made some kind of gesture. She was quiet.

Sikandar: Bossman, have a bit of roti.

—No. I want to die.

Sikandar: It's a difficult road. When you die, take me with you. Why should I live? My father won't get me married either.

Mr Shimla: He is not hungry. Nobody dies of hunger. Gandhi fasted so many times but never died.

The Nodder: Oye, don't flash your English at us. One day I'll just squish your neck. Are you some kind of British afterbirth?

Mr Shimla's Father: Now, now young man. No rages, no rages. After all, you're not well.

—Okay, I'm ill. But why are you always mocking the patients? Control your strong man there. Or I'll...

Father and son stepped out to smoke beedis. My sister refused to eat. That angered me. She was going to try and blackmail me, was she? The patients and their attendants began to doze.

I looked at my sister.

—What do you want?

—I want to go to the toilet.

—I'll get a bedpan.

—No. The toilet.

—I'll come. How will you untie your pyjama string with one hand?

—Geeta has put elastic in them.

She helped me up. Harnam Singh advised: Behenji, go with him. Stand outside.

When I was on the pot, the tube tied to my arm was outside the stall.

The door wouldn't close. Even art films have bigger toilets.

—Kanta, the door won't close.

—Leave it open, Kaka. I'm standing here.

When I had finished, I picked up the water container. It fell over and rolled to the back.

I half-turned. I lost my balance and fell over. I put one hand on the seat to get up. My hand went into the shit. I lifted it up. I half sat on the seat. One of my buttocks in the shit. I pulled up my pyjamas with the soiled hand. It got dirty. Fire erupted from my soles and reached my head. I dragged myself up. I supported myself on the door. It got dirty too. I looked at Kanta.

—I will not stay in this hospital. My hand is covered with shit. My hips are covered with shit. Take me home. I will jump from the fifth storey and kill myself. You smile. My painting is complete. There is no greater sorrow than to recall a time of happiness when in misery.*

Kanta called Harnam Singh.

—Harnam Singh. Attention. Stand still. Otherwise I will court-martial you. Bloody writer. Body covered with shit. Soul covered with shit. The joker wants to save me. I am happy in my own Hell.

Harnam Singh: Silence. Not a word. No English. That long-nosed nurse will tie you up again.

—The pipe. This pipe. I'm going to pull it out.

With all the strength in my left hand, I pulled the pipe out.

I turned. I stopped. I pulled. As the pipe came free, the skin on the back of my hand and wrist peeled away. Drops of blood.

Harnam Singh: Behenji, bring a towel and soap. A clean towel too. We'll have to bathe him.

He sat me down on the threshold of the bathroom. He opened the taps. The filth began to fall off. He soaped me thrice. Rinsed me. Took a look at my back.

Harnam Singh: All clean. Please don't speak English. Poor Behenji went pale.

He led me into the room.

Mr Shimla: Were you covered in shit?

I went to his bed. I roared:

---

* Dante Alighieri in *The Divine Comedy*. I have not been able to locate the translator.

—Bastard, stand up when you speak to Colonel Surat Singh.*

He sprang up. I took over the life of one of my characters.

—My name is Surat Singh. Colonel Surat Singh. Presiding officer of this general court martial.

The truth is always a live coal on your palm. Only once have I been unable to make the leap.

—Speak, you dog, speak. Congress, car, house, dog.

Lady Longnose came in. I swept my hand over the things on the table. Glasses broke. Bottles broke. Lady Longnose's face betrayed an eager excitement. The hunter had spotted the prey. She ordered the male attendants who were standing around:

—Tie him up. Big writer he thinks himself.

They tied me up, good and proper. The bearded Sunder respects me greatly.

—Saahab, I've tied you very loosely. You can move about a bit. Who knows what age-old enmity this nurse has for you?

I looked at Kanta. What pain my sister, a mother to me, must be feeling.

She opened the thermos—Drink some tea. And then close your eyes.

—No.

Mr Shimla spoke in Hindi for the first time—Even on a fast, you can drink tea or juice. Gandhi himself said so.

I drank some tea.

The Nodder said—Veer, how beautifully you speak Hindi. It sounds so good when you speak it.

The bath had probably made me feel weightless. My lids were heavy.

Sikandar: Bapu, when the Bossman gets angry, he might even beat me.

Bapu: No, son, the Bossman only hurts himself.

* This is a character from Swadesh Deepak's play *Court Martial.*

Sikandar: Fine. Give him a banana.

I entered my rainforest.

Kanta: Chachaji, he's been angry since his birth.

Harnam Singh: That's not anger; it's taish, a storm of rage. When a man loses it in anger, it's called taish. When a man loses control, we call it taish, a storm. A storm.

THE FUTURE

Nadira Babbar was celebrating the twentieth anniversary of her theatre group, Ekjute. She phoned. Geeta answered. I have no idea why Geeta and Nadira always speak in English.

Nadira asked after me. Geeta responded immediately: He is perfectly all right.

Geeta handed me the phone.

Nadira: Swadeshji, your wife has given you a fitness certificate. Now just come along. We've done seventy shows of *Court Martial*. And you haven't seen one!

Me: How do I come alone?

Nadira: Bring some beautiful friend along. I hear you have a fairy at your command these days. Her fragrance has wafted all the way to Bombay.

Me: I'll come by train. I'm afraid of aeroplanes.

She hung up. I said to Geeta—Don't make such definitive statements. Now I will have to go.

That morning of the seminar I got to Prithvi Theatre early.

Seeing so many familiar faces made me happy: Usha Ganguly, M.K. Raina, Dinesh Thakur, Deepa Sahi, Kirron Kher and some unknown ones too. Amal Allana, Prasanna, Govind Nihalani, Mahesh Bhatt and Dr Namwar Singh.

Nadira hugged me in greeting. I teased her:

—How bright and sparkly you look today.

Nadira: Thank you. Were it my age to blush, I should.

Usha took my face in both hands and said: Swadeshji, you're looking better and healthier than before.

The period of seven years evaporated. Usha introduced me to Amal Allana:

Amal: When you come to Delhi, do meet me. Let us do your play together.

Me: Your father Alkazi Saahab loves me very much. He goes through my manuscripts of plays.

Amal: I know. He often talks about you. He was greatly disturbed in your dark days.

M.K. Raina's voice resounded—Swadesh, are you going to spend all your time flirting? Come meet your own kind.

Raina is always full of enthusiasm; its source is the Gaumukh. He introduced me to Prasanna. I could clearly see that Prasanna had a clever vetaal seated on his face. I did not want to talk to him.

I wished Dr Namwar Singh. This was our first meeting, I think. The warmth inside him touched me.

—Now you are completely well, Swadeshji!

—What do you think?

—People love you. Their love has helped you recover. Sheilaji had indicated as much to me.

—My good luck. I suppose.

—No, it is because you write well. I spoke on Doordarshan about your play, *Sabse Udaas Kavita*.

Almost everyone in the theatre world was on the stage at Prithvi Theatre. Mahesh Bhatt, Govind Nihalani and other film people were also there. Nadira called me up. I refused. I prefer to sit in the audience.

Atul Tiwari was the compère. He speaks too sweetly. I feel afraid. I don't like it. His stomach was out to here, as if he were in the ninth month of pregnancy. Nihalani and Bhatt are his gods. He's a dialogue writer, after all.

Bhatt read out something written in English. Everyone laughed a lot. Actually he said nothing about the play.

I thought—Bloody good joker.

A doctor spoke, an actress spoke, a journalist spoke. And as if that were not enough, even Pushpa, the wife of Dr Dharamvir Bharati, spoke. She went on about *Andha Yug*, a play of the kind that has never been written in any language anywhere in the world. She actually began to weep. No one took her hand and led her back to her seat. People have grown used to this act. The morning session was delayed because of this. Atul called upon Dr Namwar Singh to preside.

Nadira: You haven't asked Swadeshji to speak.

Atul: I forgot. Because Swadeshji chose to sit in the audience.

I went up on the stage. Applause. Nadira had completed seventy shows at Prithvi Theatre. The grenade in my head began to slide around.

Swadesh: I was invited here from Ambala by Nadiraji. Some of the people who spoke had no relationship with the play at all and Tiwari Saahab forgets to invite me on stage. Perhaps I am an object to be seen. Here I am now, for a minute, standing in front of you. Take a good look.

I was silent. The audience called—Go on then, Swadeshji. Speak! Speak!

Nadira: Swadeshji, I forgot. Forgive me.

Swadesh: It was a deliberate act by Atul Tiwari. He has not apologized as yet.

Prasanna: This language of abuse, you...

Swadesh: Where have you heard any abuse yet, Mr Prasanna? I'm Punjabi. And don't dare intervene and interrupt!

Namwarji: First, let Swadeshji speak. Then you may speak.

Swadesh: Atul used insulting language to demean women and the audience. What of the audience? he asks; you can plonk them down wherever you want, as one would a wife. Anyway, they remain in darkness. When Atul does not know the language of theatre, he should not use it. An idiot does not become a sage because he's a compère on the stage. The darkness of a theatre or a cinema is a technical requirement. How can he compare that to a wife being kept in the dark? I wish your wife were here in the audience. She'd teach you a thing or two with a chappal in her hand...

Rajendra Gupta, the actor, said—The author of *Court Martial* would speak thus.

Thunderous applause.

M.K. Raina: Swadesh, that's enough. Your health won't permit...

Atul: Swadeshji, I want to apologize...

Swadesh: I do not accept your apologies. Your tail wags all the time.

Namwar Singh: By protocol, he who presides speaks last. Now when everyone seems to be speaking out of turn, I think I should intervene. Prasanna interrupted Swadesh. So, for him, this story. The Heavens are home to countless gods. They often have disagreements. Brahmaji is asked to adjudicate. Whatever his decision, after he has heard both sides, must be obeyed. Today, Prasanna seems to be playing the role of Brahma.

Applause and laughter.

Namwar Singh: Now a word of advice to Atul. You must expand your horizons. You have said twice that our literature has no mention of acting, of abhinaya. This is not only a myth but also an offensive lie about our literature. Read Bharatmuni's Natya Shastra. If you have read it, read it again. Chapters eight and nine are about acting. He speaks about four different kinds of acting. And now about forgetting to invite Swadesh Deepak to speak. At this point he is the only playwright seated among us. He has written *Court Martial* and *Sabse Udaas Kavita*. I say this to refresh your memory. It seems neither appropriate nor natural to forget him.

Now Namwar Singh turns to me. An unaffected smile. Peaceful. Gentle words. The energy of a fakir. When this man is so straightforward, why did he become a critic? He should have been a balladeer.

Namwar Singh: And now I would like to say something to Swadesh Deepak. I am not a close friend but I will say this. In Urdu, we have a saying: *Jab hum taish mein aa jaayein, toh Khuda aur maashuq donon se dar nahin lagtaa.* (When a man is in a rage, he fears neither God nor the beloved.)

He sat down.

Continuous applause.

A few months after returning home, I called Dr Namwar Singh in Delhi. Doctor Saahab, I said proudly, as if asking for his approval: Now I have control over myself. I do not get angry at all.

Namwar Singh: Rubbish. That's wrong. Do not change an iota. Stay as you were. When you are your natural self, you are at your best.

THE PRESENT: PGI, CHANDIGARH

My eyes open. Geeta is on the stool by the bed. After feeding the kids in Ambala, she comes here. By the time she gets home, it's night. On the bus, drunk men try to touch her body. She told me this only after I got home. Prabhu has given her a lovely skin. No alcohol is needed as an inducement to want to touch it.

Geeta: Tied up again?

I nod.

Geeta: Why not give up anger?

—A leopard never changes its spots.

Geeta: Kanta Didi told me everything. No wonder you got angry.

—I am a stranger in a foreign land.

Geeta: Didi said you haven't eaten. Will you let me feed you?

—A beautiful woman never asks for advice; she destroys you or is destroyed.

Geeta proffers a piece of roti she has dipped in the vegetables.

I opened my mouth. Sikandar applauds. He ate. The Bossman ate. Give me a banana.

Geeta: Is the roti cold?

—I don't know.

—You are fortunate in your ignorance.

—I was looking for the house of wine. What did I find? Matthew Arnold:

> Wandering between two worlds, one dead,
> The other powerless to be born...
>
> ('Stanzas from the Grande Chartreuse')

Dr Avneet Sharma came on evening rounds. He was shocked to see me restrained. He asked loudly—Who tied Mr Deepak up?

Lady Longnose: I did, Sir.

—Don't you know a patient can only be tied up on doctor's orders? Untie him. Right now. Never do it again.

Now the cold war with Lady Longnose will be a long one.

Avneet: What did you do, Mr Deepak?

—I was reciting lines from a play of mine.

Avneet: Begin rehearsals at once. Let's do a play in PGI.

—No. Useless. Shakespeare told me yesterday:

> Life is a tale told by an idiot
> Full of sound and fury,
> Signifying nothing.*

Avneet (to Geeta): Madam, bring Parul and Sukant to see him once or twice a week.

Geeta: They're too little.

Avneet: Children are never too little. They should meet their father. They should know the truth; they should face reality.

Sikandar: Doctor, my father doesn't give me bananas.

---

* The lines from Shakespeare's *Macbeth* read: 'Life's but a walking shadow, a poor player / That struts and frets his hour upon the stage / And then is heard no more. It is a tale / Told by an idiot, full of sound and fury, / Signifying nothing.'

Avneet: Four a day are quite enough. Or you might end up with constipation. Then we'll have to stick this tube in your backside. An enema.

Sikandar: I won't ask then. I won't eat even one.

Avneet: No, Sikandar. You eat four bananas. No harm in that.

Sikandar was happy. He asked for a banana.

Geeta: Dr Avneet Sharma said it was important to get a phone installed.

—I hate this instrument.

Geeta: The phone is not a woman that you must hate it.

—You left your smile in my mind.
My dreams smell of you.

Geeta: Whom do you talk to at night? Didi told me that you keep talking at night...

—I practice speaking.

Mayavini is a secret and a secret she will remain.

Geeta: You don't want to speak Hindi today?

—No. I am English.

Geeta: Should I bring Sukant? He wants to meet you.

—No. No. No.

Geeta: You wrote somewhere that three Nos cancel out.

—I want to sleep.

Geeta: So should I go?

—Yes. Don't let anyone come here to visit. Don't inform anyone except Sheila Sandhu. Not even Soumitra.

I entered my rainforest.

My clothes were new, my sorrows old.

Do the ghouls live in our conscience, not outside it?

Wrapped in blankets of silence and darkness, a tree said: She will come today.

A new jungle has been settled in my house.

I became a resident of two worlds. I am now only rags and scraps.

I was unsuccessful in my own defence. On my hands, locks of ice. I was being invited to dinner in a quagmire.

The disease causes many thorns to spring up in one's brain. There is a machismo in suffering in silence.

I still remember the red curves of her lips.

As time passes, pain becomes part of one.

When will you come?

My sister touched my shoulder to wake me up. In one hand ten pills, in the other a glass of water.

—First, take the pills. Then tea. I have to leave early today. Ajay will come in the night.

—Ajay who?

—My son and your nephew!

Kanta would pop a pill into my mouth and follow it with water. After a while, both stopped. The matron in charge of the ward and the other nurses had come in. This was the first time I saw her. Her features were melting. She looked the image of Mother Teresa.

Matron: Put them all in your mouth at once, Professor Saahab. Or you'll spend the day swallowing pills.

My sister: What if they get stuck?

Matron: They won't. The gullet expands and contracts according to need. Okay, give him half.

Kanta stood there confused. The matron divided up the remaining pills and picked up half.

—Mr Deepak, keep your head completely still on the pillow. I'll put the pills in your mouth and then the water. Half raise your head. They'll all go down in one gulp.

Which is what happened. Not a single pill got stuck.

Kanta gave me the rest. Once more, one gulp. Not a single pill got stuck.

Matron: Now he won't do anything. He'll make you sit by him.

—After fifteen minutes. I want to close my eyes.

—Sure. The ward boy will take you to the room.

Kanta left. The ward boy shook my shoulder.

The nurse who was on duty for the first time in the room said:

—Your wife had come. She left. You were sleeping. We didn't wake you.

I was shocked. Had Geeta turned back halfway?

—That couldn't have been my wife.

—No? She placed her hand on your head.

—Putting a hand on a man's head doesn't make you a wife.

The nurse flushed.

Sardar Harnam Singh came to my aid—*Turbyoonwali* Renu Bhainji had come.

I (to the nurse): That's Renuka Nayyar, editor of the *Daily Tribune*. She's responsible for me when I'm in Chandigarh. But she scolds me.

Nurse: Why does she scold?

—It's her hobby.

The nurse smiled. Sunder led me by the hand into Dr Verma's room. He was totally bald. No expression on his face. He signals me to sit down. My arms are bandaged. My hands dangle. He lifts up one arm. Puts it on the table. It was then that I saw that there were many pieces of wood of different sizes and shapes on the table.

Dr Verma: You must join up these pieces of wood.

—Why break them at all if they are to be joined up?

—For you to join up.

—It is stupid. I won't do it.

—Nothing is stupid in this universe. If you join them up, we will know whether your brain is developing in the direction it is supposed to.

With my hand, I scattered the pieces. I moved them about at random. By coincidence, a couple joined up.

Dr Verma: Fine. We'll join the rest up tomorrow. Now you will fill up a form.

He gave me a form. It was very long, a four-page booklet. I looked at it and then returned it to him—I'm not going to do this. Too long. Too difficult.

—You can fill in your name. Someone will walk you back to your room.

—I can go. I know the way.

—When do we ever know the way?

And Dr Verma's voice was suddenly sad.

Harnam Singh: Professor Saahab, I'm going down. Sikandar wants milky tea. Shall I get you some?

—No, I don't drink milky tea.

—Have you ever tried it?

—No.

—You should try it before you refuse it.

Shimlawala: Uncle, bring me some too.

Noddy: There you go, talking English again.

Shimlawala: Sorry, I made a mistake.

Noddy: Forgiven.

Someone came into the room. An impressive personality. A sunny smile. One of the few elderly people on whom white hair looks good. He has come to meet me. Who can he be?

—I am Virendra Mehendiratta.

I force myself to remember.

Harnam Singh: He finds it difficult to remember people.

Mehendiratta: You've forgotten, as if there was never anything between us. You live alone in your frightening and desolate world. May I remind you? Every month I have a literary salon in my home. You read your story 'Jai Hind'.

I found a thread of memory.

—Dr Virendra Mehendiratta!

—Forget the 'doctor'. I've retired.

He took a spoon from the table and opened a box he'd brought with him.

—What is it?

—Stew. Kanta* made it with her own hands. Should I introduce her now? She is my wife.

—What is stew?

—First one crushes apples. Then one boils them. And you get a stew.

—I won't have any.

—You don't need to have it all. Just two spoons. Kanta will be disappointed. She loves you so much.

He put a spoonful in my mouth. It was rather good. I drank the lot.

—Good things are always good. Swadesh, tell me what time I should come in the evening?

—No need to come at all. I don't want anyone to talk to me.

—More than the disease, it's the loneliness, the isolation that makes hospital life difficult. Maybe you don't know it but I was a patient at PGI for months.† Let's agree on one thing, we won't talk about your illness at all.

That made me happy.

—Have you told Krishnaji?

Mehendiratta knows that Krishna Sobti is a good friend of mine.

—No. No. No one else either.

—You have always been tough. When I come tomorrow, we'll walk in the verandah a little. I'll tell you stories. Don't be afraid. I won't tell you the stories I write. Now close your eyes.

I did. For a long time, he stroked my head. I did not know when Virendra Mehendiratta left. For the next five months he would come to see me without fail.

---

* Virendra Mehendiratta is a noted short story writer in Hindi. His wife Kanta Mehendiratta is also a scholar of Hindi literature.

† In 1970, Virendra Mehendiratta suffered an attack of porphyria. His wife's dedicated nursing got him through it.

Someone near my bed. I opened my eyes. Renuka Nayyar.

—Have you come here to get well or to sleep? Whenever I come, you're sleeping.

Renu shouts at me more than Geeta does. Sometimes Geeta uses Renuka as a medium for her lectures.

—What did the doctors do today?

—Nothing. Made me join some pieces of wood.

—You? Joining things? You've always broken them. Do one thing. When you're well, write a love story with a happy ending.

—Love stories never have happy endings.

Renu was silent. She has her own sorrows.

—Sikandar Kaka, there should be a knife under your pillow. Would you pass it please?

—What will you do it with it, Bhainji?

—I'll kill your Bossman. He makes everyone's life miserable.

—Then I won't give it to you.

—No, idiot. I'm going to peel apples and feed both of you.

—I'll just eat mine without peeling.

—Ah the young! Deepak's teeth are old now. First, where's your father? Let's all have tea.

Wherever Renu goes, she opens her bag and spreads a fistful of happiness around her. The silent begin to speak, the depressed come out of isolation; I had called her Prasannata Devi, The Goddess of Happiness. I never told her though.

She put a piece of apple into my mouth. I do not have the courage to refuse her.

—Listen, I know what you must be brooding about lying here all day unemployed. I've lost my job, you're thinking. You're wondering how I'll manage. Don't worry at all. When the time comes, I'll handle it all. I earn enough to run two households.

—So you will give me alms.

—No, you stinker. I'll do it out of friendship. Why do

men always take it as a personal affront if a woman wants to help them?

—My mistake.

—That's one thing I like about you. You don't try and argue your way out. Otherwise where do men admit that they're wrong, especially in a discussion with a woman? Never mind that. Which of your lady loves should I tell?

—They're all abroad.

—So what? They'll have rich husbands. They'll come by air. Who would let someone like you go?

I thought I should tell Renu about Mayavini. No. This is our personal secret. Some secrets cannot be shared, nor revealed.

—I'm off. I have an editorial to write. Shall I bring you cigarettes tomorrow?

I shook my head.

—Well, that's one good thing that came out of you being hospitalized. Or your chimney would be on all day.

Renu left. But she left a fistful of joy behind her.

Lights out at nine p.m. Before that Avneet Sharma arrives.

—Tomorrow you're scheduled for a CT scan. Nil by mouth.

—What's a CT scan?

—An x-ray of the brain. The neurologists want to see if your brain cells are damaged.

—Is this the final curtain?

—No, this is your beginning. Let me give you some good news. The clouds are dark. It's going to rain. We'll have some relief from the heat.

—The rains! She will surely come when it rains.

Dr Sharma was immediately alert.

—Who will surely come?

What could I say? What did I really know of this? She

is disembodied. She is invisible. What can be said of her? A supernatural presence?

Dr Sharma: Mr Deepak, in psychiatry it is the patient who speaks, who reveals things, not the doctor. Unlike other doctors we have no blood tests to help us. If you tell your dark secrets, I will try to understand them. And perhaps then you will be freed. Sharing with the doctor is the only way out. Perhaps you don't know that I have an MD in Psychiatry. I chose my specialization because I read literature. A book is a window opened into another person's head. But you have been hiding things right from the beginning. How can I help you? How will you be cured? You are a writer. You owe it to society. Think about this a little. God bless you. Good night.

Lights out. But they burn on the balcony still. I said to Sikandar—Listen Sikandar, I will make you Prime Minister tomorrow.

—Tomorrow. For now, Bossman, you should sleep. They're checking your brain tomorrow.

Bars on the windows. Nets too. Patients have jumped from here to their deaths. How will you die, Swadesh Deepak? A dappling of light came through the windows.

I will complain to Sheila Sandhu. But of whom?

Has my soul become paralysed? I will rest my head on her thigh. The silence of the night! Grenades bursting. Memory bursting. Memory in pieces. Who tied a talisman on my wrist? Why did it fail to protect me?

Give me my slate. I shall practise the alphabet.

The long-distance walker is dry. That is inevitable.

Do not protest. Die. Death is liberation.

Why wait for what is extinct? Now remain in the half-light. There is no ferryman. One must row one's own boat.

Make me a multi-coloured butterfly, no?

When do we dine in quicksand?

I froze before the blow fell.

Plant me a new jungle. I am the guard of incomparable sights.

Why are you deaf to my screams? You bloody bitch.

Krishna Sobti scolds me—Sleep now, you well-born bastard. Tomorrow is the day of judgment.

I was frightened. I dozed. The sound of footsteps. Three sets of footsteps. One sat down in front of me, one to my right, one to my left. Face half concealed by a white sari.

Someone put down a painting from my friend Jehangir Sabavala's mystery series in the room.

—You thought of Jehangir Saahab, didn't you?

I was frightened. How did she know? The fear vanished. She knew everything.

—I have brought two doppelgangers with me. Because you don't seem to obey one Kaamna. Today you got angry again. This rage will take your life one day.

—You've already taken it. All that is left is this disgusting body. But no complaints. *Jaan de di; di hui jiski thi** (I gave my life; but only to the one who gave it to me).

—That's Mirza Ghalib.

—You recognize the lines?

—What don't I know? These days I pray: Prabhuji, erase the storehouse of my memory.

—Uncover your face. When you leave, I will remember and curse you.

She moved her sari from her face. I felt myself begin to shine too.

—Why no earrings? A crooked nose would improve your face.

—As a little less anger might improve your personality, but how to do that? Your feudal thinking gets in the way. You want a love-slave. And the first move must be the man's.

---

* In most versions, this is: '*Jaan di; di hui usi ki thi / Haq toh yun hai ki haq adaa na hua*'.

What an innocent sentence I said: I want to see Mandu with you. But the feudal man inside you took offence and emerged. Poor me, I could only dream on. How could I ever be a friend of yours?

—That was my mistake.

The room turned into a church, my words into confession. I could feel clearly the onset of redemption. Now I would not die.

The rain began to come down. The sky poured it out in buckets.

I told Mayavini:

—You will get wet.

—Water cannot wet me; fire cannot burn me.*

—You have devastating beauty.

—How could it start raining like that?

—The clouds have stripped naked.

She looked at me without words. Abruptly, she rose. She kissed my forehead again and again. And she wept continually.

—Swadesh, my Swadesh. You are a magician of words. Why couldn't I have you? Damn you. And damn your temper.

I do not know how long she kept this up.

I do not know when her doppelgangers vanished with her.

After years, I slept the sleep of the just.

After years, I slept without nightmares.

* This may be an allusion to the Bhagwad Gita on the soul.

6. There's a Magic to Women

I screamed with my eyes.

—Love comes in through the window and leaves by the door.

—Women are stubborn. They get what they want.

—Like Hamlet, I am suspended between to-be and not-to-be. Why is there no method in my madness? I am the king of rags.

—I am waiting. But for whom?

—Take all my sunshine. But no low blows.

—I was narcissistic. I have been filleted by your infallible weapons.

—When we love, we turn cowardly.

—Love and war are similar; if you lose, you're a prisoner of war.

No more epigrams. Who is it, up so early in the morning? My younger brother, Billu.

—Veerji, I have to go to Jaipur. The bank won't grant me any more leave.

—Go.

—Veerji, you're like my father and my God. Tell me if you need anything.

—I will.

—When you get well, I want you to come to Jaipur. I have a friend who has a farmhouse. You can stay there.

—Any lions and leopards there?

—Farmhouses have humans, not wild animals.

—There are humans here as well! Why go there? How can I live with them? I am in vanaprasthaashrama.

—Geeta Bhabhi said she'd be a little late. She'd called.

—Why?

—Today is your CT scan. They are going to x-ray your brain.

—Will they tear open my head?

—I don't know. May I go, Veerji?

—Go. Don't come again.

Billu left. Sikandar got up and came to stand by my bed.

—Bossman. Don't speak English today. You'll get angry. Then that witch will tie you up again. How will they x-ray you?

—I won't speak English.

—If you're ever afraid, take the name of Waheguru in your heart.

Kanta arrived. Sikandar began to chant.

—She's here, she's here, Bhainji, it must be eight. My bananas.

Kanta gave him four bananas. I was to be given nothing.

—I'll eat three. One for Veerji after his x-ray.

Geeta came. She must have got up very early. Parul-Sukant had to be provided for; breakfast and dinner. Her face was desolate. A face without a home. Dr Avneet Sharma arrived. Geeta had a book in her hand.

They began to prepare me psychologically—The CT scan machine is huge. It's as broad as a water pipe. I looked at a dictionary in the morning. It looked like a huge drain pipe. They lie you down in it. A button is pushed. Half your body enters the tube. And your brain is x-rayed. It'll take a few seconds. Do you want to ask anything?

—What has happened to me? What disease do you...?

—We do not disclose the name of the disease in psychiatry. It's enough to say you have a mental illness. In your case, it seems as if your personality has been split into two. One part will not obey the other. And this leaves you without direction. Those who suffer from this no longer want to meet those they love; they hate talking to them. They live in a state of constant terror. Everything is an unending nightmare. That's when someone else turns up by their side. And they begin to talk to them.

Geeta said in a frightened voice—It sounds like a very strange and difficult disease.

Avneet: Neither strange nor difficult. But we need the patient's cooperation. Deepakji is not helping us. In psychiatry, the patient speaks and we listen. He's hiding something. He won't open even a tiny window to let us peep in. We are helpless.

Before I could say a word, Mayavini said in my ear: Say nothing. We will become impure.

I said nothing.

A crowd outside the room. All oddballs. Four benches in the verandah. On all of them, patients lying down. The people with them looked at me, astonished. No head wounds, two women with him. What is he doing here? When someone joins a crowd, those who are already there resent him. Maybe his arrival will delay our turn. I leaned on the wall and we waited for an hour, standing there. On one side, Kanta; the other, Geeta. An hour passes. Thirst.

—Water.

Kanta: No, my beloved son, no water for you.

I am in Rajasthan now. In the vortex of a sand dune. I began to dig a well. Someone has stolen my camel. As much sand as I dig out, the sand-soaked wind drops back into the hole. I keep digging, for hope is a bitch; it keeps the possibility of getting something alive. I am now in a folk tale by Vijaydan Detha.* My death is predestined.

I ask Faiz Saahab: *Janaab, shaam-e firaaq aa toh gayi; talti kyon nahin?* (Sir, the night of separation came at last; why does it not pass?)†

In a voice that was barely audible, he said that for the likes of me, the time of separation from the beloved would be long and pain-flecked.

---

* Vijaydan Detha's renditions of Rajasthani folk tales are available in English translation and have formed the basis of films like *Duvidha* (1973), *Charandas Chor* (1975), and *Paheli* (2005).

† A reference to Faiz Ahmad Faiz's famous ghazal: '*Shaam-e firaaq ab naa pooch, aayi aur aake tal gayi / Dil tha ki phir bahal gaya; jaan thi ki phir sambhal gayi*' (The night of parting came, and having come, it passed; / My heart recovered and my world settled back into place).

Three hours.

The doctor opens the door a crack and calls someone else's name, not mine. She is my enemy. A woman, after all.

—I want a glass of water.

Kanta was startled; then her face turned to stone.

—Kaka, don't speak English. Not a word. If you do, I'll leave right now. And I promise on my son, I will never see your face again. You will only see my face in death.

Her patience is infinite. She must change three buses from Panchkula to come and see me. Her five-year-old granddaughter must be left in the charge of neighbours. Perhaps her hope has now been shaken. From where did she acquire such long-suffering patience?

The old man sitting near Kanta said to her:

—There's no use getting angry at the ill. It's not their fault, is it? He has been standing there since morning. From all over the Punjab, Haryana and Himachal Pradesh, accident cases come here. The emergency cases who have serious head injuries are given preference. Because they must often be operated on immediately.

As soon as he said the word 'emergency', I knew he was Indira Gandhi's stooge. I was terrified.

Geeta: What he has brought upon himself! And upon us!

Kanta: Prabhuji makes these decisions. How brave he was. As a child he never cried, no matter how badly he was hurt. Remember when our father died? His eyes were dry, even as he lit the pyre. And our father was his friend. Our mother yearned to see him weep so she could console him, but her wish was never fulfilled.

They brought the warrior back to the house of death.

A warrior is cold and hard as stone outside, but inside as well.

A horse, a horse, for my kingdom.* Richard III's plea when his horse is killed under him in battle echoes down the

* Shakespeare's line: 'A horse, a horse! My kingdom for a horse!'

centuries. When I was very young, a woman raped me. I have only told Krishna Sobti this incident. The magician of language said—Swadesh, even today anyone might want to rape you.

When Mayavini locked me away, I could no longer share anything with Sobti. We were no longer on speaking terms, thanks to Hashmat.

How was that evening of parting, Faiz Saahab? *Aayi aur tal bhi gayi?* It did come and it did pass...but what of my evening? It crawled on, an unending snake. You had once come to Ambala. I met you. I had recited some of your own couplets to you. You were surprised. For people my age were no longer supposed to be able to speak Urdu. They'd begun to study Hindustani instead. When I told you how I came to know Urdu, you burst out laughing. You kissed my forehead and said—Swadesh, you are a handsome scoundrel.

For a while you were silent. Sad too. You warned me of the danger that was imminent.

—You will suffer much at the hands of women. But why fear? Mirza too suffered much. May Allah protect you. But you are fated to suffer.

A true poet can see the future. Faiz Saahab saw it.

... This time the doctor came out of the room. She came up to Geeta: Dr Avneet from the psychiatric ward has called me twice. I do know that Mr Deepak has been standing here, hungry and thirsty, since the morning. I can't help it. There's just been a stream of serious patients.

—I must be a non-serious patient then.

—I am really sorry. I never meant it that way.

—What time does the tiger arrive?

She was shocked. She hurried inside.

Rajendra Yadav is also afraid of my tigers. What had he said once—You must wonder why I haven't used you in my writing. You're the king of the beasts. How many stories with cheetahs, tigers, foxes, vultures? If I were to live in a zoo for a few months, I could write about you. Anyway women are mad about your writing. Do you know why? Because they like animals *and* the writer Swadesh who writes about animals too. How many violent beasts do you have inside you?

I am never offended by what Rajendra says. He starts in jest and ends on a serious note.

—Here you go. Now the ball is in your court.

Virendra Mehendiratta came there. Geeta was startled.

—Doctor Saahab, how did you get to know that Deepak was...

—Deepak's fans find him out. I went to the ward. They told me he was here. An x-ray of the brain. What will they get? We've never got anything all these years.

Kanta: Today has been bad for him. Not a drop since the morning...

Mehendiratta: He may have suffered but I'm sure he's not so much as murmured. Sometimes I believe he has Karna's armour.

He took my hand, pressed it gently. A warmth began to invade my body.

Mehendiratta: Geeta beti, go home. The children have been alone since morning. It will be night by the time you get home.

Geeta: I'll see Deepak back to his room and leave.

By now Mehendiratta knows that Geeta is as good as her word.

—I want to tell you a story by Premchand today.

—Premchand, who?

—Premchand, the first great Hindi writer.

—Where is he now?

—It's been a long time since he died.

—He's lucky. It's those who want to live that are unfortunate.

The doctor came out. She took me by the hand and led me into the room. She put me into a tunnel. The CT scan was taken. From 10 a.m. to seven in the evening. Bloody scan.

Kanta: Kaka, the Red Cross canteen is nearby. Have some tea.

—No.

—Some water?

—No.

Geeta knew I had drawn the pin of the grenade.

She was completely silent. I went into the room and sat on the bed. Avneet came in. He stood quietly by me. He thought a bit. Then he said:

—We'll have to do the CT scan again. The doctor called me. She is not happy with the results.

The lurking cheetah roared. It sprang.

—No. No. No. I should have slept with that bloody woman. She's killing me by inches.

I screamed, a seven-year-long scream. In my soul, a seven-year-long scream of sorrow, trapped. The glass in the windows cracked. As the scream reached Mayavini, it began to pant. The patients shot up in shock. There was a crowd of patients at the door too. I was thrashing about on the bed. Dr Sharma took a glass of water from the nurse's hand. He brought it to my mouth.

I shook my head.

—Drink it. In one go.

Dr Avneet Sharma had never spoken in such stern accents before.

I drank it in one gulp. Sikandar complained—Bossman. I still have the banana that was brought for you in the morning. Please eat it.

Mayavini said in my ear—Why did you scream, Swadesh? I have just brought you a blessing. From Ma Kali's temple. I will come by in the night. Now you seem to like me. So why abuse me—bloody woman? In the night, we'll chat at our ease. Say something.

—We'll talk like T.S. Eliot's women do:

In the room the women come and go
Talking of Michelangelo

('The Love Song of J. Alfred Prufrock')

There is no cure for my malaise, nowhere in the world. The green shoots have dried up in my brain. No birds either.

Once Geeta asked if she should write to Nirmalji. He might come.

Nirmal Verma is the elite author of all elite authors. He does not go the houses of writers who are smaller than him, nor does he call them to his house.

Krishna Sobti's dictionary is free of words like big and small. She listens to everyone as an eager child might. One day, she came over on her way to Delhi. I could not even rise to greet her.

—Sheilaji told me over the phone that I should not come. I thought Swadeshji is not a jailor. And so here I am.

Geeta came out and greeted her. Krishna looked at her closely and said:

—I have seen your nose ring. It shines with a fine light.

Geeta went to get water. Krishna looked at me and smiled. I knew she was going to say something naughty.

—Yaar, to look at her taut body, you'd think you hadn't even raised the wedding veil.

—She's your Mitro Marjani.

—If she had been, she would have eased all your knots and twists.

Krishnaji is clever. She has depth and breadth. Not once did she mention my illness.

She knows one must wrestle with one's own angels. Parul and Sukant came out. They recognized her immediately. It was not that they had read her books. It was her national mourning dress. In good times, I had teased her.

—Krishnaji, more people know you for these mourning clothes than for your books.

—Swadesh Saahab, you're not just a well-born scoundrel but a swine too.

These shameless exchanges did not offend us. Krishnaji is not a Hindi behenji. Once Soumitra had asked:

—Is *Surajmukhi Andhere Ke** autobiographical?

—Every book is autobiographical.

Geeta came out of the kitchen and asked:

—What will you have?

—We bachelors can have no wishes; we eat what we get. I'll have lunch here. I'll carry my dinner to Delhi. Pack me something.

Krishnaji looked into my room, the unpainted walls, the flaking clay, a terrifying poster of Richard Burton in his role as Hamlet and on the other wall, Ma Durga. Nothing else. Krishna did not look at the books.

—It's the room of some destitute feudal overlord.

—May I recite two lines from Adam Saahab?†

—Go on then.

Dil khush hua hai masjidein veeran dekhkar
Chalo meri tarah Khuda ka bhi khaana kharaab hai‡
(I rejoiced to see mosques in ruins
For God's home is as wretched as mine).

Krishna: Have an affair, Deepak. A woman will restore your lost powers.

—I hate them.

—Actually, those we say we hate, we love without limits. This will be beyond you. Because of that he-man image you have of yourself.

---

* This has been translated as *Sunflowers of the Dark* ,by Pamela Manasi (Katha, 2008).

† Deepak refers here to Abdul Hamid Adam (1910–1981).

‡ More ordinarily seen as '*Dil khush hua hai masjid-e-veeran ko dekh kar, / Meri tarah Khuda ka bhi khaana kharaab hai*'.

On the way out, she asked:

—Should I tell Soumitra anything if I meet him?

—Nothing at all. Stop him from coming if he tries.

Krishnaji let loose a barb.

—That job is reserved for your Delhi-based ambassador Sheila Sandhu. If Soumitra asks, I will tell him. It's our friends who hurt for us, not our relatives.

I went back to my jail.

When she put her hand on my head, I knew she had come. After all, she is disembodied. A sari the colour of a red flower in flames. A face as sad as sadness itself.

—I heard your scream 1,573 kilometres away in my city. I felt the glass house inside me first shiver and then crumble. When I looked through your eyes, I bled for you.

—My scream was as long as my suffering.

—You have been washed clean inside. I was frightened, I shrank and I was happy when Ma Kali said: Swadesh is yours. Do not hurt him. Which is why I'm wearing the clothes of a bride.

—If I were Othello...

—You would have strangled me.

—What sanguine happiness there is in killing someone. You are beautiful and you are dangerous.

The moon was visible in the window. What I said angered her.

I was in a state of samaadhi.

That woman was now near me. I asked:

—Where will we go when I am well?

—The Sunderbans. There are lots of tigers there. The house of Royal Bengal Tigers.

—Where will you stay?

—We have a guesthouse there. In the nights, the tigers will roar. I will play the tigress in our room. We will walk away from the world.

Has my death warrant been withdrawn? I could see them. Will they hunt me, those horsemen in the dark river, the ones with their lances raised? Insomnia breeds black dreams. The last rites would be conducted for me. My body would burn. And what would be left of colour and scent?

From your purse, sprinkle a handful of spring on my bed. Look, do not break your promises. I will listen to you roar like a tigress. Eliot said: In my end is my beginning.

Clinging to your hand, I fell asleep. I was in the Sunderbans now.

Dr Chari came with his platoon of juniors.

Dr Naidu gave him the charts. He read them.

—Congratulations, Professor. The wounds on your chest and back have begun to dry up. No bandages there now. But your arm, your right arm...

He turned questioning eyes on Dr Naidu.

—Grafting, Sir.

—It's early. Not now.

—Yes, Sir.

To Lady Longnose:

—From today, six eggs and two kilos of milk a day for him.

—I cannot drink that much milk. I'm not Dara Singh.

—You can. You will. We have our ways to feed you, if you refuse. We will turn you into Dara Singh. I have read five of your stories. You behave in the same terrifying way as you describe in your stories.

I always hated milk. After marriage, Geeta terrorized me into drinking it. But she always added something that changed its colour.

Harnam Singh: A little piece of advice: drink your milk quietly or they'll tubefeed it to you. And that hurts.

Sikandar: Bossman. Don't worry. I'll quietly drink half of it.

I was brought to Dr Verma's room. I greeted him with a Namaste. Something sparkled in his empty eyes for a moment.

—Today we won't join up bits of wood. There's a board on the table with different coloured holes. And there are coloured pegs. Fit the same coloured peg into the hole.

—I've been admitted to the kindergarten apparently.

—Kindergarten is where we all start.

The test wasn't as easy as it seemed. One wrong peg in the wrong socket and you had to start again. And when all the sockets were filled, one was still empty. I began to get angry.

—I really have gone mad. Such a simple game...

—You're not mad. Your concentration is divided. The last peg is in your right fist.

—Why didn't you tell me that in the first place?

—You didn't ask. Asking for assistance is a natural social thing to do.

He came with me to my room. Dr Verma asked:

—Do you believe in God?

—No. But now I believe in doctors.

—Doctors are God's ambassadors.

THE PAST

Faiz Saahab had asked: Young man, how do you know Urdu? You probably studied in Hindustan.

He was staying at Rajendra Malhotra's home. Malhotra has a Wills cigarette agency and is an aficionado of Urdu poetry. He started a Sham-e-Jahaan mushaira in Ambala. He would take part in Indo-Pak poetry festivals. His dogs won prizes at dog shows all over the country. The foreign breeds were kept in air-conditioned rooms.

Nirupama Dutt had come to Chandigarh to cover the event. She came over and said:

—This time I want to write the piece in Hindi. I've even thought of the headline: 'The Man Who Loved Poetry and

Dogs'. But the newspaper people are backward. They will change it.

That desire remained unfulfilled in Niru's heart.

Faiz Saahab came to Ambala. Malhotra sent word asking me to come and see him. He had been surrounded by business types who wanted to talk to him about films. Faiz Saahab was speaking so softly, so slowly that it seemed his words would fall on the floor and splinter. When Malhotra Saahab introduced me as a writer and a professor of English, a spark of hope lit up Faiz Saahab's face.

—Khushwant Singh and many others say you should win the Nobel Prize.

—To go to jail for one's country is the greatest reward of all. Right, tell me this. You have been educated in India. How is it you know Urdu?

I: My father was a scholar of Urdu. He was a friend of Adam Saahab when he lived in Rawalpindi. He was a veritable dictionary of Urdu shaayari.

Faiz: Did he teach you?

I: No, Sir. After Partition, we were in a refugee camp, in Kurukshetra. Father would write messages in Urdu on pieces of paper and send me with them to his lover or mistress. He knew I could not read Urdu. My mother insisted that I should get the letters read by the munshi who sat under the mango tree and then tell her their contents. The wife generally takes revenge on an errant husband through the children. My mother beat me without mercy.

As always, the mango-tree munshi was abusing the Congress. Seeing me, he extended his hand:

—Give it here, let's read what a lover's tears have wrought.

I gave him the sheet of paper. Before beginning the munshi said:

—Kaka, learn to read Urdu from me. Your father is going to have these affairs up to his death. And when I go, who will you get to read them?

He read the message. And shot to his feet. He picked up his slipper.

—Wait, you spawn of sin! In your old age, you dare to write such filth. Me a pandit and your mother…

I: Uncle, tell me what he's saying. Or Ma will beat me.

The mango-tree munshi knew my mother was a demon. He said in a voice of flame.

—The pandit has asked me to give some hair-removal powder. To your father's mistress, that black bitch. She may be black but she can't get enough.

—Uncle, what does hair-removal powder mean?

—Spawn of sin, shall I tell you what it is? It is your mother's head between her legs. Run, you sister-fucker. I'm just going to sit here and abuse the Congress which took away my small home so that it could rule in Delhi.

And so I learned to read Urdu from the mango-tree munshi.

Faiz Saahab burst out laughing. He kissed my head.

—What a beautiful and interesting way to learn a language, but you are also a lovable rascal.

And he became a little sad.

—Swadesh, you will be hurt by women. It is written on your forehead.

—But I don't even look at them, never mind talking to them.

—That is why they will hurt you. God himself shaped women, his finest creation, his Taj Mahal. One looks, one admires, one loves. You are Narcissus. You are fated to suffer at the hands of woman. May Allah protect you.

I should not have smiled; but then these words seemed without foundation.

—Faiz Saahab, should such a time of hopelessness befall me, I will remember you. And my courage will increase.

Dil na-ummeed toh nahin, naakaam hi toh hai
Lambi hai gham ki shaam, magar shaam hi toh hai

(My heart is not without hope, it only lacks agency
What if the evening of sorrows be long? It is still but an evening.)

Faiz Saahab was silent. He was also sad.

THE PRESENT

In the evening, Geeta came, a letter in hand.

Geeta: It's from Rajendra Yadav. He's asking about you, about your illness. The first letter from any author. How did he find out?

For no particular reason, we haven't spoken or corresponded in the last ten years but he will allow no complaints about this nor will he remember it as women would. His heart is unguarded, his tongue sharp.

Me: Rajendra Yadav is omniscient; bad news makes its way to him.

Geeta: Any answer?

Me: Please reply. Say Deepak is fine. Do not come to see him.

Geeta: It surprises me that you don't want to meet even your good friends. You've even warned Sheilaji and Krishnaji not to come.

Me: My kingdom has been looted. Everyone has forgotten me, save for a few. In such memories as I live, I am a storyteller. I do not want anyone to see me in this vulnerable state. I am like quicksilver. I can't even talk. A woman has driven Swadesh mad.

Geeta: Don't let yourself believe in these false dreams. A woman drive you mad? You would drive any woman foolish enough to spend any time with you mad. You are a sadist. A cruel sadist. You cannot strike a balance between pain and pleasure.

Geeta is right. Outside my characters, I cannot share anyone else's pain. Not even my own. Which is why I send people back when they come to visit. Visitors with transparent polythene bags which contain a few apples. Everyone can see that they have brought fruit for the patient. That they've done their social duty.

In these seven years I have not wept nor have I begged for anyone's help. Nor have I written about my terrifying condition to any of my friends. I have wiped out spineless words like 'mercy' and 'misery'. I will die on my own terms. And only then could I draw strength from the line in 'Aatma Vaktavya' ('Soul Statement') by that Sultan of Akavita, of Unpoetry, Soumitra:

Main tumhaari sahaanubhooti par thookta hoon.

(I spit upon your sympathy.)

THE FUTURE

After I was released from the hospital, Soumitra came to Ambala. He had wanted to come earlier but Krishnaji prohibited it. In Delhi, Geeta's brother Brajendra Mehta also stopped him. Geeta's mother told him sternly that Deepakji meets no one. After all, what disease could be greater than love? Was it AIDS? No, Deepak could not have that one. He even hesitates to sleep with his own wife.

My first question was: Written any poems?

Soumitra: No, ever since you disappeared, I haven't written anything. I just didn't feel like it.

No one is as cruel and merciless towards his poetry as Soumitra is. If he gets stuck at a word, the whole enterprise is finished. He often dismisses his own work with his favourite epithet—raddi, waste paper. If only some other poets would establish such censor boards for their own work. Then we would not be subjected to this flood of poetry. Soumitra Mohan is a total poet.

Soumitra: If you will, tell me about it. I'll keep taking pictures.

When I told him about Mayavini, about the seven-year revenge exacted, there was no doubt in his eyes. He always trusts his friends.

Soumitra: I think such a thing is possible, probable even, and this is because you told me about it. But what can be surprising about it? There's a certain magic to women.

Me: But...

Soumitra: But what? The seductress made her romantic approach and you answered with abuse. You've always been afraid of women; you've always run from them. Why? How can I tell? Some kink, I suppose.

Swadesh: But such a terrible, long sentence!

Soumitra: Mayavini let you off lightly. If she wanted, she would have turned you into her baa-lamb and kept you with her. She would have walked ahead with a bunch of green grass and you would have trailed behind after her. Mayavini can do anything.

Soumitra was withdrawing into his ludicrous absurd world of poetry.

THE PAST

After eating and taking some pills, I began to doze. My eyes were open. On the bench to the right was Vikas Narayan Rai.

—I had gone home. Allahabad. I returned last night.

I was silent.

—Did the fire happen by accident or...?

—I set myself ablaze. The fire said: I am your friend. It lied.

Now Vikas was silent.

—Don't come. I hate visitors.

—I will definitely visit. I won't talk. I'll sit here quietly.

Three men came into the room. Healthy men. In the itch-inducing heat of the fag end of September they were in suits with ties. Definitely government cattle. They walked around my bed, surveying me with measuring eyes.

Vikas saw the terror in my face.

Vikas: Who are you?

His soft but firm tones convinced them he was an important officer. He was DIG then.

One: We are from the Haryana Sahitya Akademi.

Two: Our Director Saahab has sent us.

Three: He will come tomorrow. With a journalist and a photographer.

One: He will give Swadesh Deepak economic assistance.

Vikas: How much?

All three: Sir, five hundred rupees.

When he is angry, Vikas's face is expressive but even so he does not raise his voice.

—Clear out, right now. And do not let your director come.

—Yes, Sir.

They left, shoulders slumped.

Vikas: This is the ethos of political power. Your life has been valued at five hundred rupees. No doubt, an ordinary person's life would be five rupees. All these are like Captain Kapoor in your play.

Geeta came in. Vikas gave her a phone number.

—This is my office number. Someone is always on duty at any time of the day or night. If you ever need anything just call. I will explain everything to my reader.

Vikas and Geeta went out to the verandah to talk.

Geeta sees Vikas as my most capable and responsible friend. She came in and took a small comb from her purse and ran it through my hair.

Geeta: Today I'm going to bathe you. And change your clothes.

Me: No, I'm not going to be naked in front of you.

Geeta: Yaar, I've seen you nude often enough.

She smiled a crooked smile. For the first time, I began to feel sure I would get well again.

Geeta's best characteristic is that she says very little.

In her presence, I can still think, I can still slip into my crippled dream world. What does all that I have achieved amount to?

Madness. Tigress. Doctor. Medicine. Terror. Rebirth.

Fear. Lame hopes. Madame Bovary. And. And. And. Lukman Ali.

Dr Chari came, his platoon behind him. Lady Longnose gave him the chart. He looked at it. He grew angry. When he is in a temper, his moustaches quiver.

—Just two eggs and half a kilo of milk. Why?

—I gave them to him. He refused. He's very troublesome.

Dr Chari: You didn't give him anything; the government of India gave it to him. What did you think, a psychiatric patient is going to sing for you? You had better shift him to some other branch. Whatever he eats, even tea or water, must be noted on the chart. I will check every morning.

—Yes, Sir.

The doctors with him were stunned. Dr Chari looked at Dr Naidu.

Dr Chari: Take Mr Deepak to the surgery ward. Show him how patients are force-fed. Do it today.

Dr Chari sat on a stool close by the bed. Deeply sad.

Dr Chari: You have disappointed me deeply. The characters in your stories are so powerful. They are warriors. Our war has not begun and you've thrown down arms. If you refuse the nutrition we give you, your arm will always remain twisted. You will not be able to hold anything. How will you write? How will you brush your teeth? Shave? How will you wash off your shit? How will you eat? Fight back? For God's sake, fight back, Mr Deepak. Give us a fair chance.

When he had gone, all the patients were cowering.

Lady Longnose came in and addressed Geeta. Geeta's face reddened. Her words dripped poison.

—Whenever this man asks for anything to eat or drink, bring him to my room. He will eat in front of me. I have no idea why the doctors think so much of such a disgusting, dirty and ugly man. Some cheap mad writer.

Geeta's face flushed. She could easily have put Lady Longnose in her place but hospitals make cowards of us all.

—Deepu, look at how much disrespect we have to bear because of you.

I got up on the bed. Colonel Surat Singh from *Court Martial* entered the room. One by one, the destructive powers I had had conferred on me at birth began to awaken. I turned into a cheetah. A cheetah, behind a tree, its body shrunk into itself. Before it makes the death-dealing leap, a cheetah pours its power into its limbs, marshals its strength. William Blake's big cat.

Tiger, tiger, burning bright
In the forest of the night.

Lady Longnose marched out. The cat sprang:

—Come back, you bloody bitch. Why is your tongue always suffering from dysentery? If you ever raise your voice, I will strangle you to death. You should know that the law doesn't prosecute psychiatric patients. Doctors don't scold you because you are inefficient. Don't ever think that I will even complain against a worm like you. Get lost...

—I'm sorry. I made a mistake.

—I made a mistake, Sir.

—Sir, I'm sorry.

—So go to your room. Why are you standing here?

She left. Geeta said:

—You shouldn't have abused so much.

—A shoe in the face is the only cure for the wag-tongue.

I fell back into bed. My arms and legs move continuously, like an animal crushed by a bus. It was not totally dead. Dribble on its neck. Kanta wipes it away with a towel. The attendants in the room by the bed. All silent.

—Tell me the address. My home address. I am homeless. Where is my Russian cat? Bring it to me. All the doctors are enemies. I'll beat them when I'm dead. I'll marry Madhubala. Why can't I remember Mrinal Pande's face?

Now time was no longer my interlocutor.

No one has pity for the old and the mad.

Now it would be completely impossible to investigate the self.

The butterflies that live in my soul began to fly away, one by one.

Why did I think of Mir—*Aksar hamaare saath ke beemaar mar gaye.**

Sleep did not come. Nor did Mayavini. Would she now come? Who would create murder and mayhem then?

In the morning, I was tied to the bed. Sikandar said that another doctor had come in the night. He ordered me to be tied up.

—You spoke a lot of English in the night, Baabyo.

Vikas Rai came. Seeing me tied up he asked—Broke some things? Beat someone up?

I shook my head.

Sikandar: The nurse said some rude thing to Bossman here. Babaji got angry in English.

Vikas: Count up to ten when you're angry, the sage advice goes. You'll get control of it.

Me: When is Ebrahim Alkazi going to present *Jalta Hua Rath*?

Vikas (surprised): How would I know?

Me: You were with me when I met him.

Vikas: No one was with you. You met him alone. Yes, you did tell us.

Me: Okay. I'll ask him when I meet him next.

But even when I met him, I did not ask.

THE FUTURE

I am in Delhi these days. Under Vikas Rai's supervision in Vikas's home. Vikas is returning my self-confidence to me by degrees. One morning I said:

---

* The lines are from Mir Taqi Mir (1722–1810): '*Jin jin ko tha yeh ishq ka aazaar mar gaye, / Aksar hamaare saath ke beemar mar gaye.*' (All those who were struck by that disease called love died / Those who were stricken along with me, died too.)

—I'm going to meet Ebrahim Alkazi.

—Alone?

I nodded. Vikas's face was thoughtful. His daughter, Misha, looked at me angrily. She is now my daughter too. She scolds me a lot.

—Papa, don't send this fool alone. He may land up on the moon.

—I'll send the car for you after I get to the office.

—I'll walk.

—In Delhi the walker never reaches.

There are two Vikases. One is an officer; the other is a poet; the poet falls to my lot.

—Papa, don't send him alone.

—I'll send a commando along.

—Send four. For this freak of a man.

Misha left for college after giving me several dozen instructions. Only one commando in the car. When we reached Triveni, the commando gave me one further instruction:

—I will be at the gate. When you come out, come straight to me. Those are the DIG's orders.

I said to the receptionist:

—Tell Alkazi Saahab that Swadesh Deepak has come from Ambala.

Perhaps he heard my voice. He came out almost at a run. He hugged me. His back was shaking. I was frightened. Was he crying? Alkazi is made of sterner stuff. No sentiments. No emotions. He pulled back, looked at me.

—The same Swadesh after seven years. The sun on the face.

He called out to his wife Roshan.

She came out and said:

—What did I tell you seven years back after reading *Jalta Hua Rath*?

—You said Swadesh will either go mad or commit suicide.

—Look, look again. Swadesh has defeated both death and madness. He belongs to mythology.

Roshan left. We drank tea.

—Why are you sad, Swadesh?

—I cannot write.

He set his cup down. In his eyes, a little anger:

—What did you say? You have come out of the well of loneliness and you want to write. You are just demonic. Give yourself rest. Recover your inner energy. Do you have friends in Delhi?

—Yes, but she doesn't read nor does the theatre interest…

—You don't need a critic for a friend. Does she have a car?

—Yes. She has a car and she has time.

—Good. Go and be a flâneur with her. Wander about as actors do. Drink tea at roadside stalls. Go to art galleries. See those worthless Hindi films. Pamper her. Flirt with her. Is there a word for 'flirtation' in Hindi?

—Ishqbaazi.

—Better than flirt. Remember. Remember it always. A woman is the greatest and purest source of inner energy.

Alkazi Saahab was right. I went off to renew myself with my friend, naughty Nidhi. How did I meet Nidhi?

A production of *Jalta Hua Rath* was on at Shri Ram Centre. I read that Nirmal Verma had disliked the play from the very beginning because the fire in it consumes everything. It does not cook. It does not help in refining gold. I did not tell Nirmal that fire has only one dharma: to burn. The director, Suresh Sharma, said that Nirmal came to see the play twice.

I arrived a little while before the play ended. I did not have the courage to see my own play again. Then it ended.

A woman broke free from a picture and stopped by me. I have no idea why she was convinced I was Swadesh Deepak.

—I have seen *Jalta Hua Rath* five times.

Without thinking I said:

—Are you mad? This terribly dark play is bad enough once.

—You have no idea what you've written.

—You tell me.

—When the blind Munna tells Baba that someone has betrayed her, his reply—Where would you have the good fortune to be betrayed by someone?—is the reason I come back again and again. For this sentence alone.

I could smell her blood. I thought of D.H. Lawrence. Call of blood for blood.

I donned my protective armour, my kavach and kundal, immediately. Now to lie.

—I will phone you tomorrow.

—There are no phones where I'm staying. (And this when Vikas has three.)

—Let me give you my card. Call me, please?

She gave me her card. I put it in my pocket without reading it. I do not call women.

—You haven't even asked my name. I am Nidhi.

I refused to say I was happy to meet her. I wasn't. Just then Alok Dhanva* arrived. We had met a few days earlier. He is constantly trying to become a miniature version of Nirala. He looked at Nidhi. And kept looking at her. When he sees a lovely woman, he is immediately ravenous though his digestion is poor.

—Swadeshji, introduce us!

I was silent. How should I introduce someone I didn't know? Nidhi found a way out of this difficulty:

—I am Swadeshji's second wife.

The poet suffered a lightning bolt.

—I had no idea.

Nidhi: It's not the kind of thing to talk about.

Hunger—and thirst—wiped out, he left.

---

* Alok Dhanva (b. 1948) is a Hindi poet and critic.

I was surprised, worried too, that these silly sentiments did not anger me.

—Why did you tell Alok Dhanva you were my second wife?

—It's the best way to cut a man off. Tell him you're married.

—You could have told him your husband's name.

She burst out laughing.

—I don't have one.

She was staring her fill, smiling. I suddenly understood. She has a true friendship with the smile. She wore no ornaments. Some people do not need them. They are ornaments in themselves.

—Can I ask you something, Swadeshji? Why are you always tense? Why do you seem to be afraid?

—I went through a seven-year eclipse.

Nidhi was speechless. Perhaps she didn't understand.

—What happened…?

—Some stories must stay hidden. Their listeners may be cursed too.

—But I…

—I have no language in which to express my pain. It is no longer possible to investigate the self.

—Sharing sorrow…

—That's a meaningless phrase. The soul's sorrows can never be shared. I am a man condemned by God. Time is no longer an interlocutor.

—You are the strangest man I have ever come across.

—Yes. I am the strangest living man. Goodbye. I am tired. We shall never meet again in thunder, lightning or in rain. Shakespeare. Macbeth, opening lines.

I started off. Behind me, a voice:

—You will call?

—Yes.

I lied and left the spring behind as I walked away. After dinner, Vikas went to his room. He had some reading and writing to do.

Misha: Why are you looking like a sad monkey, you old man?

I told her about Nidhi. Misha gives no quarter.

Misha: Who made you professor of English literature? You are a moron with no sense of humour. Do you know what is humour? When a beautiful woman teases, you should enjoy it. You're a lucky bastard.

—Why did she say she was my second...

Misha: Don't worry. No sensible woman would marry you. I am always surprised that Geeta Aunty loved you and then married you! Is Nidhi beautiful?

—Yes. She is.

Misha clapped her hands.

—Let us make her a member of our Abnormal Group. Cops, poets, painters, playwrights, actors, comrades, singers, photographers and beautiful Nidhi.

Very soon Nidhi became part of our group. My wounds began to heal with her, for she was not Mayavini but a gust of summer breeze. And Soumitra Mohan became her biggest supporter.

THE PAST

What have I achieved in life?

A crippled brain. And no liberation.

My carers are tiring. A long illness. A long curse.

Shelley lied when he said: If Winter comes, can Spring be far behind?*

Spring, for me, had been locked away in her purse for seven years.

Thc falsc harbingers of recovery can be painful.

Now I have no army, no banner. All I have is a prayer.

One of Geeta's friends said after reading a book by me:

—Deepakji, you have not been touched by the flame of love. Or you might have turned God.

* From 'Ode to the West Wind'.

Now I am totally homeless. I walk with the support of others.

But nothing changed in my situation.

The moon wanes. Me. Hospital. Bed. Stink. Impossible hopes.

Yeats has not come for many days. He must not have received his visa.

Instead Lady Longnose came. No greetings, no Ram Ram, no good morning.

She poked the thermometer at my mouth. A stream burst out as if from a mountain.

—Sister, I beg your pardon with folded hands. I am a teacher. I should not have used such words. I can't think. I can't understand. That Mayavini has left me disarmed.

Her features melted. I bathed in the stream.

—You should not apologize. You are my elder. And then this illness is like that; one does not know what one is doing.

How could I tell her that I had never known what I was doing? I have always been self-absorbed. Someone said: I'd like to see Mandu with you. I replied with abuse.

Beautiful women always take revenge; their bodies are their weapons.

You understand this too late. Love and war have the same methods.

Now there is no single reality in my head. Countless elements. Bodily pain from a limb does not reach the brain. Neither extreme cold nor extreme heat affects me.

This is what bothers the doctors.

I experience things that are beyond my ego and my reality. Bad health, a disorder in the heart and mind and a sense of grandeur. It's an arbitrary and directionless weirdness. Then the 'I' so precious to individualism experiences radical changes in thought and feeling.

Now I was a Prima Donna.

If you know everything, do something. In this disease, thoughts do not turn into actions.

I was in a state of heat. A continuous illusion: paranoid.

My enemy was always out in the open.

She had a 360-degree view of the space.

Constraints all around me.

Constantly waiting. But for whom?

Sorrows become friends. And then one gets completely self-absorbed in one's world of madness.

Much later Dr Namwar Singh explained:

—Swadesh, in Hindi we have a word: 'vikshep'. It indicates extreme fraughtness, terrible distress. Things not fitting inside one. The anarchy of breakdown. This has not happened to you.

I felt bad that he hadn't told me this before.

How could he have? We had never so much as set eyes on each other.

Today, my arm will be bandaged. Kanta told me to get up. I refused. Harnam Singh brought in the attendant from the next room. A near-demon of a man. Oil dripping from his hair but a dry beard.

—Will you go or should we carry you?

I discovered that demons can also speak sweetly.

Dr Naidu wet the entire arm with water. He waited a little. He took hold of a strip and pulled. For the first time: pain. I almost screamed. Dr Naidu applauded happily.

—Your recovery has begun, Writer Saahab. Signals have begun to reach the brain from the arm. Congratulations.

Kanta: Why don't you take them off slowly, Doctor Saahab? He'll feel less pain that way.

Dr Naidu: No, the slower you go, the greater the pain.

I escaped to the moon. But whatever I did, there was no avoiding the pain.

Me: When will the arm recover?

Dr Naidu: At least three months more.

I got angry with myself. Fool, I berated myself, you wouldn't have to go through this shame if you'd got it right and died.

Dr Naidu: Deepakji, burns take time to heal. The new skin appears very slowly. We'll do a skin graft.

Kanta: Oh God, how much more suffering…

Dr Naidu: Don't complain. God has a plan for his cure.

One day I will ask Dr Naidu. Doesn't he feel revulsion, dealing with these burned bodies? How does he keep smiling?

I closed my eyes almost as soon as I lay down. My sister asked: Tired, Kaka? I'll go for a cup of tea. Shall I get you something?

—A handful of happiness. If that's not on offer, poison.

—Don't talk like that. Is this how you repay your poor old sister for taking care of you? You who were never afraid of sorrows. You were a warrior. Remain one.

The sound of footsteps by the bed. I opened my eyes. Dr Avneet Sharma and another person: Dr Pratap Sharan, who has searching eyes in an expressionless face. As if he had spent his life diving into the ocean for pearls. He asked about me. Before Dr Avneet could reply, I said:

—I have a strong death wish. I can no longer live in this world of hostile circumstances. The very centre is missing and I am drowned and dead. My outer and inner force is paralysed. I followed an inaccurate map and I'm lost. This feeling of inadequacy gives birth to impotent fear that robs my courage and cripples my reasoning.

I was silent. Dr Pratap Sharan was quite stunned.

He asked Dr Avneet:

—How does he know so much? And then English…

—Sir, Swadesh Deepak is a writer and a professor of English too.

Dr Sharma plunged into the deeps. He emerged with a single sentence for me.

—It is always difficult to understand those who have understanding. We will have a tough time with Mr Deepak.

They left. I closed my eyes. I know that no one will believe what I say, what I write.

No one believed Kafka either.

I can see the future. When I finally commit my words to paper, I know that you will not believe them. May God never require you to walk the path I have so that you may understand.

This unbalanced terror. The crippling of the ability to discuss things, to debate them.

They want to think what pleases them. They will not look for proof nor will they refute this belief. Our loved ones begin to be unlovable.

Fleeing reality makes one happy and it's easy too.

Geeta came early today. The nurse gave her a slip for another test. From the fifth to the second floor, we must go. The nurse said there was a lift.

—Shall we use the lift?

—No. What if we get stuck?

Geeta doesn't try to convince me. She knows that each day a new fear is born in me.

As we climb down, floor after floor, terror rises in me though Geeta supports me. If I should fall…

—Wipe your forehead.

I searched the left pocket of my kurta. Empty.

—You never have a handkerchief.

Even as she said something so ordinary, her voice was sad…was she spent? Not even a nurse can keep serving you for seven years as she has. You don't get patience from outside. It comes from within, and if it is used constantly, it can be exhausted… Has Prabhuji written a dark destiny for her? She married against all opposition. And she got me for her pains. When I was fine, I had a tough ego. Now I was neither physically nor mentally fit. Dr Avneet said: Mr Deepak, you are lucky to have a wife with such strong values. In these cases, generally the women desert their husbands.

We got to the room for the test. Seeing so many healthy people made me hate them.

They said nothing to me. They sat me down and tied me to the chair. On both my palms they poured a great deal of cream.

—What's this for?

—To put in your hair.

—No! I've never put anything in my hair up to now. Free my hands.

Geeta: Deepak, stop it. Why are you putting this cream on him?

—So that the electrodes will be easy to put on. Then we make a graph and a chart of his brain.

—Well, put it on then. But you should explain it to the patient first.

They set up electrodes. For a long time, it was as if worms were writhing in my head.

I got up. Geeta offered me a glass of water. Out of habit, I tried to take it with my right hand. It fell out of my hand. Had Geeta ever dreamed of seeing me so helpless? A very tough man turning into a vegetable.

—Oh Deepak! My poor Deepak. How much more suffering is there in store for you?

She took my hand. We climbed the stairs in silence. Perhaps we had nothing left to say to each other.

Where had those clothes gone? That style? Right from the beginning Geeta had liked to dress me up stylishly. One of her close friends had teased her:

—You always keep him dressed to the nines. What if someone steals him?

—Who would?

—What if I steal him? Forever.

Then Geeta would look at me proudly, and now...

Why does the seductress only come at night? The queen of a dark kingdom. And now what is left? Some broken images.

At that moment Eliot came to mind—I will show you fear in a handful of dust.*

—The dogs are sharpening their teeth. Why do no children's voices emerge from the gardens?

Why is this room as quiet as a desert?

Has anyone ever opened my book?

How did these familiar scenes become strange?

Black clouds have abducted the sun. Total darkness, let us sleep.

I don't know when I heard the sound of her footsteps. My Mayavini. My eyes opened.

The lady came with three white leopards.†

She took my right hand in hers. My blood sang.

The three white leopards fell asleep, their heads resting on their forepaws.

—Aren't you scared of them?

—Me? I know how to tame the wild.

—As with Swadesh.

—No. I tried. I failed. *I* was tamed.

I saw a tree swaying. Constantly swaying.

—When you're better, I'll call you. We'll see Mandu together. What will happen then?

—Then our bodies will smell of each other. You will bleed. Your body will be ripped. I am a very violent lover.

—When will this poor woman see that day?

—I will sit by you and tell you stories. Your body, your soul will be in the seventh heaven. But what do I do about

---

* From 'The Waste Land'.

† These may or may not be the three white leopards of Eliot's 'Ash Wednesday':

> 'Lady, three white leopards sat under a juniper-tree
> In the cool of the day, having fed to satiety
> On my legs my heart my liver and that which had been contained
> In the hollow round of my skull. And God said
> Shall these bones live? shall these
> Bones live?...'

the fear that is in front of me in the afternoon and behind me afterwards?

Hearing the word 'fear' the white leopards opened their eyes. Now they were red.

—What fear? Fear of whom?

—Shall I tell you? In Eliot's words:

*I will show you fear in a handful of dust.**

Mayavini was nowhere to be seen. Her white cheetahs nowhere.

Now it's me.

For the past year they have been telling my stories, sitting by my bed.

* From 'The Waste Land'.

7. 'Now No One Will Come Here, No One At All'

'Nothing happens, nobody comes, nobody goes, it's awful.'*

—Beckett

Why don't I die?

Geeta: Because I won't let you. I have to face my share of sorrows too. And you know, your powers have been transferred to me.

So many words from a laconic woman? Even in the stormy days of our love affair, she would say only a line or two. The opposition always took fright at this. She was a lover of discipline. After we married, all my neglect of my person, my food and my writing vanished. Her friends would tease her: Geeta has tamed a tiger. If she has set her mind on my living, I will not be allowed to die. She is a wild rose, who will not wither if exposed to a little sun. She is my wife.

—I'll just go meet Dr Avneet Sharma.

Geeta left, I got up. I am in my classroom. I read *Waiting for Godot* as a performer would. Beckett's play cannot be understood if it is not enacted. Without preamble, I begin to teach:

—Don't question me! The blind have no notion of time. The things of time are hidden from them too.†

The reading was lifeless. There was no energy inside me at all. I came back to my room in the psychiatric ward.

Sunday. The nurse called me to her room. I climbed onto the scales. I got off. Sister noted my weight. She compared it with last week's weight. She looked alarmed.

—Oh God. In one week, you've lost five kilos.

---

* From *Waiting for Godot* by Samuel Beckett.

† Ibid.

Do not ask me questions. I am Godot.

—Why do you ask me questions? The blind have no sense of time. Things concerned with time are hidden from them. All they can do is wait endlessly. For Godot. Who's that? Don't know. When will he arrive? Don't know. What then? You must wait.

The nurse paged Dr Sharma. He came in kurta-pyjama. Sister showed him the weight chart. He looked worried. He looked at me.

—I forgot to wish you a good morning, Mr Deepak. No need to worry. I'll call your physician right away.

—When I get to zero, I'll fly away.

—Where will you fly to?

—The Sunderbans.

—There are tigers there.

—No. My tigress is there. Her ceaseless cry. Is the mating season upon us?

Dr Gautam of the Medicine Department arrives. He is very fair. A well-groomed long beard. About six feet tall. A Greek god.

He asked the nurse: How long has he been losing weight?

—Three weeks. He's lost fifteen kilos.

—What was his original weight?

—58 kilos.

—If you hadn't weighed him a few more weeks, he'd have disappeared.

Dr Avneet showed him the list of medicines I was being given.

Dr Gautam was quiet a while, looking at me.

—You know how important writers are to society. You are a totally negative person. You have to give us some help. How many rotis do you eat?

I was silent. Sardar Harnam Singh replied:

—Half in the day, half in the night.

Dr Sharma thought for a while. Then he said:

—The desire to sacrifice oneself is actually suicide. The other does not benefit and one does not survive. I don't believe in force-feeding. From half a roti, can you make it one? Do you know why you are losing weight at such an alarming rate? Because your body is consuming itself. The body will do just about anything to stay alive. I'll come again tomorrow. Think about it.

Me: You have so much hair in your ears. I hope you can hear.

He stopped and smiled. He looked like a mystic poet.

—Do you read?

—No. Books seem false to me. They think one thing and say another.

—*Court Martial* tells no lies. I've seen it twice.

—That bloody *Court Martial*. The root of all evil. She saw it and became the hand of death. A crouching white leopard.

I would be shifted to a sick room. The sour smell vanished. The wilted patients left. I entered my dream world. The trees have colourful fish hanging from them, not flowers. A vegetarian tiger nibbles grass. The wolf has a pen and paper in his paws. He asked:

—Why do beautiful women cause pain?

—Beauty makes them fatal. And they turn into the apocalypse.

The wolf: You're mad. You know nothing. Beautiful women give birth to beautiful children.

The grass-eating tiger raised its head. A subdued growl.

—My wolf child, I have not turned so vegetarian that I would not be able to kill you. One does not talk to writers disrespectfully. They will take a rag and turn it into happiness.

Me: At first, write patriotic poems. They're easy. And they make you famous.

Wolf: Teach me, oh master.

Me: How do I teach? She took all my poetry away.

The wolf was sad. I was sad. The tiger concentrated on the grass.

I am sitting under an Ashoka tree. Its long leaves are a hand fan. But there is no rustle, no breeze. I think of new ways to die.

—If I stop breathing—no, that's not possible.

—What if I spread a blue bedcover? Nothing will happen. No man loses his masculinity from spreading a blue bedcover.

Strangle someone. That will mean the noose.

No. The mentally ill do not get capital punishment. Just incarceration in a mental hospital.

Then what can I do? Why does no one hear my plea?

Three white leopards, Mayavini's bodyguards, come to me.

All three sit down, placing their heads on their paws.

All three sad, all three silent, all three distracted.

One: Today Swamini could not come. A proposal has come for her daughter.

Me: Her daughter is very young.

Two: Swamini was also young when she married. Only sixteen.

The birds flew away in terror of the leopards. The animals fled. My part of the jungle emptied. Don't they know anything? White leopards are non-violent and herbivorous too.

The tree said: Get up. Go. I'm sleepy.

All three leopards: We'll escort you to your room.

When the illusion abandoned me, I was in the hospital.

Geeta: How fast you're losing weight. Don't become the Invisible Man.

—All my clothes will get loose.

—Don't worry about this nonsense. Haven't I always got your clothes stitched? I'll get these done too. Try and eat some more.

—Three white leopards escorted me to my room. I was wandering near the jungle.

Geeta was startled. She realized my parallel world was taking birth. And now she wanted to keep me in this one.

—In a little while Kamleshwar Sinha, the associate editor of *The Tribune* will be here. He helped us a great deal when we had to admit you. Please recognize him.

But first Renuka Nayyar arrived. She hugged Geeta. Renu looked at me. Mischief blossomed on her face.

—I want to hug you too. But if you take a reclining man in your arms, the whole meaning of the scene changes.

Renu is like a fresh breeze. I smiled.

—Look Geeta, Deepak can smile. I really ought to take him in my arms. He might even laugh.

Geeta: Give it a rest. These days he's a regular touch-me-not. If you touch him, he's in pain.

Kamleshwar Sinha arrived. He is every inch the sage. He studied at Santiniketan and some of that peace is still part of him. He put his hand on my head: You will recover totally, Swadesh. The body is a machine. When things go wrong, God puts us to bed for a while.

He was the only person who had complete faith that I would get well.

Kamleshwar: Geetaji, from time to time bring Parul and Sukant to see him. The children should know that their father is walking through this river of sorrow. Their ability to face tough times will grow.

Renu: Let's go down to the canteen.

Me: And what will you do there?

Renu: We'll drink beer. Shall I bring a couple of bottles for you? Close your eyes. Be a good child.

Matron came into the room. She touched my head.

—Today our writer looks happy. You should talk to your guests. The burdens get lighter.

I closed my eyes.

Matron (to Geeta): The night attendant you hired is an alcoholic. He just sleeps all night. The patient kept asking for water. I've sacked the attendant. You'd better find...

Renu: We can find someone tomorrow. Today Deepak can be alone...

Matron: No. You have to have a night attendant. It's a rule in the psychiatric ward.

Geeta: Renu, let's go downstairs, we can call Vikas Rai.

Renu: We'll have a cup of tea and come back. Why has your face fallen? We'll bring you back yours as well.

She left. For the last twenty-five years, Renu has been a member of our family. She has an amazing self-confidence and influence. She is the only woman in Hindustan who can shout at me.

Harnam Singh said sweetly:

—May Waheguru give everyone a friend like Renu Bhainji. She comes into the room and immediately asks after everyone's health.

Sikandar: And she loves me lots.

Me: You are lovable.

Sikandar: Bossman, you're not entirely lovable. You fly into terrible rages. That's why they tie you up.

Harnam: Son, you shouldn't talk like that. He's your elder brother, no?

Sikandar: If he's my elder brother, why doesn't he give me bananas?

I wanted to close my eyes. I closed them. Vikas Rai was on tour. Of the three white leopards, one had perhaps become my friend. I will tell it to slash my windpipe. Her daughter's wedding. Mother-in-law. A change in life-roles. Will she feel ashamed about coming to see me? She will definitely come. This time I will throw down all my weapons and make an offer of friendship. I cannot fight any longer. Tomorrow a session with Dr Verma. Let's see what games he invents for me this time. I want to eat a carrot à la Godot. Why don't the letters of the alphabet work for me now? What happened to the musical notes? What food is this? I'll tell Geeta to get me a slate. I'll write on it. I'll revert to childhood. Why do I hate myself so much? Have you ever heard of a warrior, helpless for seven years? How many people told me, pray, say Ram Ram in your heart. How? When no inch of it was left empty? My entire heart was Mayavini's kingdom. She'll destroy me, she'll make me whole.

I'll start with the alphabet. What are the musical notes? Tell me and tell me how to cook.

You have to fulfil the hopes that people have in you. You have to smile. You have to keep them happy. Tell them nothing. Smiles are born inside. They do not come from outside to sit on one's lips.

It is the desert. A burning forest of stars. She is like a green hill.

I underrate myself. For things do not change.

Meaning is lost. Friends turn into enemies.

Every moment spent in self-excoriation. I turn the accusation on my own pride. And then I begin to tally all the sins of my past.

Who am I? A constant search for meaning and relevance.

I believe only that about myself which I wish to believe.

I do not even look for proof. Our best-loved beliefs suffer no criticism. We look for no evidence for them.

Thus fleeing reality is easy. Easier than confrontation. Which is why my Mayavini is a paralysis brought by the wind. A tree begins to sway. Beneath, three white leopards sit. For the last fifty years they have been sitting by me, reading me my stories.

Why did I wake from a doze? The heavy tramp of boots outside the door.

My eyes opened. Renu was sitting on a stool near me. Her eyes were on the door.

Two commandos from Haryana came in. Not an ounce of superfluous flesh on either one. Ready to kill or be killed.

Mr Shimla let out a squeak. Two patients scuttled out.

One: DIG Saahab sent us.

Me: Why has Vikas sent you?

Renu: Be quiet. You can't remember what happened seconds ago. Geeta called Rai Saahab.

Hearing the commotion, the nurse hurried in.

The sight of two uniformed and armed guards stopped her in her tracks.

Nurse: Who are you? What are you doing here?

Two: We are Professor Saahab's relatives. We're going to stay with him through the day and night.

Nurse: You shouldn't have brought your weapons in here. You frightened the patients.

One: You keep them, Sister. We'll retrieve them when we leave.

Nurse: No. What if they vanish?

The nurse left. The patients calmed down.

Renu: If you need tea or snacks, the second floor...

Two: We'll find out everything, Madam.

They left the room. The tea trolley came by. Renu took two cups.

Renu said: Deepak, you shouldn't talk about death in front of Geeta. She's desperate. For the last seven years, she's been your mother, not your wife; she's bathed you and dressed you and fed you.

I said: I won't.

—I know you. You agree immediately and then do what you want. When she knows it all, what is there to say? I wanted to ask: will the moon rise today?

Renu said: You must get well. You face every challenge. My man-child. Don't get well for us. Do it for yourself. You have to write another *Court Martial.*

—I will not be able to write anything now.

—You're some kind of seer who can tell the future? Acknowledge your strength. You can do anything you want. When you get well and write your first book, I'll give you a packet of cigarettes.

THE FUTURE

Cigarettes remind me of Nidhi.

After I met her the first time, perhaps a month passed before there was an opportunity to go to Delhi: an exhibition of my old and dear friend Neeraj Goswami's* paintings. He insisted I come for the launch. I did. Many people there. I was introduced to Ajeet and Arpana Caur. Something happens to Jagdeep as soon as he sees me. He begins to take pictures. That evening too he began to do that.

I said—Enough already. What will I do with them?

Jagdeep—I'll distribute them among your lovers. Absolutely free.

Nidhi came up with some people I didn't know. Her first question was why I hadn't called her.

—I didn't have your number.

—I gave you my card.

—I tore it up that very evening.

She paled. She looked at me for a while. Then she burst out laughing. These days I use small gestures of disrespect to put people off.

Nidhi said she'd never met as strange a man as me. These things should be said privately.

I said beautiful women often get used to sycophants and bootlickers.

She teased: You must have a weapons factory inside you somewhere.

I smiled. She clapped.

* Neeraj Goswami (b. 1964) is an Indian abstract painter, alumnus of the Delhi College of Art.

—I got you to laugh. Jagdeep said you never smile. But you look nice when you smile.

The pure light in her eyes reduced my fear.

My mind explained that even if one woman is a despot, it did not follow that all women must be white leopards. Nidhi said that I must have tea with her the next day. At home or outside?

I told her I never went to people's houses.

The woman turned into a naughty child. She touched her throat and said: I promise not to touch you if you come home.

I touched her forehead. I grew calm. Nidhi could not be ill-starred. I was the ill-omened person. The jinxed man.

—You don't even know how to tease.

—I knew once. I've forgotten now.

On her face, an evergreen smile. She assured me—I'll help you remember it all. Jagdeep says you have a vile temper. Rage at me whenever you want. I love it.

Happy with each other, we kept drinking tea.

When night fell, I went to sleep.

After a long time I discovered this truth: that all women are not tyrants. All women do not suffer from the hungers of the body. I was now in the world of smells. We spoke in silences to each other. I began to feel her voice. I don't hear and my light is not cold. Warmth too and touch as well. How fate has brought us together. Not fate: destiny. Could it be that a woman is also a cell in a church? First one accepts one's wrongdoing. Confession. And finally freedom from sin. Redemption.

Alkazi Saahab was right: Wander like a loafer with your girlfriend but make sure you bring those wonderful days back. The mornings were not redolent with perfume nor had the candles of beauty been lit.

THE PAST
PGI, CHANDIGARH

My younger sister Sarita came with her husband Pradip Sharda. Pradip was born to serve people. He is this era's Shravan.* After he greeted me, he asked everyone for their lists and money. He would get what they needed.

I closed my mouth tight and shook my head. Pradip complained that though he had come three or four times a month, I had never asked for anything. Pradip works in the technology department of PGI. He went to get the other patients medicines.

Sarita sat down on a nearby stool and asked why my mouth was closed.

Sikandar replied: Bhainji, Bossman is eating the newspaper.

Sarita pressed my cheeks with her fingers. I opened my mouth. She put in a finger and pulled out some pieces.

—Were you hungry, Veerji?

I shook my head.

Sikandar told her some more frightening news.

—The Bossman sometimes says he wants to eat the bedsheets. With great difficulty, he makes do with the newspaper. If he's hungry why doesn't he eat roti?

Harnam Singh came in with Sikandar's bananas. Sarita asked:

—Uncle, what will happen to my brother?

—Akaal-purakh† will save him.

—Veerji, what should I get for you to eat tomorrow?

—Bring something. I'll eat it.

—Would you like a shawl? Winter's coming on.

---

* Shravan is seen as the epitome of filial piety. Since his aged parents wanted to go on a pilgrimage, he carried them on his shoulders to the forty places of pilgrimage.

† Akaal-purakh is a Sikh name for God. Literally it means: the timeless one, or the one outside time.

I shook my head.

—Veerji, you'd better give up this bad habit of shaking your head. We long to hear your voice.

Dr Mehendiratta came in. He sent Pradip and Sarita off. They left.

—Deepak, get up. Let's go into the gallery.

—I'll get tired.

—Then we'll come back. Give you a hand?

I shook my head.

—Right. When have you ever let anyone help you?

As we walked in the gallery he read the story 'Namak ka Daroga'* ('The Salt Guard'). When he had finished Premchand's story, we walked a while in silence.

—Who is the hero of the story?

—The zamindar.

Mehendiratta was startled—Premchand makes the guard the hero…

—Wrong. He was weak; a coward too. He is overwhelmed by the zamindar's kindness and accepts a job with the zamindar who got him sacked in the first place. This is a eulogy to the zamindar.

Mehendiratta knew that the mentally ill often have moments of clarity.

I returned to my sick world.

Tired now. The room. The bed.

THE PAST

Together we went to see Neeraj Goswami's pictures. Neeraj explained some of them.

One painting had the faces of a man and a woman almost overlapping each other and yet they seemed separated as if

---

* A story by Munshi Premchand. Vanshidar, a salt tax official tries to stop a zamindar smuggling salt. The zamindar perverts justice and Vanshidar is sacked. But then the zamindar hires Vanshidar for his honesty.

each were on the opposing banks of a river. Their bodies were together, their minds miles apart. The images turned to stone.

—Neeraj, if I ever write again I will use this painting on the cover.

—Do you think I should title it?

—No need. A title would limit its possible meanings.

Many years later, this painting would be the cover of *Kaal Kothri*. Vani Prakashan's lack of attention to detail meant that Neeraj Goswami's name appeared nowhere.

Nidhi asked—When do I come to fetch you for tea tomorrow?

I said—When you feel like it, but first ask Vikas.

She stared at me with full eyes:

—Why? Is Vikas your keeper? Jagdeep was also saying you seem to be in his clutches. What is it with you? You are a perfectly healthy man.

—Nothing wrong with me. Vikas likes to look after his friends.

She clapped happily.

—Then I'll look after you too. That'll be fun.

How easy it is to please this thirty-two-year-old girl!

As we drank our tea, the conversation turned to the question of why some artists never achieve success. Jagdeep said: Gurudev will tell us.

—More poets and writers have been destroyed by their wives than by prostitutes.

Nidhi: Neeraj, you should paint me. Maybe I could be on the cover of Sir's book too.

Neeraj: Five Jehangir Sabavalas would not suffice to paint you. And I am only a child.

Jagdeep, a habitual offender, added:

—Madam, if you keep calling Gurudev here this government-style 'Sir', you don't have much of a chance of being his cover girl. Think of another relationship.

I escorted Nidhi to her car. I had no idea Vikas was

behind us. At the door she turned to me. She seemed to be waiting. I was thinking, making a decision.

Then I decided to voice my suspicions.

—There was a sandalwood tree in my courtyard. It's not there now. Did you take it?

She was speechless, motionless as a stone. Neeraj Goswami had only to touch his brush and she had gone pale.

Vikas took my arm, said to Nidhi—Let's go. Deepakji must be tired.

Vikas had realized that I had gone back to my accursed history.

THE PAST
BEFORE ADMISSION TO HOSPITAL

Parul, my daughter, reads the papers. She gives me the news in brief in Hindi. Geeta whirls out of the toilet and plants herself in front of me…

—When you go for a shit, what do you do in there? The whole seat is filthy. You don't use any water to clean it. Half the day I spend with a wet brush cleaning it up. Will you turn me into a sweeper now? You do this deliberately to torment me. What sins have I committed in some past life?

Sukant—And why do you let your pyjama string dangle? What do you want to prove?

Parul is like me. She lives on the edge of a volcano. She slammed the newspaper on the table and said in a cold loud voice.

—Shut up. Just shut up. Why are you after his blood? And Sukant. Is this the way to talk to your father? You must really be a bastard.

Everyone is afraid of Parul.

Geeta: Parul, if you were in my place…

Parul: You know what I'd do? I'd divorce him or let him die in peace. I would never become a savage.

Everyone retreated to their bedrooms. I came out to the verandah.

—You are real. Did my diseased dreams give birth to you?

—When I am free of you, I will be able to free myself from myself.

—Can it be so easy freeing oneself from one's shadow?

—I have never been in a black cab. I have always been in search of meaning.

—I am a loser in love. She takes me swimming at night.

—In the echoing screams, we speak in approximations of silences.

—Swadeshji, stay with me. I will help you recover. The scent of my body will become medicine for you. I will tell you my story.

—I am in the shadow of every light. I am the Hamlet of my age.

Is your existence a trick? Only an illusion? We will live in a cave. We will have no desire to know anything. We will sing the old ballads to each other... Outside our cave, the wind will carve out maidans for us. Even in that darkness we will be able to see each other... You will touch me and free me from my spell... I will begin some long stories... In the hollows of your neck, I will check your temperature with my lips... After that we will sprinkle greenness about... You will fold your hands and beg... Get angry at me, Swadesh... I am a cold woman... I am a moon man... I will not be angry. I will torment you. And language, shamed, will leave the cave. Our bodies will speak to each other. You will burble with happiness... Perhaps you will open the cage and let me fly away... But I won't fly away... Yours is a happy prison... For your body is the guard... The language of the body admits of no grammar.

Sunday again. My day of sorrow. Many visitors. God bless them. Bringers of advice. Dr Gautam has cut the hair in his ears. Now he has hairless ears.

The nurse proffers the weight chart. He looks at it.

—Five kilos down again. What was his weight at admission?

—57 kilos.

Dr Gautam sat down on a stool.

—Deepakji, get yourself a thermos. You can fill it with water from the cooler outside. Where do you get water from when you're thirsty?

—I summon up my river.

His face fell. Nothing is as easy as it seems. The road to Heaven is not straight. Urvashi and Maneka haunt the path.

—You will lose more weight now. A reaction to the medicines. To the psychiatric medication. As fast as you lose weight, you will recover. Don't worry.

—My worries do not live with me. They reside in the Sunderbans.

—A good place for them. But to live, you will again have to mould yourself.

—When it rains, the tigers in the Sunderbans romp about. They often recite the poetry of Nirala.

—I've read some of your stories.

—In all of them, the ink-dark jungle squats in the middle.

Dr Gautam got up—If you want any books, let me know.

—Now I will not sin by reading. Wisdom destroys.

Holidays are days of sorrow for me. The sisters will come. Renu will come. Geeta too. All of them will preach—Be brave. Not one of them buys me some bravery from the market.

—You will have to conquer the past. Then you can control the future.

—But how can an aged hawk spread his wings?

—Blind eyes may be cured. Not a blind soul.

—Someone else's image peers out of the mirror. Beautiful and terrifying.

—She will spread greenery in my arid world.

—Nothing happens. No one comes. No one goes. It's terrifying.

Beckett came, sat on a stool, his overcoat smelling of words. His eyes are cruel for they have seen the ultimate truth: the meaninglessness of life.

—Are you also waiting for Godot?

I thought it wise to be silent. I have still not understood his play. He turned into an actor. Don't question me. The blind have no notion of time. The things of time are hidden.

Beckett ran his hand over my bandaged right arm.

—You are a good playwright, Swadesh. But you are a bad lover. I'll go now.

Your Prime Minister has invited me to lunch. I'm off to the President's House. Beckett touched my head. I closed my eyes. Announcement:

*TIME HAS STOPPED.**

Renu arrived. Her Namaste was a bit haggard.

—You should at least smile when you greet me. Mummy's come from Ludhiana. She's brought halwa for you.

—I don't eat sweets.

—My fault, Veera. I forgot to read the Constitution. It must be written there that Swadesh doesn't eat sweets. Everything is 'no'. Learn to say 'yes'. People like to hear 'yes es'.

Renu gave Sikandar some halwa. I ate some too.

Sikandar: It's so tasty. Did you make it, Bhainji?

Renu: Heaven forfend. Kiddo, do I look like the halwa-making type? Listen, I hear you're after your father to get you married. Marriage means you have to work.

—My wife will work. I'll just sit around and watch.

—That's right, Sikandar. When it comes to a woman, man is a bull gone wild. Why do you want to marry?

* From *Waiting for Godot* by Samuel Beckett.

—Bhainji, I love children.

—So all you have to do is offer that love to the children of your area.

Sikandar's eyes lit up. He guffawed.

—Great idea, Bhainji. I won't marry and play with the children of my area. A new child to love every day. That's a great idea.

Sikandar withdrew to a community of his dreams where he began to play with children.

Renu took my left hand. On her face, diffidence.

Renu: Listen, don't feel bad, but tell me who do you talk to in the night? Who comes to you? Dr Avneet complained to Geeta. There's a secret Deepak is keeping from us. How can we help him? Harnam Uncle has also heard you speaking.

In a second, Mayavini is at my side—Say nothing. Tell them nothing.

—I talk to the wind.

—That's what you do in your stories. I'm talking of the here and now.

—Renu, some secrets stay personal. Or one might be cursed...

Renu never insists. She is familiar with stories of sorrow.

Renu: Geeta will be here shortly. I'll take her to see a film. Poor thing, she needs a break from this dark world. Can we go?

—I have never stopped her from doing anything. Now she has become a cold breeze.

Today, Sukant is with Geeta. He's grown taller. His eyes are fearful as he looks at the patients in their beds. Renu told him to sit down but he would not.

—He is reduced to a skeleton. Will he die soon?

Renu: Don't say such dreadful things. And listen: English is forbidden in hospital.

—Okay. Papa, should I take you for a walk?

Geeta: Don't go downstairs. Stay in the gallery.

After two rounds, he asked:

—Did you fall ill because you get angry, so angry?

I was silent. Out of the mouths of babes.

—Why don't you want to live? You attempted suicide. Why set yourself alight?

—I had no reason left to live.

—Your student Bhagwant Singh comes twice a week from his village on a motorcycle. He brings vegetables. Nani told him not to visit you.

Bhagwant is a small mountain of a man, so strong that up to now no one has dared to fight with him.

—I read your stories. They're all tragic. I didn't understand them.

—Some sorrows can only be understood with age.

—But why do so many people die?

—Death is a final truth and a final mystery.

—Mummy says everyone is afraid of you.

—And now I'm afraid of everyone. Bloody sissy.

We were silent. Conversation at an end. Now Sukant's face was without fear.

—Papa, I will stay with you on the weekends. I'm not afraid of the hospital now. I'll bring you cigarettes on the sly. You can smoke them in the loo.

I leaned on the wall. Sukant does not hate me. We should take our children into confidence. My mistake.

—Why does Renumausi say we can't speak English in the hospital?

—She's teasing. But better not to. It frightens people.

—Why?

—Everyone's afraid of the language of the ruling class.

I was on the bed. Geeta proffered a letter.

—I don't want to read it.

—Read it. It's from Jehangir Sabavala. He's very worried. You haven't replied for four years.

Jehangir writes one letter every year. And I send my reply.

Kamleshwar* was then with *Sarika*.† I sent him my first story 'Ashwarohi' ('The Horsemen'). I told him the title came from Sabavala's '*The Riders*'.

In those days, editors didn't play politics. They worked hard. Kamleshwar got hold of a photograph of the painting somehow and printed it with the story. One of his friends told Jehangir about this. He was very happy. Jehangir Sabavala could not read Hindi.

Rajkamal agreed to do my selected stories.

Sheila Sandhu thought it would be a good idea if Sabavala would agree to have '*The Riders*' on the cover. She warned me that he did not usually allow his paintings for book covers.

I wrote him a letter. His reply arrived with a transparency of '*The Riders*'. And a friendship began.

Not that we've ever met. Or even seen each other.

Geeta and Renu came back after the film.

Geeta: Sukant, get those shoes on. We're off to Ambala.

Sukant: No, I will stay with Papa.

Geeta and Renu were almost shocked.

—You'll be scared here in the night.

—No. Who will frighten me? The patients? They're helpless.

—And what will you eat? Hospital food?

Harnam Singh: Bhainji, they give so much food, three people can eat it. And this is the age when one develops courage.

* Kamleshwar Prasad Saxena (1932–2007) was one of the foremost of post-Independence Hindi writers, along with such figures as Mohan Rakesh and Nirmal Verma.

† Hindi literary magazine. Kamleshwar was editor between 1967 and 1978.

Someone brought a pillow, someone a bed sheet. Sukant made a bed on a bench.

Geeta: The doctor says we should have a phone in the house. Should I apply? You've never allowed us to have one. You seem to hate the device. But now...

—Apply. But not in my name. Apply in yours.

Geeta went out. Renu lifted a corner of the sheet and slipped something underneath.

Renu: Just a little money.

—Why? What will I do with it?

—Do what? Order in some beer, big brain! You never know when you'll need money in a police station or in a hospital. Get off your high horse, won't you?

Renu left. Harnam Singh said to Sukant—Come on then, Kaka. Let's go down for a walk. We'll get your dad some milky tea.

Sukant asked Sikandar—Uncle, should I get you something?

Sikandar looked at him for a moment and then clapped his hands.

—Bapu, I've become an uncle. I'm grown up. Get me bananas.

They went out. I wondered why my son and I have been near-enemies. Of course, I had never talked to him much, other than saying No. I wanted him to sit with me but could never bring myself to ask. I didn't know that adolescence is a time when children alternate between great understanding and complete callousness. My close friend Om Prakash Verma had explained it to me.

—Professor, when a man's feet fit into his father's shoes, they become equals. That's when we should begin to share our sorrows with our sons. They cannot figure those things out for themselves. We do not tell them what we expect but we want it done anyway. The pride of becoming a father turns a son into a stranger. Sukant is very smart. Tell him your troubles.

A book in Sukant's hands. I asked which one.

—*Madame Bovary*. I took it from your book rack.

—It's not appropriate for your age.

—I'm old enough. I'm sixteen. I'm going to read in the gallery. I sleep late.

Geeta is terrified that Sukant may also become a writer like me. And that too a Hindi writer.

I fell into a doze. She did not come. Busy with her daughter's wedding, I expect.

The sound of footsteps, a young police officer. Two commandos. A woman ripe with youth and beauty.

Officer: Sir, I'm Ashwini Sharma, Station House Officer, Sector 17. Do you recognize this fatty?

I shook my head.

Officer: The fatty is Meera, your student and my wife. When I woke up this morning she was in tears. I asked her what happened and she said, Deepak Sir is ill. He's in hospital. At PGI. I was shocked. Meera, these days no one even weeps over the death of a lover. You're crying over a professor who's ill? So I brought her here.

Meera put her hand on my head. Sir, you will get well soon. How did this happen?

—I fought a duel with a tigress.

Meera: But Professor, you...

Sukant: He talks in metaphors.

Meera: I'll come and see you again.

—Don't come. I'm afraid of writers and leopards.

They left. Sukant said:

—You must be tired, after sitting in the verandah. Try and sleep.

My eyes began to close. This was the beginning of the nightmare time. Those who are nowhere will come here. Again the questions-and-answers and again I will drown in the river of sorrow.

—She is the heroine of one of the old ballads. You can see her in the dark.

—Those wrists. The neck, taut, at an angle. Those three breasts. My Kama Sutra...

—The entry of the wind is prohibited in my house. She sits on the skylight and wails her laments.

—Fear consumes strength. Then one even loses the power to debate.

—I have become a waning moon. No interlocutors for me.

—Writing was my shield and my sword. The seductress took them away.

—She asks, why doesn't Swadesh Deepak know how to cry?

—What peace, what happiness, if I could just strangle her, kill her.

—Every morning, she stops my breath. My weak world vanishes and I am paralysed.

—Sometimes I labour under the misapprehension that she is not the enemy, that she is my green jungle.

—When I rest my head on her thigh, no phantasms lurk. The scent of a female body.

—This is the tragedy of your cowardice. You fear her and you want her too.

As yet we are not fated for the final meeting. Then I will drive her mad.

Sister told me to sit in her room and read. Go to sleep. I was made to fear for nothing. Now I will spend weekends with you. He lay down. Sorrow makes us big and gives us understanding. What a fate is yours! A sixteen-year-old son must look after you.

THE PRESENT
THESE VERY DAYS

A trunk call. Late at night. Sukant picks up. He says:

—For you. Some lady. She wants to talk to you. Very husky voice.

—Who is it?

—I asked. She didn't say. Don't get angry.

I took the phone and said: Swadesh speaking.

—I'm calling from Trivandrum, Kerala. May I speak in English?

—Go on.

—I am reading your fractured memoirs in *Kathadesh*.

—Yes.

—*Maine Mandu Nahin Dekha* has given me the key to your suffering.

—Yes.

—The seductress who drives you to madness is very powerful. Your soul is still in her custody.

Now I was alert and on guard.

—I am a more powerful seductress. I can save you from her black powers. Come and stay with me for three months.

I lied:

—But I'm going to America for three months. Where did you get my number from?

She said in Hindi:

—I know everything.

Seeing that I had lost colour, Sukant asked:

—Who was it? What did she say?

—Someone from Kerala. How did she get my number?

—She must have got it from *Kathadesh*. Ask them.

I phoned them. Harinarayan said that he had given no woman from Kerala my number.

I was thrown back into my world of terror. Sukant now shares my secret. He's wise. I share everything with him. He never laughs at me.

—Tomorrow go to PGI. Tell Dr Pratap Sharan everything. Don't tell Mama. She will be disturbed.

PGI, CHANDIGARH
NEXT MORNING

I told Dr Pratap Sharan everything. His face was expressionless. But his eyes deepened and it was clear that he had got some insight.

—Where did she get my phone number?

—You're giving that far too much importance. Anyone can find out anyone else's number.

—How can a woman I don't even know ask me to stay with her for three months?

—Disturbed and abnormal women seem attracted to you.

—But I do not wish to enter that fathomless cave.

—Construct a defence. Do not let that woman in.

I was silent. I did not get up. Dr Sharan got it. I was hesitating to tell him something. He waited in silence too.

—I think about Mayavini often.

—She does not show up?

—No.

—No harm missing her. But we should try and think of the good things about those we love.

I got up. Dr Sharan offered some advice—Even if you're slightly disturbed, come and see me.

Outside, I seemed almost free of my fear of the Kerala resident.

THE PAST

Lying on the bed, I can hear the moon's footsteps through the window.

My Kaamna is sitting near me in the Sunderbans. All day we talk nonsense. My Mayavini. In my dream, the branches vibrate like the pinions of an eagle.

I am turning to stone again. I am neither dead nor alive.

This is it, Swadesh. Does enduring humiliation become a habit? Sometimes I see myself through the eyes of those I love. I turned into a lazy, dozy cat who will not move even to catch a rat. Now I want some ugly girl to become a friend. At least she will cause no pain. Why doesn't the trembling of my feet end? No, why don't I end? You should wear slightly bigger earrings. When they move, their shadows will reach your nose. My fear has no direction and no limits. Fear now has a tangible form. Will I have to hold someone's hand for the rest of my life? I am a lame tiger. Have I become Madame Bovary? All my dreams of happiness have turned into nightmares. I want to die. That would be a happy ending.

Kanta came in the morning. I did not answer her Namaste.

—What happened, Kaka? Not a word in greeting?

I was silent. She asked Harnam Singh what happened.

—Bhainji, who knows what happened to him? No tea even.

—I gave him a banana. He didn't take it.

Kanta put her hand on my head—Won't you tell your mother?

—I dirtied my pyjamas in the night.

After some thought—You didn't get up or you didn't realize it?

—Didn't realize it. Took them off. Burn them.

—How many do I burn? I'll wash them. When you took them off, your legs must have also been soiled?

I did not answer.

In an almost defeated voice to Harnam Singh:

—What is going to happen, Bhai Saahab? What do I do?

—What can we do? Appeal to the mercy of God. I'll take Professor to the bathroom. Bring some fresh clothes there.

Harnam told me to keep my eyes closed. He scrubbed me down, bathed me and dressed me in fresh clothes. I drank a cup of steaming tea. I ate a banana from Sikandar. Both refreshed me.

My eyes drifted shut.

There were sounds by my bed. I opened my eyes. Dr Pratap Sharan.

He studied the chart the nurse gave him. And cancelled something.

—I've removed eight pills. The other four to continue.

I made a Namaste.

—How are you? A nice early bath today, I see. After a while, go sit in the gallery. Spend some time on the terrace.

—I don't feel like it.

—The body and mind are not independent of each other. We're fighting a disease here. You have to care for your body too. If you keep on lying down, your body will forget how to walk.

I was silent.

—Day after tomorrow there will be a medical conference on your case. About a hundred doctors and MD students will attend. You will too.

—What is going to happen?

—I'll tell you there. Tell your wife to come too.

—What will Geeta do there?

—I'll tell her there as well. We'll have a conversation. All these doctors will study your case together.

Dr Chari came with his entire team. He asked the nurse:

—Is he taking his eggs and milk?

—Yes, Sir.

He pulled away the sheet. He turned my arm around and his moustaches twitched.

He told Dr Naidu that there had been no improvement.

—Sir, I fear there is some infection.

He touched the burnt flesh and thought for a bit.

—Okay, Dr Naidu. Get an early date in the operation theatre. We will do grafting.

He saw my face. The terror on it. He explained:

—We'll take skin from your thigh and graft it on the burnt area of your arm. It will quicken the healing process. There is nothing to worry. Your arm will become almost new.

Everyone says: No cause to worry. My body, my mind... so many sounds... Why are the panes of the windows shaking?... If I go to her door, I will lose words again... I am the hero of a Greek tragedy... But scarecrows don't make tragedies... Everything is evanescent... Everything has vanished... I was the hero of my own illusions... Roopvati confined me to bed...her subject... What is she... Surely not a mere phantom... A revolt is out of the question... One more suicide attempt... What will I get from this paralysed mind and body?... When will I rest upon her thigh?... What is she?... Women curse me... Why does the wind roar all the time? I remember nothing from Faiz Saahab... Geeta sold her bangles. There's a hole in the bank account... My illness... Depression... Subsidence... Everything dull, downcast... An incessant sadness... Finding oneself deeply alone... No one in the world is happy... All the colours are black. Nothing is meaningful... We can only wait for bad news... Every question answered in monosyllables...all language in one note... I never ask a question...I shy away from people... Without life, without enthusiasm... My shoulders bowed, my expression defeated... Some huge crime has been committed... The verdict is 'guilty'... My sins are unforgivable... He has no right to live... Everyone has abandoned him... He is destined to die a lonely death...

These are the signs of my sickness. But the sickness has not been diagnosed yet.

Dr Verma's classroom. Huge letters on a chart.

—Deepakji, make a sentence starting with these letters. A meaningful sentence.

—If it is a sentence, it will have a meaning.

—No. I saw a horse. I take a roti. These we do not think of as meaningful. You do not have to do them in order. Start anywhere you want.

I thought a while. Asked—What happens when I make a sentence?

—We will try and discern the order of your thought process.

D—Donkeys do not eat mangoes.

Dr Verma: How do you know?

—Mirza Ghalib says so.*

K—Kaamna is my weapon.

Dr Verma: That sentence has no meaning.

—My life's entire meaning is summed up in it.

P—Prime ministers should not write poetry.

R—The ruling class is spurious and illusory.

B—Bullocks sing bhajans.

Dr Verma: How can that happen?

—That's called unpoetry.

W—When it rains in the Sunderbans, white leopards sing ghazals.

R—Rajendra Yadav wins the Nobel Prize. The Hindiwalas are filled with dismay.

S—Soumitra Mohan does not write poetry but is nonetheless a poet.

D—Deepak, Swadesh is the worst writer in the world.

G—Gone is the glitter of the stars.

K—Kshatriyas open tea stalls.

---

* This refers to the story in which Ghalib has thrown mango peels out of his house and a donkey, having sniffed them, moved on. A passerby is said to have remarked: 'Look, donkeys don't eat mangoes.' To which Ghalib, who once wrote an ode to the mango ('Dar sifat-e Amba'), reportedly said: 'Yes, only donkeys don't eat mangoes.'

I—I have no reason left to live.

Y—You left your smile in my mind.

Dr Verma—In Hindi please.

—That line can only be written in English.

I set the pen down on the table. Dr Verma asked, won't you write more?

I shook my head. He got up to escort me back.

—No need. I remember the way.

—I like walking you back. You've lost a lot of weight.

—If I lose some more, I can fly out of the window into the sky.

He stopped. Troubled. Then happy.

—You can even use a plane to fly.

I stopped, surprised, then happy.

—No one told me. Now I'll use a plane.

The Conference Hall. All the doctors in place. Avneet Sharma says:

—First your medical case history will be read. Up to that point, you will not be there. Then you will be called. Questions will be asked of Deepakji. Madam, you will not be allowed to speak or to help him answer.

Avneet went in. Geeta took both my hands in hers.

Geeta: Answer whatever is asked of you. Perhaps they'll find a way…

—What possible way is left?

Geeta: You stare into the souls of your characters. Have you ever…

—I am the dead soul of Gogol.*

We were both silent. We were lost, not in each other, but

* Nikolai Gogol (1809–1852) wrote *Dead Souls* (1842), a Homeric and picaresque novel in verse. The 'souls' of the title refers to the serfs that Russian landowners owned; the term was used as a measure. 'Six souls of serfs for sale', for instance.

in ourselves. Mayavini advised me gently—Say nothing about us. Or I will grow old immediately.

Is Mayavini Rider Haggard's *She*?*

We were in the hall. Professor Kulhara, Head of the Department of Psychiatry, is in the chair. He explains the rules.

—Swadeshji, no doctor will be allowed to ask you more than two questions. Answer only if wish. You may choose to be silent. You may take no part in the conference. You may leave now if you so desire.

I began to move. Geeta realized I was going to leave. She grabbed my knee and held me down.

Professor Kulhara: For twenty-six years, Swadesh Deepak has been a professor of English. He writes in Hindi. He has written ten books including the play *Court Martial*.

Right now it is being shown in Chandigarh. Deepakji, we will call a halt as soon as you are tired.

Pens came out of pockets. Notebooks were opened.

Dr Ajit Avasthi: What kind of books are you reading these days?

—Detective fiction and thrillers.

Dr Avasthi: You mean cheap books.

—No. Such books are called popular literature. Not cheap books.

Professor Kulhara: We should not forget Deepakji is a professor of English.

If he wants, he might take a class with us right now.

Scattered laughter. My tension lessens.

Dr Avasthi: How much do you remember of what you read?

---

* H. Rider Haggard (1856–1925) wrote several overwrought potboilers of which *She: A History of Adventure* is still the best remembered, for it is here that we meet the eternal Ayesha, a white queen in 'Darkest Africa' who is worshipped as 'She who must be obeyed'. It is a measure of Deepak's disorder that he can slip and slide from Gogol to Haggard. Or is it?

—Nothing. I read books several times over.

Some other doctor: Do you feel there is a mirage behind the phantasm?

—When memory begins to vanish, any home, one's own home can become a betrayal.

The same doctor: Then how do you recognize what's yours?

—Only by a desperate desire to acquire that which is inaccessible, that which is problematic. The morning is silent and the wind, a deep roar.

Professor Kulhara: Try not to reply with such difficult poetry. After all, we are only doctors.

Some other doctor: Do you not love your own folks?

—No, not when they give advice. When they are close, I feel paralysed. Read scripture. Chant the holy name of Ram. Count to ten.

Doctor: What do you think about?

—That I've lost my way, I lack direction. A spiritual drifter like Robert Frost.

Professor Kulhara: You seem out of breath. You can be silent for a while.

—I'm not smoking these days. I will lose breath.

Some doctor: Who do you talk to in the night?

I was silent. Geeta nudged me. Tell them.

—If you ask me such personal questions, I will start telling lies.

Doctor: Your home could be wrecked. Have you considered that?

—No, these days I think Adam Saahab was right when he wrote:

Dil khush hua masjidein veeraan dekhkar
Chalo meri tarah Khuda ka bhi khaana kharaab hai.

Doctor: What kind of dreams do you have?

—The cat could have a heart attack at the terrifying dreams of the rat.

Geeta: Answer the question directly.

Professor Kulhara: Madam, please do not help him.

Doctor: Why do you always write tragedies?

—Tragedy is the only truth of life. The wordless one who is always with me says: You were born to write tragedies.

Doctor: Don't you like women?

—I fear women.

Doctor: What would you like to be in your next life?

—A dozy cat. I will walk noiselessly with the moon.

Someone put a cup of tea on the little table by my side. Geeta said: Drink it. Who knows how many more questions they'll ask? Are you tired? Should we go? Don't get angry today. For my sake.

Wild dogs crawling towards me. Their stomachs on the ground. Wild dogs with their eyes on me. Their tongues loll, saliva drips continuously from them. Am I their food? The doors of fear fly open. Will she who stole my shield come to rescue me? I asked Geeta—When will day break? Why doesn't the night end? She understood. I was about to return to my excited world. She took my hand and pressed it. I stopped at the door. In those seven years, my body had learnt to read the signs.

Doctor: Why haven't you written in so many years?

—She robbed my dictionary.

Doctor: Why do you wish to die?

—Physical liberation is on the far side of the barbed wire.

I was tired. The questions were so meaningless. I was answering like a telephone. I kept sitting there. I was in a country where no one spoke my language. I could not understand their language.

Doctor, if nothing else, you should read the newspapers. For the diversion.

—Why listen to the echoes of screams? Have you ever touched cold light?

Doctor: Do you have any focus?

—I would like to head to the green mountains.

A tension spread in the conference room. The doctors realized I had left the room.

Doctor: You will have to decide to fight this disease.

—No. I am a damned Hamlet. The prince of hesitation.

Geeta said: Don't speak English.

I said: I told you I don't know Hindi.

My body began to absent itself from there.

Doctor: Have you figured out why you fell ill? Do you hate someone?

—Not now. She smiles and she weeps.

Doctor: Is there some reason you like her now?

—Flowers drying out quietly. My betrayal. I have been cast out. Bread cast upon the waters... Insomnia...dark experiences...a black spring... Wordless, sinless... Seven years...a noose...my neck...a rope...pull the rope.

Geeta silenced me by pressing my knee. Sitting there, I began to hyperventilate.

Professor Kulhara: Deepakji is tired. Only questions that are truly vital.

Dr Avneet: I think we should close here. My patient is tired.

Professor Kulhara was silent. This was his way of permitting more questions.

Doctor: One does not live for oneself alone. You have children, a son and daughter.

—My children have drowned in a river of sorrows. A contagious disease. They will not stay near me. Now I converse with God. He said they are all dead for you.

I see bottles bobbing in the sea. They hold secret messages for me. People talk through their knees. My dead father says: follow me. My wife. My shroud. The voices say—Do not stay with your own. Why do I not have three children? I, the king. My ministers. My courtiers. Now my kingdom of the mad. I am in Pushkar.

My festival of camels. My brain under lock and key... I stink from head to toe.

A farce of mercy. I am not fated to meet her...the prayers of one's own.

Why don't I die? I'll take them with me... There is no woman like me... Smart, brainy, beautiful, sexy and fatal. Don't ask me for my address...where has my piano gone? All the sentences have crumbled. Words have divorced the dictionary. Life is an illusion... I am a moral leper... I am a disaster...for everyone... When will my end come?

Geeta wiped my lips, my neck. I was dripping spit. She said forcefully—Now not another word. What kind of questions you've been asking him! You are bone-tired.

Doctor: If you are...

Swadesh: Words, words, words. Am I a criminal? Being grilled and unclothed. Beware. Beware of her burning eyes. She will come with her white leopards. She will kill.

Her buttocks are a little large, a little heavy, very sexy. Am I Kafka? Am I the hero of *The Trial*? Is this a court? Any fractured soul on trial? Swadesh Deepak. Public Exhibit Number One. My grief is suspect. The doom is only truth. There is no motivation. There are one hundred prosecutors. Where is my defence counsel?

Everyone began to get worried. Geeta wiped up the flying drops of saliva.

A doctor slowly stood up in his place. He was very fair. His hair was tightly drawn back. The body of a Greek god. He said: I am Partha Choudhury. Defence counsel for Swadesh Deepak.

8. The Wanderings of a Darkling Autumn

This was my climactic moment.

No, it was the climactic moment of a broken man.

Time said: There is no reason for you to be. And it took away my place of refuge.

Why do I have no meaning? Why am I of no consequence?

Memory, crouched in a corner of my soul, began to doze.

My memory was gone, all gone.

Even my nails are tired...

From a shoe shop, the smell of sweets. The women are tired.

In the afternoon, Geeta asked: May I leave early? Parul goes to Delhi tomorrow.

Had she read what was written in my eyes?

—Did you forget? Parul has been selected by the Taj Group of Hotels. She starts training soon.

Sentences took shape inside me.

My daughter to work in a hotel. But the words would not take the shape of sound.

—Go. Prepare her. Her return is improbable.

Geeta's eyes fill with fear. Has Deepak returned to his city?

—You're not pleased? If you want, I can stop her from going.

—Those who go to Delhi never return.

Geeta left, her shoulders bowed further. Chacha Harnam Singh stared at me constantly. His lips moved in prayer.

His son Sikandar had been admitted again, the third time to PGI. Chachaji was now familiar with the signs.

Kanta said she had to go early too. Her granddaughter's birthday.

I was now in a jungle full of booby traps. Hunters build these snares out of fresh young bamboo.

Her back is silvern. She came and sat by me.

I began to climb up a sheer rockface. No one saw me.

Kanta said again that it was her granddaughter's...

—Go. Don't give me reasons. You're with your brother, not in jail. Give me no rigmaroles.

Kanta sat down again. She began to cry quietly. Then she regained control of herself—Now your elder sister gives you rigmaroles.

Chacha took her hand and said—Chalo Bhainji, let me get you to a bus.

Kanta saw the fear in his eyes and went quietly with him.

Sikandar: Bossman, you're scaring me. Don't talk in English. Here, eat a banana and you'll be fine.

In a moment, the kingdom of fear began to spread. When the war begins in Punjab, the trenches are dug in Calcutta. The patients and their attendants got wind of this. The lights go out. On the stage of the soul, the play begins. Harnam Chacha sat down on a stool near me.

—Professor Saahab, today let me tell you a story about Shri Krishna who was as great a warrior as a thinker and intellectual. He knew every tactic of warfare. He forged an army out of farmers and milk vendors. He uprooted a strong and cruel ruler like Kamsa so completely that no other Kamsa could take root. Once there was a war. The enemy's army was inflicting much damage. Shri Krishna realized the enemy would defeat him and kill him too. He had to survive that day if he wanted to fight another day. And so he took his army and retreated. And so another name for Shri Krishna is Ranchhodji.

Sikandar: Bapu, why tell Bossman that story? He is not Shri Krishna.

Harnam Singh: Son, in each one of us there is a small part of Guru Maharaj. The sons of Guru Gobind Singh were walled up alive. Seeing the women and children weeping, Guru Gobind Singh roared: Stop that weeping. Two of my sons are dead. What of it? Countless sons of mine are still alive. Into their hands will I put the scimitar. They say the tears dried in people's eyes. And flames flickered in them. Professor Saahab here has lost a battle. But he will win the next one. Our Guru Maharaj will be at his side. Shoulder to shoulder, they will take on the enemy.

Ranchhodji did not arrive with reinforcements. Soorma Guru Gobind Singh did not come. I searched both sides of the bed but she had stolen my weapons. War had been announced and I descended onto the battlefield without arms.

Sound the siren. You lazy bastards. The enemy planes have crossed the border.

The patients ducked under their sheets.

She came. Three white leopards. She will kill me. She will kill me.

Outside, Vikas's two commandos heard the word 'kill'. In a blink they were at my bedside, one on either side, their automatic weapons at the ready; in their ears, the sound of sanguine words.

—Who's come to kill you? We'll rip them apart.

—Saahab, don't worry. God himself would not be able to come in.

—Dalvir, full alert. I'm going to call DIG Saahab.

—No Vikas. No V.N. Rai. He has joined the enemy.

Harnam Singh explained that there was no real and present danger—His nightmares have begun. Go back to your places.

—Sardarji, we are going to stay right here. We won't move unless we get orders from the DIG or the doctor.

They began to scan the room, their heads turning by degrees, looking for a murderer.

Dig me a trench. The bombardment has begun.

Mr Shimla screamed that someone should get this bastard out of the room. The professor has gone completely mad.

Satbir Singh went to his bed.

—Young man, one does not abuse one's elders. I think you should shut up now. If we shut you up, you may never speak again.

The Defence Minister himself revealed this frightening secret, that your seductress shaves her legs of brown hair every Sunday with a safety razor. She does not understand the difference between A and B.

On the lawn, an old chair. Whose dentures are those lying on it?

How do I resolve all these sorrows at once? To me the most fraudulent words in the world are: You will get well.

Sikandar: Bapu, enough now. Bossman will die.

Bapu: He won't die. The Guru is by his side. The golden arrow has been nocked. What force can touch the professor now?

I got up and circumambulated the iron bed.

Harnam Singh: Well then, we shall pay for it. Get some milky tea for you?

—Bring me a bucket of that one's blood. I'll drink it in a gulp. Maud Gonne is here. She's come. From Ireland. She comes every day. She lies. She will make you well. Every day a ship of mine is lost at sea. She is Helen of Troy. The first fatal woman. The curse of men. Chachaji. All my ships have been sunk. How shall I cross the ocean? There is no one with me in this calamity.

A huge iron rod was lying near the pillows. The horses of winter had begun to gallop. The long red tongues of goats. Shouts of victory. Long live Krishna Baldev. To break the rod I hit my head with it. The rod does not break. My head does not break. No blood runs. The head is thick in the middle.

Sikandar shouted: Bapu, his head has a bump on it.

—Harnam Chacha. Tell them. Tell them all. If I get them, I will rip them with my spear.

Second collision. My horse! My horse. Run for it. Bring me my horse. I declare war.

Sister came in. Sister ran out.

Harnam Singh reassured the patients that she would page thc doctor.

Today I will kill her. I will kill the bitch-goddess.

Sikandar said: Bossman, you have no weapons, none at all. The two of us will wring her neck. That should be fun.

Between my legs, a rat. A scrawny rat. I was frightened. I began to cry.

Sister came. With a long, tall, dark man.

The patients were happy. The doctor was in. Now the monster will be silent.

He stood in front of me. I stopped running.

From Bengal. So he speaks chaste Hindi.

—Swadeshji, tell me my name.

Psychiatrists know this: a name links you to things outside.

—Suryakant Tripathi Nirala.

—I wish it were my good fortune to be named after such a great poet. Mine is such an easy name. And yet you always forget it. How about a clue? It's a name from the Mahabharata.

—The second femme fatale: Draupadi.

—No. My name is Shantanu Gosain.

I had my chance now. I could split my head open with a rod. Some people got up to restrain me. Defeated by her own ego, Draupadi issued a royal order.

—Be seated. No one will take hold of Swadeshji.

I began to climb the sheer rockface. I walked without my feet touching the earth.

—I can phone Geetaji and have her here in an hour…

—Geeta cannot come. She has gone to Pakistan. To meet the President. She wants permission to pray for Deepak and get the pirs and fakirs of Pakistan to intercede on his behalf. The pirs and fakirs of your country are legendary.

Sister advised Draupadi—Please call Dr Avneet. Professor is running high temperature. His body is burning.

—Sister, get the thermometer. I'll call Avneet Sir.

Terrified, the nurse inserted the thermometer.

—Professor Saahab, I'm like your younger sister. You won't bite the thermometer and break it, no?

—Use it on Sikandar. He's the one with the fever. I am this iron rod.

Third collision. Nothing happens to the rod. One more bump. Mr Shimla sobbed.

—Professor Sir. Your suffering is endless. You must die. I will pray.

He looked at Noddy. Fear, silence.

—Brother, use English if you must. All languages are permitted to express sorrow.

Every language fails to express the grief of man.

—Deepak Sir, please be quiet. No one shares their sorrows. Everyone laughs if you do. Be quiet.

I stopped flogging this dead horse. I mounted another one. I saw her coming towards the room. What illusion was this that had taken on the form of Mayavini?

—Do not come in. Not a step... I will... You ghoul...I will eat your heart out in front of everyone. I will have sex with you...and your daughter...will get pregnant. How much have you paid for my soul? The moment I saw you. The moment I realized your hobby is collecting souls. Don't ever dare to think that poets and writers are simpletons. Go back to your den. The leopard now knows your sex scent. It has arrived... The whole forest will throb with your cries of pain and pleasure, you bloody rich bitch.

Today, she is frightened. She turns and flees, her head on the ground, her feet in the air. No one wipes the spit from my neck. Geeta in Ambala. The piano played with burning hands. No sweet sounds. No cacophony. The piano is offended.

Shantanu, Gautam and Avneet Sharma arrive all together. This is the first time I have seen doctors in kurta-pyjamas. Enter the demonic attendant. They have confining ropes in their hands. They watch me with crooked eyes and peripheral gazes.

—Welcome. Everybody welcome to the theatre of Beckett.

Avneet: Tell us the name of the play.

—Beautiful murderesses do not hang.

Avneet: Wrong. Capital punishment means they hang too.

—Wrong. She will appeal to the President for mercy and the President will look at a picture of her and forgive. After all, he's a human too. And a man as well.

Dr Gautam looked at the terrified nurse. From her trembling hands he took the trembling thermometer.

—Deepakji, it's me, Dr Gautam. Your bodyguard. May I use the thermometer? You won't crunch it in your teeth? I'll lose my job. My polio-stricken child will die of hunger.

I opened my mouth. Thermometer in. Out again. He looks at it, looks again, returns it to its plastic home, closes the box. He puts on its cap.

Dr Avneet: How much?

Dr Gautam says nothing.

Sikandar: One hundred forty.

Mr Shimla: Shut up. At a hundred forty, wouldn't his head have melted?

Sikandar: Shut up yourself. This is the Bossman. Is he going to have some small-time fever?

Dr Gautam: 105 degrees. It might rise. Immediate shift to medical ward, I think. Please call for a stretcher.

Dr Avneet: Mr Deepak will not be moved. He is my patient. I will take the decision.

Dr Gautam: A sick person is everyone's patient. If the fever increases, his brain might be compromised. Perhaps you don't know how the medical department works. Emergency calls are noted. The doctor on call writes down what the patient has and the medicine has to be given. He gives his advice. In an emergency, the emergency doctor is in charge. It is called medical law and medical ethics.

Dr Avneet: You're getting angry for no reason. He always hides things. In this mental state, he might reveal something. Then his treatment...

Dr Gautam: Why do you psychiatrists always see

yourselves as so superior? Swadesh Deepak is in a state of delirium. He is raving. He is on the edge of madness. He can take the jump any moment. I'm going. You don't need me. This poor helpless patient needs me. I will put all this down in my report. And if something happens to him, God himself will not be able to protect you from the law and the courts. Please believe me. I will be the state witness against you.

For a little while, I came out of the world of delirium. I am in the habit of writing long dialogue, just as Gautam was speaking now. Perhaps he has learned my dialogue by heart. He could have been a tense actor like Piyush Mishra.

I have completed my renunciation. I was secure in my beloved personal world of delirium.

I turned into a ceiling fan with broken blades, something to be tossed into the corner of a room, whether the psychiatric ward or the medical one. What difference did it make to me? Both were fatal.

I am an indeterminate and dim mausoleum.

My brain began to throb again. Please God. My brain has started throbbing.

I asked Dr Avneet why women's stomachs swell when the winter comes. Harnam Chacha wiped the spit from my cheeks.

—I remember her yellow cat so well. Cats are not loyal as dogs are. They go where they will be petted.

—The fat women raise their arms to do their hair. Why don't they do the hair in their armpits?

Dr Gautam: Your patient will go any minute. Brain paralysis is setting in. We have lost the only chance of shifting him to the medical ward. Who...

Avneet: Dr Gautam, don't take on so. This is not brain fever. We call this the climactic moment. It is a distressing time for the patient. But it is often a priceless moment for us. Psychiatry recognizes this as a bipolar disorder. Patients live between two extremes. Dr Pratap Sharan's thesis is that hardened criminals and bipolar patients have secrets they never reveal. In psychiatry, machines are so helpless.

Dr Gautam: Sorry, Dr Avneet. For a moment I lost my cool. In fact I like Swadesh...

Dr Avneet: This might be his tragedy—many people love him. Deepakji is now convinced that he is special. He was not born of a mother, God himself brought him to earth for us.

He gestured to the demonic attendant that I should be made to lie down on the bed.

He had to bend down to lift me up. Dr Avneet said that first the rod should be taken from my hands.

First he pulled gently at it. Mayavini had poured all her powers into my hands. The demon went red in the face. In front of so many people, to be unable to free a rod from my grip!

He took hold of one of my fingers and began to bend it backwards. The pain began to run into the fingers.

Noddy the engineer's head stopped moving. He asked from his seat on the bed:

—Hey, strongman, do you want to break his fingers? Blow in his ears instead. His fingers will relax. You may be fat but you're not strong.

Dr Gautam blew in my ear. The rod dropped from my hand. The engineer began nodding again. Dr Gautam looked at him questioningly.

—Sir, I'm an engineer by trade. We often start machines by blowing into them.

Swadesh recumbent. A drip in his arm. A drop of glucose falls from the bottle. It runs through the rubber tube and then... drop by drop it conjures up his life.

Dr Avneet asks Harnam Chacha whether Deepak has had dinner.

Avneet: Why didn't you eat dinner?

—Because I was very hungry.

Avneet: Tell me an incident from your childhood.

—I was young. I went to the temple to give the pujari some food. I saw him with his back to the tree, masturbating.

Avneet: At this moment what would you like to do?

—Paint a giraffe. Give me a big canvas and a small ladder.

Avneet: Why do people love you so much? You made Dr Gautam lose his temper.

—My good fortune. By rights, they should spit on me, a low ugly person, a worthless writer.

Avneet: In your sleep you often say—She will not let me go. Who says this?

—Krishna Sobti.

Avneet: Wrong. Totally wrong. However good a writer Sobti is, she is an even better person. She could never harm someone. Your diseased dreams...

—Krishnaji did not say it. Sobti would never even in her dreams wish someone ill. Maya Bakhshi said it.

Avneet: Who is Maya Bakhshi? (Pause.) The one from your story, 'Kisi Ek Pedh Ka Naam Lo'? That is your darkest story.

—I read it to Krishnaji. She raised her head. It was night but it was as if the sun were bright on her face. She said:

—Swadesh Saahab...

When Krishnaji suffixes your name with 'Saahab', you have to wake up. She can turn even a flower into a weapon.

—Swadesh Saahab! You let Maya and Ajay have three days together. The playful Maya falls in love with the stern Ajay. You give Maya no warning, no omens of disaster. And her last meeting with him is on Death Row. Why? I'll tell you why. Because you're not just a well-born bastard, you are also a wicked person. Now Maya Bakhshi will have her way. She will revenge herself, somehow or the other. She won't spare you.

Many years later, I realized that Krishnaji can divine the future. She was right. Maya Bakhshi would not let me go. She only changed her name. Mayavini.

Avneet: Who is Mayavini?

—No one. A European literary prototype. A seductress. Mayavini is the translation of that word.

Avneet understood that I had slipped away just before giving him a vital clue.

Avneet: Your imaginary...

—No, not at all, these are not phony meetings.

Avneet: Why don't you try and sleep?

—If I sleep, I will be captured.

Avneet: You could try...

—When a man dies inside, he must walk a dark tunnel for the rest of his life. Dr Sharma, my disease is out of your cure or control. Have you heard of mercy killing? Sometimes it is a blessing. Please bless me.

Dr Sharma knows that when I speak English, I am lost.

Avneet: Psychiatrists never admit defeat. You've begun to recover in patches. This is priceless for us. We will renew you.

Dr Gautam: I've read your case history. Why such a volcanic temper?

—The castrated can only resort to rage.

Avneet: How did Sukant's fear of staying here leave him? When we suggested he visit, he would refuse. Now he insists on spending the night.

—In a night, I increased his age by ten years. I introduced him to pain. From sixteen, he became twenty-six in one twinkle of an eye. Sorrow makes you tough, and cruel to yourself too. From a teenager, he became a man of twenty-six. Tough, mentally strong and a man of his word. When we protect our children for too long, we make them weak and cowardly. This truth my tantrik guru taught me. I would go and stay at her ashram when I felt like it. Even as she saw me, she would fall silent for she would be sad. Her sadness was occasioned by her gift of foresight. She was damned because she could foresee the future. She decided to die and she died.

Avneet does not speak in English. But sometimes one's own language may prove inadequate.

—How did this metamorphosis take place in Sukant?

THE PAST

That night, the moon suddenly changed its time-table. The moon is mad, as lovers are; and careless, again as lovers are. It forgot to spin its light during the day. Now how could it emerge from its room?

It had failed to make any moonlight. It writhed on its bed for it could not turn over. It could see the struggle between silence and speech play out on my face. I was in a state of indecision.

—Papa, do you want to say something? Why not say it? Why are you scared?

A few days earlier, Sukant had been asked to try and speak to me in Hindi. Our own language gives us strength. We do not share such stories with our friends as will weaken them. My closest friend is Soumitra Mohan. I told him nothing. I did not let Jehangir Sabavala find out a thing. Rajendra Yadav, Krishna Sobti, Nirmal Verma, no one knew a thing. This was not pride. When I knew this to be the kind of disease in which no one could do a thing, what was the point of making one's pain public? Telling Sheila Sandhu was important. She is made of iron. She would be able to stop those who loved me from coming to see me. Look. No one came except for Krishnaji. No one can stop Krishna Sobti. She came. The powers of all the winds are hers.

Sukant: Tell me, I'll do what's right. I'm not scared now.

I signalled that he take me outside. He got angry. He has strength now but no patience.

—Why can't you speak in the room?

—This is no place for inauspicious words.

We were in the long gallery.

—Give me a cigarette.

Sukant: I don't...

—Don't lie. At your age, all boys smoke and hide it. I did too.

Sukant gave me a cigarette. He looked scared.

—What if the nurse sees? The attendants might...

Swadesh came back for a moment. And with him, the poison.

—Fuck them. Sometimes you must fuck everybody. Light the bloody cigarette!

I held it in the fingers of my right hand. I raised it to take a drag. The cigarette fell on the floor. The fingers have no practice in picking things up. He picked it up. And brought it to my lips.

—Here. I'll hold it. Oh God. My poor father. My helpless father.

He was close to tears.

—I'll smoke it myself. And don't you ever use words like poor or helpless when you're talking about me. Those milksop words are not meant for me. In the dictionary only two words apply: bloody bastard.

And he began to become a man.

—If I die in hospital, cremate me in Chandigarh. No point taking the body back to Ambala. Fire will burn you the same in every city. That is the dharma of fire. No need to tell anyone either.

Not my relations. Not my brother and sisters. Or your mother's siblings, for that matter. Don't use words like 'final rites' for me. They don't apply to the bastard Swadesh. If you run into trouble ask the municipal corporation to help. They're kind, those municipal workers. They cremate dead animals and they'll burn me free. There'll be some opposition. They'll abuse you. If Geeta is in Ambala, don't call her. I've terrorized that good woman enough. Don't be afraid. Don't fear at all. It is your legal right to do all this. I could have told Parul. She's strong. She makes snap decisions. But she is still only my daughter.

In the gallery, the wind begins to pick up. The wind cannot fly in the dome. Dizzy, it collides with the circular walls. The wind began to sough.

Sukant was silent. I felt a moment of remorse. On his slender shoulders, this monstrous burden.

—Sukant, do not for a moment imagine that this is my madness speaking. If you want, you can ignore my words. After death, who feels pain? Who has worries? But do not lie. You will fall in your own eyes. That's what I did. My father said: Don't go to Haridwar for me. I did not. He died in bed. I performed no rituals to make sure he would enter Heaven. He is very happy now. He was in the habit of using abuse as encouragement. When he meets me he lays his hand on my head and laughs: Truly my son, my bastard boy.

The wind began aiming its cold spears at us. I could clearly see Sukant shivering. I have written a lot about all kinds of wind. The wind is now a friend. She gives me advance warning: I'm hot today. Today I'm cold. Today I shall march, tomorrow I'll sashay, swinging my hips. Only once did she get angry—when I named a short story 'Kyonki Hawa Padh Nahin Sakti'. For four days, I had a cold. Geeta said I should get a doctor friend of hers to recommend medication. He's an old man, he teases. Geeta made his prognosis all the more alarming—After a chill, you get a fever. And that will linger for ten–eleven days. And then you can hop about. Fever fears nothing, not even the filthiest abuse. And how dismal your gopis will be when you cannot go to college.

I went to Dr Vijender Singh. Geeta always mistakes a cold to be the precursor of throat cancer. I have been going to Dr Vijender Singh for thirty years. Experience has taught me that one should not change one's doctor or one's lover. It saves a lot of foolish questions.

When I told him I had a cough, he started laughing and would not stop.

—Geeta beti must have twisted your arm to come.

—She's a scaredy-cat.

—No, Deepakji, some wives are extra-careful when they have husbands like you. The reason for that is yours to know. Why should I want to know? I'm seventy years old now. I'll prescribe something. You should be okay by evening.

His compounder put a whole lot of pills in a screw of paper.

—If I'll get better by the evening, why so many pills?

—The pills are for two days. That will keep Geeta happy. Indian husbands have forgotten the art of keeping their wives happy. My wife is very happy. Which is why we have five children. Otherwise an educated wife won't let you get close once you've had two.

I took the pills for a day. The rest I consigned to a watery grave.

I learnt my lesson. I do not bad-mouth the wind now. I have my ways of preserving the self. Back to the wall. Now the wind cannot freeze me in the round.

—Are you tired? Shall we go in?

—I'm not tired. The wind warns us—It says I should walk in the room. Banalata Sen* has come.

—Who is Banalata Sen?

—I'm meeting her for the first time. I'll tell you later.

—It's a Bengali-sounding name.

—It's a French-sounding name.

Sukant stopped. He stared at me. He asked: Papa, are you entering the kingdom of the mad?

—Son, my son. I have already entered the kingdom of madness.

The wind sneered: Sukant is smart. One should not tell the entire truth.

At first I thought I should shout: The truth is always a whole. But I did not scold the wind. It is, after all, a good friend. In the days that I was writing, how much I would talk to it.

I began to search for myself. Perhaps Banalata Sen could give me some clues to freeing myself, to mukti. Yes, the same

* Banalata Sen is the heroine of a legendary lyric poem by Bengali poet Jibananda Das (1899–1954), a poet often described as the most loved after Rabindranath Tagore.

one—the one who Jibananda Das introduced to us in his poetry.

I lay down. She sponged my face and head with a damp towel.

—Swadeshji, who stole your colour?

Banalata Sen is angry. The world is angry.

—Don't tell me if you don't feel like it. I can carry on both sides of the conversation. It is the season of drying up and weeping in silence.

—Jibananda Das is disappointed in you, he's angry with you.

My breath was taken from me. I will go to my cave now.

—Do you know why he likes you? Whether you like what they write or not, a reader becomes a spirit. And you enter into a conversation. He was deliberately ignored all his life. He had become a challenge to the rich, to the great poets of the bhadralok. You did not follow the formulae prescribed by the critics. Perhaps no one has been defeated for as simple a reason as you were. This cruelty, this feudal pride, are you sure it isn't all a front? My poet doesn't get it.

—But then you are from Bengal!

The words came out of my mouth without forethought.

The sea leapt out of her eyes.

And a live volcano leapt into its place.

Seeing Banalata Sen in a rage was magnificent. She tossed the hair that had been lying on her shoulders behind her. She grew taller than I.

—Do not say such unpleasant and hateful things again. Bengal has its own holy culture. Even if a poet or an author or an artist leads a foul personal life, they are revered as if they are gods. They are not treated as if insane. Mayavini is the poisonous blood of your state. What is unattainable must be destroyed. Her grandfather migrated to Bengal from here. She has those poisonous seeds in her.

She was as reticent as her poet. She grew tired. Her breast rose and fell as a bird's does. Her hair was once again on her shoulders.

Like the ants, I began an incessant investigation.

Would the next curse come from Banalata Sen?

I began to frighten the fishes.

I went to the graveyard and forgot the way back. I have been living there ever since. My river has vanished. Here and there pools of stagnant water. Who broke the stems of the flowers?

—That Mayavini, her powers...

—Don't call her Mayavini. Other than her fatal beauty, she has nothing. If there is a Mayavini, it is your wife Geeta. In seven years she has turned into a fortress. Any other woman would have left you. Who allows a neurotic to live in this society? She dropped all illusion and would not allow herself a single word of disrespect about you. You gave the royal command and she did not allow any of your friends to see you. She wrote Jehangir Sabavala that you were well. You tried to kill yourself three times. She kept that from Parul-Sukant. She knows that children do not like a coward for a father. Swadeshji, you...

Banalata Sen could not complete her sentence. She was crying too hard. She was crying silently. Her shoulders were shaking. She was a river of sorrow in spate.

What if her name were Sarayu Sharma? I shivered uncontrollably. The poet himself once said to me: Two heroines never weep. One is my Banalata; the other your Maya Bakhshi.

I did not have a handkerchief. How was I to wipe her tear-wet face? What do you have to do with good manners?

I got angry. Why would Banalata not understand? My life was on the line. My lease had run out.

All my dreams were lost. This is not intentional.

My grief. My disease-stricken soul. I began to scorch in the fever of my dreams. My entire body was languid. A seven-year-long battle. How much longer could I fight?

I have no aim in life. There is no fish-eye. I must shoot. Then why is everyone after me? Why does Banalata Sen of the long hair and weeping eyes want me? I should have a prime aim. What should I say? What can I say to get out of her enchanted castle?

The volcano blazed again in Banalata's eyes.

—What enchanted castle? This is one of your diseased dreams. Every man is not for sale. Jibananda Das was not for sale. When you're dying, fight it alone. No relation, no beloved can come…

She filled her lungs, in her voice a conch sounded.

—Why are you living this apology of a life? Ignoring your faults, you think of yourself as a hero. Once my poet said—Swadesh has no complete dream. He is good in bits.

In her voice nagaaras began to roll.

—You are no more a warrior. Jump. Take a meaningful jump like my poet. Your ego. Your masculine pride. The stupidity of men. Your homegrown Mayavini, Geeta has built such a strong citadel that death has been repulsed three times from its battlements. You will go to Bengal to search for your seductress…

—Where would I find the courage…

—Now I will say that courage is not to be bought at the grocer's. Swadesh, oh Swadesh. I hate spiritual cowards. Good bye. Good night. When I tell my poet Jibananda Das—Swadesh is dead, he was always a fake warrior… Then my poet will no longer mourn for you. You could not possibly be the man who wrote *Court Martial.*

The frightening drum rolls of the nagaara. Banalata Sen got up. From the empty space she left behind the nagaaras still sounded.

THE PRESENT

In the morning, Geeta came early. From today, electric shocks. After the medical conference, there was a consultation about me—Dr Partha Choudhury recommended shocks. Dr Avneet Sharma opposed this on the grounds that his patient had a weak heart. The risk…

Dr Partha Choudhury said that if there were a danger, Swadesh Deepak should be allowed to die.

A vegetable for the rest of his life. Why should anyone be left in a state like that? In London, seventy-five-year-old patients had been recommended for shocks. And recovered too. The British doctors with me would call me Mad Partha Choudhury.

Giving Swadesh shocks could have two possible outcomes: he can come out of the diseased world. Or he could die. Both results would be good for him.

Dr Partha Choudhury's arguments carried the day.

So Geeta came early. No greeting, no good morning, no Ram Ram, no Namaste.

If we had greeted each other, it would have been a lie. I saw three lines on her forehead. She was silent. The General of a long-running war. No use asking anything. Sikandar gave her his news enthusiastically.

—The Bossman was speaking English. He scared everyone; they were crying. The Bossman tried to break his own head open with an iron rod. And such rage. More English and one more bang on the head. The nurse came. The junior doctor came. And the fat messenger of Yamraj. The Bossman hit himself again. A third lump. More doctors. But Veerji kept talking in English.

Sikandar stopped to eat his bananas. Mr Shimla said in a scared voice:

—Madam, your husband is really mad. Tell the doctors to kill him. You can have a second husband.

Geeta said a dry thank-you. The accountant shut up.

—When you know it causes problems, why talk in English?

—The words are imprisoned in the dictionary. I would free them. The words of one language must cohabit with words of another language. Decent people do not say 'fuck'. Words are wild animals. Terrifying. Angry. Frightening and beautiful. When a genuine poet has sex he becomes 'nirala' (different). *Juhi ki Kali* and *Ram ki Shakti Puja*.* A great poet has sex and becomes Maithilisharan Gupt.† A national poet is always mala fide.

—And what happens to Deepak?

—Deepak becomes Virginia Woolf. A wolf who is always advancing into the depths of the sea. And the sea frees it. How shallow is my sea. It reaches only my knees.

—If you really wanted to die, why did you sell the .22 rifle? The sea liberated Woolf? Well, Geeta will liberate you. I cannot bear to watch you die by inches. Who took away your panache? Now a physical cripple, a mental cripple. You must die. My Deepak must die. I will change my prayers to God. Now I will pray for you to die. As long as I live, you must not be forced to beg for mercy. Sukant has begun telling his school friends that you're not his father, you're his relative. Now, like a pig, I love to wallow in filth.

This woman whose name is Geeta Mehta has gone over to the enemy camp.

I will marry royal words and common words. French words, English words, German and Black Negro words will all live in a commune. As little as possible will be asked of a word's past. That princess is actually in love with her beautiful sexy servant girl. Every night, a samudramanthan, a churning of the sea.

I am Virginia Woolf speaking. This is not Swadesh Deepak.

Geeta: I remember how scared you were of rats. Even taking a rat caught in a trap outside would set you off. I would get angry and in my head I'd say—what a lion-heart is my Deepak. Snakes would wander into those old colonial

* These are the names of short stories by Nirala. In English: 'Jasmine Bud' and 'Ram Performs Shakti Puja' respectively.

† Padma Bhushan Maithilisharan Gupt (1886–1964) was called Rashtra Kavi by Mahatma Gandhi. Which may explain where Deeepak's riff takes him in the next line.

houses. You would break their backs with your heavy boots. They could not free themselves. Then you would crush their heads. And you'd explain it to the children—first break the back and make movement impossible. The best weapon is a hockey stick. Now even Sukant kills snakes with ease.

She looked at me and the memory of those snakes and rats gave her a context within which to ask:

—Now I'm hearing a woman drove you mad. How did a woman's shadow manage to get close enough to fall on you?

Why is she talking so much today? She has always had a problem with my harsh voice. On the first morning after we got married, I wished her good morning and she said:

—Listen, Deepu, I think it would be best if you didn't greet me. Your 'good morning' sounds like a threat.

What sorrow must I display for this obstinate girl? She loved my savage weapons, admired them.

—*Geeta daachiwaala muhaare kaise mod le!** The reservoir of my scent has dried up. The swans came and went back thirsty. As evening falls, no dervish comes, no knock sounds. The renunciate stays with me all night. Dawn comes but she does not meet my eyes. Manjeet asks questions. I cannot answer.

Crooked teeth flashed. A curtain-raiser. Rage.

—Do not speak to me in poetry. Poetry has destroyed you; poetry has driven you mad. I hate your Eliot, your Yeats. I hate your Soumitra Mohan. Will poetry feed your children, or me?

She was silent. Poetry begged, hands folded—I am a daily-wage labourer. Give me some work to do.

Today Geeta is wearing the clothes of bees.

The female eagle was tired. Her slow fluttering wings khankhach, khankhach. How am I to explain? Our monotonous life is at a sorrowful end. And what is left is the scent of poetry.

---

* This has reference to a Punjabi folk song in which a woman asks her lover, the leader of the caravan of camels, to turn back.

THE PAST

Kirti Nagar, Delhi. Perhaps thirty years ago. Some friends said, come on let's introduce you to Soumitra Mohan. He lives around here. We found his home.

He was entertaining a toddler by pretending to be a cockerel. He went on cock-a-doodle-do-ing despite our presence. The child gave him no quarter either. A woman came hurriedly into the room, whipped the child up into her arms and vanished inside. No doubt his wife. Splendid men often have such wives written into their destinies. After being introduced, his first question—Do you like Dharamvir Bharati's poetry very much?

I was annoyed. He ought to offer a context. A friend reminded me that my long story 'Ashwarohi' had some lines by Dharamvir Bharati in it.

—The lines by Bharati were what the story demanded. We prose writers use lines of poetry as our birthright.

Soumitra ran a hand over his 1930s-style hair. I realized that in conversation both body and mind were always alert.

I wanted to ask this good-looking poet whether he could only transform himself into a corpse. Could he growl? Could he roar? Could he ambush? I did not ask.

—Have you read any of my work?

—No. I live in Ambala. The little magazines do not get to little towns.

Soumitra looked at me with curiosity—You're a swine.

His mouth opened, a guffaw came out and whirled up to the roof. One of my friends can guffaw for so long too; she prides herself on being the world's ugliest woman. She challenges any man to have the courage to marry her.

When I go out with her, to see a film or have a cup of tea or visit a book shop, people stare at me, not her. When we come back to the house, she abuses me, and lets loose a poisonous barb—You're a man like a girl.

Soumitra gave me a slender-looking book.

—My chapbook of poems—*Chaaku Se Khelte Huey* ('Playing with a Knife').

I thought I should tell him the term 'chaaku' was also used as a euphemism for the penis. I didn't tell him. It was the first time I had heard the word 'chapbook': a soft word, delicate. I had no idea how to take hold of it. It was a 'handle-with-care' word. Never mind, now to get rid of it.

—Deepak, I know you teach English. Which Hindi poets have you read?

—Mahadevi Pant and Sumitranandan Verma.

A variety of expressions flitted across Soumitra's face.

—Those names are not...

—What does it matter who's Verma, who's Pant? The world's largest country had the world's biggest revolution for independence. The great Hindi poets had nothing to do with the hopes and fears of the ordinary blood-soaked people. They stood behind the Shikhandi* screen of their natures. The decision about whether an author is great or not is made in the future. These two poets have a very short future, limited to school and college textbooks.

Soumitra asked warily—Are you a comrade or something?

He had liked my interchanging of the names. He guffawed. This time it did not touch the ceiling. From behind the door, a military voice—Do not laugh so loudly. The child will get up. This is the undeniable truth about children. When they are awake, they turn you into a rooster; when they are asleep,

---

* Kidnapped by Bhishma Pitamah for Vichitravirya, Amba refuses to marry him as she is already in love with Salva. But when Bhishma takes her to Salva, he rejects her. When Bhishma takes her back to Vichitravirya, he rejects her too. She promises to destroy Bhishma for this; upon being told that she cannot do it in this life, she immolates herself to speed up the process. When she is reborn, in some versions, she is a man. But when faced with this 'man', Bhishma is aware of her having been a woman and so cannot fire on her, therefore Arjun can use 'her' as a shield. Hence the use of Shikhandi as a metaphor for a shield.

laughter is forbidden. I remember to this day that he did not offer us tea. Now I understand that his sthaayi bhava, his permanent aesthetic mode, is a fear of his wife.

THE PRESENT
HOSPITAL

Today I am afraid of Geeta. Why is she suddenly so angry? I have always been in the habit of lying down. I've always been dependent on others. Is that why? No, she isn't that small. There are no alpha males in my jungle.

Icy tears in the eyes of my visitors. They speak of courage and warmth.

I find it difficult to talk for any length of time.

I am in the last layer of muck. And sinking fast.

Geeta: They do not keep patients in the psychiatric ward for more than three months. It's a rule. Where will you go if I don't take you home? No one wants a sick man at home.

—I will stay with Geeta Mehta. She'll take me.

Geeta: You impossible madman. I am Geeta Mehta. I am Geeta Deepak. You have torn a woman into two.

Dr Avneet Sharma came in. He heard Geeta's complaints. He saw her despair.

Dr Avneet: You are getting angry at a man whose mental age is one.

Geeta: What show did he put on last night?

Avneet: He did what a patient does. We don't want a silent stone of a patient who won't let us in to even a small corner of himself. This writhing is not just external, it is internal too. This sudden commotion startles us doctors. You should...

Geeta: My curse. I have no strength left. Either he dies or I should.

Avneet: Wishes don't make horses. You have to share the curse and live on. How can you escape your share?

Today I fear my wife. What have I done? I am lying on my bed of pain. This woman, who has forgotten my great betrayals, is angry for no reason today. Well, never mind. How would I understand?

I won. I won handily. Now to disarm.

I will continue to walk in this endless tunnel. My personal curse. She took my picture away. What will Geeta do with the empty frame?

Mayavini said it will snow tonight. My footsteps will not show. When a girl writes poetry, her menses begin. But then she wants a man, not a poem. In how many paces will I measure the earth? Climbing the marble stairs of your home makes me tremble. Under the pretext of holding my hand, you have sought and found me.

Smoke stands at the door, waiting to get in. God sent a message from Heaven—Beware of dangerous beauty.

Now when she comes, she will be cross-eyed. In your vagina, a withered rose. Why do the dogs howl? Why doesn't Swadesh Deepak howl? He's lost it, my brother.

Avneet Sharma came. He sees Geeta is angry with me.

—You are angry with him. Why? Hasn't someone told you that it is as if you have given birth? His mental age can be counted in months. Now you must look after a third child.

—I'm defeated. I'm tired. When he was well, he was violent. Now he's ill and violent too.

—One does not abandon a naughty child. You have to do some supplementary work.

Looking at Geeta's wet eyes, my new friend Banalata Sen advises me not to let her cry. It will destroy the children, if they find out. Geetaji is now the man of the house.

I looked at Geeta, without blinking. She became alert. And the cannons were rolled out.

—If you must cry, go out and do it. I fuck tears. Suffering is upon us. Fuck the neighbours. Go on then, count my enemies. When we cry then the real mercy...

—Shut up, Deepak. Please. Enough. I am not crying

because I fear hard times. I cried to think of the magnificent days we shared.

Dr Avneet said I would be given my first electric shock. A total of ten over alternate days. First a sedative to make you unconscious. Then the shock. There will be no pain. You'll be lying on your side and you will sleep for two hours. The male attendants fitted my hands into iron bands and tightened the screws. A doctor came. Dark-skinned. Parul in dark make up?

—Swadeshji, I Dr Vasantha.*

—Speak correctly. I'm Dr Vasantha. You are Parul. You are not Vasantha.

Geeta told her our daughter's name is Parul.

—Here in PGI, I changed my name, Papa. Vasantha is as good as Parul.

I turned my hand into a fist. With all my force, I bore down. My veins will stand out. Geeta began to go out. Vasantha said:

—You can stay back, Ma'am. You must watch the suffering of Swadeshji in its most brutal form.

Another doctor came in. Geeta said it was Dr Partha Choudhury.

He put his hand on my forehead, teased—This is the temporary death warrant I signed.

Vasantha inserted a piece of rubber between my teeth. I clamped my jaws down. She put on the hood that looked like something out of a moon voyage.

The injection.

I gave up the world of blood and bone. After that I knew nothing.

Oblivion.

Later Geeta said that the shocks set off spasms that sent my body up a couple of inches in the air. My hands struggled

* Dr Vasantha presented a problem as a translator. She speaks bad Hindi. But her relationship with her patient/surrogate father is based on language and so I chose to transliterate it.

desperately with the iron bands. Dr Partha pressed down on my knees to hold me down.

When Dr Vasantha moved the hood away, her face was white. A daughter giving her father electric shocks…

Dr Partha Choudhury said, in a voice gone suddenly hard: Dr Vasantha, I will kill all his demons. Swadesh may die in the process.

—Oh Deepak. Such pain. I won't go into that room again. It was torture.

—Sweetheart, I knew nothing. I was in complete oblivion. It was like being in the yogic state of vismaran.

Back in the room. All my companions worried. Nothing happened. No broken bones, no burn marks. There are lots of terrifying things associated with electric shocks. Sikandar erupted. He gave me a banana and a hug.

—Bapu. Veerji. Big Brother has taken bigger shocks than me. He's a bigger madman than I am.

Harnam Chacha said: Geeta beta. Let's go to the canteen. A cup of tea. And an omelette for him.

Geeta asked me how I was feeling. I thought for a bit. Then said:

—Something new happening inside me. Tell them to put green chillies in my omelette. I seem to be swimming in the wind. She had stood up. She sits down again. Now she is crying.

I don't know whether she's crying or whether it is the winter wind.

I know she's thinking of the days of my good health, when my omelette would be green with chillies. Perhaps she feels the dust-covered mirror of the self* is being cleaned at last.

---

* This may be a reference to Ghalib: '*Umar bhar Ghalib, yahi bhool karta raha / Dhool chehre par thi, aur aaina saaf karta raha.*' (All his life Ghalib made the same mistake / He kept cleaning the mirror when the dust was on his face.)

Was her time of desperation coming to an end? Would the cats in the house saunter about again? The two of them went to the canteen. Noddy said:

—Veerji, did it hurt?

—I felt nothing. Two hours of deep sleep.

—Veerji, maybe I should have shocks. I don't get sleep only. I keep thinking about my wife. She hasn't come even once to the hospital. She told my father in English—I am scared of hospitals. Saali conventi kutti.* And he began nodding again.

The doctor came. A long-stemmed flower in her hand. She put it on the pillow.

—Parul! When did you develop a liking for flowers? You called it sentimental nonsense.

She sat down on the stool. Completely silent. She was preparing her words:

—Sir, I've read your case history. Heart: weak. Mind: sick. After giving you two shocks, my hands shook. If something had happened... *Main bahut dar gaya tha.*† (I was very frightened.)

—Not 'dar gaya', dar *gayi thi*. When you marry words, you must act with care.

—Sir, please continue to correct my Hindi. I will pray to Prabhuji to cure you. He's my friend.

—Please, Vasantha. Show me Prabhuji's face. I will rake it with my nails.

---

* This wonderful adjective 'conventi' was too good to pass up. In much of India, an English-medium school is a convent school, regardless of whether Christians of any denomination are involved or not. Thus a 'conventi kutti' would be a bitch who has been educated in English. It was not only Swadesh Deepak in his mania who had a tormented relationship with the English language and its products.

† Dr Vasantha uses the masculine form of the verb. Deepak corrects her in the next sentence.

Parul put her hand on mine. She was despondent.

—Sir, Prabhu is in all of us. *Aap saat saal se chehra noch rahi.* (You have been raking at His face for seven years.)

I did not want to correct her by saying 'noch raha', not 'noch rahi'.

Dr Avneet came. All happy and excited, although that's not in his nature at all.

—You were scared for nothing. Dr Partha Choudhury's gamble has paid off. He was in London for three years on deputation. The doctors with him used to call him 'The Indian Magician' to tease him. He is very happy. He has seen the spark of life. You slept for two hours and he sat by you for two hours. He is trying to enter your dark self.

After aeons, I tried to tease someone.

—It's winter. How has the psychiatry ward filled up with so many flowers?

Dr Avneet replied in kind:

—Your readers must have sent them.

Dr Partha Choudhury came. He pulled the stool close to the head of the bed and sat down. He was vibrant with energy. On his polka-dotted tie tiny flowers bloomed. One day I will ask him why he combs his hair like a woman. Partha Choudhury cannot be a Bengali. His name is Bengali though. And his skin the colour of white marble.

—I saw *Court Martial* in Calcutta. Usha Ganguly's production. I don't know another text so full of social and political comment.

—How did you manage to see it?

—I go home to Calcutta for the holidays. You probably don't think of me as a Bengali because of the colour of my skin, right? God gave this skin colour to people of other states to break the pride of the pale faces of your state.

I smiled. Partha Choudhury inflicts small wounds with

his remarks just as the characters of my plays do. If he should ever become a character, his words would become swords.

—It is summer. The birds have aged. Swadesh has aged too.

—No. No. The writer of *Court Martial* will die before he ages.

—In the season of flowering, Swadesh Deepak withers, he withers.

—This disease has built a fence around you. No one will be allowed to enter. No friends. No loved ones. No sunshine. No breeze. Everything withers away. Together we must dismantle this fence.

—The cat is tired of miaowing. No moonlight enters the bedroom.

—Swadesh, just one question. Do not think before you answer or it will be useless. All this began in Calcutta, no?

I thought I'd say nothing. Then I thought, I should tell him. Partha Choudhury is no Sherlock Holmes to be able to find out all the secrets while sitting in a room.

—Yes. In Calcutta. How do you know?

—I'm mad about theatre. The theatre folks of Calcutta love me deeply. At the first show, Kriti Verma was sitting next to you. After the play, 'she' was standing next to you. Suddenly, you took offence and went back to the guesthouse. You did not meet the audience. You did not meet the journalists. Why?

—Who is this Kriti…?

—You know. Tell me. And roll this boulder away.

I was silent. Partha Choudhury is a hunter. This is an ambush.

Geeta came in. With her a man, dark of skin, slender of body. Total army type.

—His name is Suresh. He will stay with you. Chatterjee of the Ambala Cantonment Board has sent him to look after you.

—Will you obey me?

—I will obey reasonable commands. Mem Saahab has given me a list of jobs.

—He seems to be very rude.

—Just an ex-army man. I won't do what's wrong.

Partha Choudhury got up. He smiled.

—Careful, Swadesh. A character out of *Court Martial* arrives.

Where have my companions gone? Dogs. I told them nothing. I did not let them come to see me. My arrogance could not be broken. Even as I died by inches. My father was right.

He said: You only get such a cruel bastard with great difficulty and after much praying. At this age, men play with women; this one plays with words.

My father was an aficionado of ghazals—a romantic.

He had no idea of the power of words. As someone said—I have not seen Mandu. First, I became a fakir. Then a dervish: above sorrow, above happiness.

My clothes were on fire. I continued smoking a cigarette. The fire kept doing its work. I did mine. The result—PGI, Chandigarh.

Every author and poet has a favourite word that opens windows and lets her look in. Soumitra Mohan's was 'raddi'. Soumitra's creative process is also unique. And honest. He writes a poem and then locks it away in a drawer. He believes the poem will correct itself.

After a few months, the poem comes out of the drawer. It's still the same. Surgery now begins. Soumitra is an expert surgeon. He wants only the specific word that the poem needs. A synonym will not work. This is why his poems never suffer from diarrhoea. He has only one collection to his credit—*Lukman Ali*—while his contemporaries have dozens, all assembly-line poems from the same factory.

Out of a hundred poems, Soumitra rips up ninety as raddi.

I do not take the risk of asking him to read anything before it is published. He might declare them raddi and me a ruin. If he disagrees with someone, Soumitra dismisses him with—Never mind. He's a raddi fellow.

Some time ago he sent me his poem, 'Adh-likhi Kitabein aur Patjhad' ('Half-written Books and Autumn') to read. I called—When did this happen?

—About 1990, I think.

—So long ago!

—It's a poem, not a foetus to take nine months.

The first lines of the poem gave this chapter of mine its title: Behind closed eyes / the wanderings of a darkling autumn.

THE PAST

I have known Rajendra Yadav before he became the powerful editor of *Hans*.

His nature is that of an Urduwala: gossipy, mischievous, the king of devilry. Because we Hindiwalas have no sense of humour at all, sometimes he ends up in a soup, which is why his word of choice is 'ghapla' (mess).

I got married a few days before the Indo-Pak War of 1971 broke out. Later when we met he said, you had a ghapla: here a marriage, there a war. It couldn't have been easy.

—What? When evening fell, the sirens would ring, the blackout would begin. Geeta and I would get into bed and she would cling to me as the sirens yowled.

—Rogue, Geeta must have found that rough going.

—True. She got pregnant immediately afterwards.

Yadav changed his spectacles, lit his pipe and became Sherlock Holmes, the world's smartest man, who doesn't need to leave his home to discover the truth. Perhaps he grew a little sad.

—You Punjabis are rogues; you find a way to enjoy yourselves, whatever happens.

Rajendra's favourite word for poets: 'naraadham' (villain).

These days 'ghapla' does not suffice for him and so he uses 'neech' (low) and 'sooar' (swine). He wrote: 'Hona/Sona ek khoobsurat dushman ke saath' ('To be with/To sleep with a beautiful enemy')* and found himself in the middle of a storm.

Yadav is a good writer and editor but he does not have the military tactics necessary to deal with women. Instead of beautiful, if he had used the word 'ugly' no woman would have objected for no woman sees herself as ugly.

Men are stupid, spending so much time chasing beautiful women when ugly women are so much more progressive in certain important areas.

I have not read such an account anywhere else about how men in every age have formed groups, used women and turned them into sex slaves. In a single piece on the exploitation of women, he did what hundreds of pieces could not do. But writing that was not enough for him. Such an essay Namwar Singh could have written just as well.

He used the names of body parts of women which they protect with great care. He had forgotten that Hindi has just begun to become a language in which sexuality can be expressed. It does not yet understand the importance of expletives as ornament.

Thus began a countrywide agitation against Rajendra Yadav. He was very happy to find his life a success. At a literary festival, a Rajkamal event, Rajendra was chairman. Also present were Sudha Arora, Mrinal Pande and Nirmal. All Rajkamal's crown jewels. Mrinal and I were blabbering. No one excels at the art of conversation as Mrinal does. She turned her sights on Nirmal and me.

—Nirmalji, this disease Swadesh is supposed to have had is obviously a conspiracy between you. You can't tell he's been ill at all, looking at him.

---

* This is an essay from his collection *Aadmi ki Nigaah mein Aurat* ('Woman in the Eyes of Man') (Rajkamal, 2006).

Rajendra was irritated. The chairman cannot indulge in the pleasure of idle conversation. The chairman is the meekest animal of all in Hindi.

Then a woman walked in. She could have had it stamped on her head—I teach Hindi.

With no preamble, she attacked Rajendra.

Rajendra made another tactical error. He tried to reply.

When a woman turns into a termagant, just be silent. When she is tired, when she has fallen silent, use that most false of all masculine falsehoods: You're even more beautiful when you are angry. But our Sherlock Holmes is an ignoramus in the ways of women.

I began to get angry. I almost stood up... Mrinal Pande pulled me down again.

—Sit down. You see a Punjabi woman and you get ready to interfere.

The woman let loose an arrow that never fails.

—Come to Mathura some time. I will show you...

Rajendra himself does not know what an innocent child he is. In his innocence, he ends up telling the truth:

—What need to come to Mathura? You can show me whatever you want right here.

That woman must have run out of the event, out of the Rajkamal stall, out of the literary festival.

My favourite word: Fuck off. My daughter Parul's favourite word: Fuck off. Geeta's favourite word was: Deepak the hooligan.

Even after many meetings, I have not been able to discern what Nirmal Verma's favourite word is. Because he loves every word in the dictionary. Perhaps because of the restraint in his writing, words stand in front of him like slaves.

THE PRESENT
IN THE HOSPITAL

The beginning of winter. I need only a shawl. My twisted arm won't let a pull-over go over. My kurtas are now gowns.

Whoever wants may play toss skirt at will.

Explorers' delight.

When I recover, maybe I can go to college... No. I do not think I will ever be able to teach again. My ability to think rationally is finished. But I know only how to teach. You are condemned forever.

I imagine I have a begging bowl in my hand. I must seem like a felonious beggar.

I should write to the President. Ask him to make me a governor. The governor has nothing to do. He just has to sit around, looking good. He's not part of the rat race. Getting well might be dangerous. Seven years in bed. In the same place. Dirty feudal blood. I should have been Shrikant Verma, Indira Gandhi's balladeer. In the habit of cleaning his ears with a matchstick. When he went to stay at the Taj Bombay, the hotel presented him with large matchsticks that might penetrate deeper, offer him more pleasure. These five-star fellows know how to make their guests happy. They'd sell their mothers on commission. This story of the matches came to the ears of Ashok Vajpeyi through the poet's wife and he printed it in some government newspaper. Truly it is said—wives have done more damage to poets than any number of critics or prostitutes. Now I can no longer even read the poems in *Magadh*.* The recurrent image: a besmeared matchstick.

Someone at the head of my bed. I open my eyes. Suresh. He offers me a glass of warm water.

—Gargle. Clean your mouth. Then tea.

—Bed tea does not need a clean...

—That's a bad habit the British have. Our officers adopted it. In the night, the saliva stays in the mouth...

I did as I was told. I gargled. My mouth tasted clean.

—I have the Hindi papers here. Should I read to you?

* Shrikant Verma's *Magadh* was translated by Rahul Soni (Almost Island, 2013).

—No murders, riots or rapes. Anything else will do.

He did not open the newspaper.

—That's about all the news there is.

The patients began to get up and go. Suresh made their beds.

He offered me my morning nutriments. Pills.

—After breakfast.

He took Geeta's instructions from his pocket.

—Saahab, the pills are to be taken first.

I took them.

—Let's go brush your teeth. And shave.

—I'll use my finger and tooth paste. I can't hold a brush…

—In your right hand? I know. That's why God gave us bilateral bodies. If one half stops working, we can use the other half. Saahab, it does not become a man to give up.

—Okay. But no shave. The barber talks too much. Blood oozes for hours afterwards from my mole.

—Saahab, I am with you. The barber will neither nick your mole nor will he speak. He should know that when an army man hits you, you stay hit. Even his mother will feel the pain.

A staircase descending. A broad one. A crowd ascending. A stream descending. No one looking at anyone else. No one stopping for anyone else.

Citizens of Hades, the half-dead.

In the crowd of ascendants, I spot a familiar face. Spectacles. Long hair. Mischief on the lips.

Dr Gyan Chaturvedi: Not a doctor of letters, a medical doctor. Always a joke at the ready. A dear friend. His wife Shashi is also a doctor. She's from Ambala. My student. But even so she has great respect for me. Odd but true.

I shouted at the top of my lungs. Gyan!

He looked back. Immediately he joined the descenders. He saw my strapped-up arm. And he had one of his jokes ready:

—Your arm is the spear of a Nihang. People will get out

of your way. But then who ever had the courage to get in your way?

The barber on the footpath is busy today.

—Gyan, this illness has taken forever.

—When you write long stories, how could you hope for a short illness?

—She hasn't given up yet.

—How could she? You've given birth to a powerful character yourself. Then you married her. But you've gone very thin. Don't lose any more weight. You'll turn into a desirable girl. Your women friends will have heart attacks.

I was delighted. Gyan is such a scoundrel. He never talks about sad things.

—How is that Nimmi? The one who has turned into Meera for your sake?

Gyan remembers Nimmi because whenever he came to Ambala, she would ask for advice on her ailments. Her cold. Her dry hair. Her depression. Gyan has never prescribed any medicine. I asked him once.

—Gyan, what's wrong with Nimmi?

—Nothing, Sir. The ills of a faint-hearted girl. She has the makings of a Meera but not the courage. To climb a pyre of sandalwood and fire, you need total determination.

And he had fallen silent suddenly as if someone had said something to hurt him. Now I told Gyan Nimmi had married and gone abroad. She had not come to see me.

—Oh she will. She probably doesn't know about your illness. A girl with a perennial cold never forgets her loves.

Remembering Nimmi's idiocies made us smile.

Now I am on a piece of sacking. The barber began to soap my face. Suresh said:

—Do not touch his mole. It bleeds.

—There's hair around the mole. When I...

—Don't use the blade there. Use a small scissors instead. Nobody can produce as much blood as you take with each shave.

Gyan's store of jokes must have been stolen. He must be thinking back to those moments in Ambala. The naughty MA English girls who would come home during the day got to know him. Each one developed some ailment or the other. Gyan would conduct a veritable dispensary in my home. I'd scold them. Don't worry him. Get on with you. Make some tea. One of them asked:

—Why are Deepak Sir's cheeks so red while ours are not?

—Two reasons. He does not sit in the sun. And he's always angry.

He would come in the evening, around the time senior Air Force and Army officers such as Wing Commander Wahi would also visit. They would bring things to eat and drink. Gyan was in awe of the fighter pilots. He asked:

—Aren't you afraid in one of those planes?

—I'm more afraid of my wife. When I'm going to fly, she gives me advice on how I should fly slowly.

—Don't you object?

—Not at all. Only foolish men take offence at what women say. Like Deepak here. How often he's shouted at Nimmi in front of me. She should leave this brute.

—I won't leave him. I am *mantramugdha*.

—What is this fucking mantramugdha?

I explained: Cursed by a spell.

Once Wahi came with a very senior officer, an Air Commodore. A grand-looking Sikh. All my topics of conversation failed. I had to drink beer. He drank whisky and beer and was getting rather high. The Sikh Commodore got onto his high horse.

—Mr Deepak. Wahi here says you're a writer. Come to the air force station at Hindon. I am the commanding officer. It's a very peaceful place and close to Delhi.

—No. Hindon is near Saharanpur.*

* Just for the record, Delhi is 35 km from Hindon and 174 km from Saharanpur.

—What nonsense. I am the CO. Would I not know it's close to Delhi?

—No, it's near Saharanpur. My girlfriend's brother works there. Why should she tell a lie? Wahi said to him: Give up, Sir. A beautiful woman is never in the wrong. Confronted with this efficacious weapon, the Air Commodore laid down arms:

—Deepak Sir, come to Hindon. It's near Saharanpur. I'm the CO Air Commodore Brar.

The party ended on a peaceful note. They left. Gyan teased:

—Sir, you're quite something. You even rewrote geography. Poor Brar.

—Brar was drunk, Gyan. Hindon is where Nimmi says it is. After all, her brother works there and why would she lie to me? Her nose...

—Leave it. It's a delicate nose. If you broke it, what would she do when she caught a cold?

THE PRESENT

Gyan outside the hospital. On the footpath. The mischievous smile missing. Everything freezes. I'm on a piece of sacking, being shaved.

Gyan and I have had so many moments together; some naughty, some intimate, some that mixed laughter and anger in equal measure. What must he be thinking now? What heights Swadesh has fallen from, to be sitting on sacking on the street to be shaved.

Gyan has no idea. I'm an orphan now.

Gyan Chaturvedi's specialty is his teasing, his happiness. He doesn't offer insults wrapped up in words.

Once I told him off: Don't call me Sir.

His answer: Some faces command respect just as some faces are worthy of love.

His advice: Sir, you're living life too fast. Take thought.

I told him nothing about Mayavini. What would he think? This is the man I look up to. Now this smart fellow has made a hole in the wall.

The stable door was open. The horse had bolted. By the time I found out, it was too late.

All those warm moments have vanished. Only the cold that makes your teeth chatter remains.

Now I am forever going to be speechless. I am the question. I am the answer.

The courtesans' bodies hurt. They tire, they doze, they snore.

This scent, this fecund scent, which tree oozes it? A tree that stands on the periphery of Hades. You cannot tell a fool until he opens his mouth. Shut up, Swadesh.

Love is a misunderstanding between two fools.* The man is the bigger fool. Like Swadesh.

People run with the hares. They hunt with the hounds. I did nothing wrong, knowingly or unknowingly. And yet this curse of madness.

Today I will abuse Bhagwan. In which language? Punjabi will be the most poisonous.

Gyan took my left hand and raised it.

—Let's go back to the ward, Sir, your face is so wan. You seem fated to suffer.

I began to head towards my familiar bottomless pit. Gyan changed my route:

—All this is that Common-Cold-Nimmi's doing. She stole your joy and hooked off abroad.

—Gyan, Nimmi was a fine person, no?

—This you did not say to her in eight years. When she was talking about her coughs and colds and the dryness of her hair, she was talking of another kind of suffering. But you were sitting upon your throne. And an enthroned king does not understand anyone else's sorrows.

We got to the open terrace of the ward. Many patients were sitting in the sun. All silent. No one talking to anyone else. Everyone lost in the memory of their halcyon days.

---

* The line appears in *Kaal Kothri.*

—Why don't you sit in the sun for a while? I'll meet with your doctor.

—Not in the sun. The room...

—You never sat in the sun, did you? You'd wash your hands in cold water and hold them out of the verandah. Like a teenage girl, you were scared of getting tanned.

Suresh tucked me into bed. He took Gyan to the doctors' room and came back.

—Saahab, you're very quiet today. As if you're sad. Should I phone Madam?

I shook my head. Madam did not have all the answers. She gets angry and curses her destiny. Once, I said to her:

—Geeta, your worst piece of luck was falling in love with me. The second was marrying me.

—Shut up. Just shut up. I am not a character out of your stories.

What do I do about my ugly thoughts? She pities me. She does what she does for me out of a sense of it being a social duty. Which is why she takes such good care of me during this terrible time. She has every right to want to exhale a deep sigh of relief, after these seven years.

But this relief would only come with my death. Which comes but does not come.

Swadesh is Brihannala*—a castrato. The duration of the curse: the rest of my life. Then I will learn to write. No. Just hard work does not make a writer.

I am a living embodiment of bibhatsa rasa.† The other rasas she has in her bank locker. She has the key. I am in a constant state of doubt.

---

* Arjuna, the epitome of male beauty and the greatest Pandava warrior, must spend some part of his exile in concealment; he takes on the guise of a eunuch, Brihannala. Deepak's own self-image as a man seems to be implicated in this transformation.

† A reference to Rasa Theory in Sanskrit aesthetics. The Natya Shastra identifies nine rasas or emotional states which may be found in a work of art. Bibhatsa represents disgust.

Everyone is praying for my death.

One must have some reason to like a person. Why would she sacrifice her life without a reason?

Do not lie. The Lord of the Bow, Kamadeva, had my style in his sights when he sent someone to cure me.

THE SHINING FUTURE

Delhi. To Nidhi's house. For a cup of tea. The first time. As the car stopped, she said, Sir, stay where you are. I realized she was going to tease me terribly. She opened my door. She bowed, taking on the attitude of the doorman of a five-star hotel. I got out to stand next to her.

—Sir, you are very tall.

—Idiot, you are very short.

My gaze fell on the nameplate. I was bewildered by her surname. People with this surname are generally very low. They will cast public doubt upon their own paternity for no reason at all and will do it with great pride. This is only to demonstrate what bastards they are.

She lived in the first-floor flat. As we climbed the stairs, she grabbed my hand.

When we reached the flat, I asked why she took my hand. I had needed no help with those stairs.

—Sirji, I needed an excuse. Otherwise I thought you might have got angry. So what could I do? Perhaps you should wear a placard: Touch Me Not.

Nidhi was neither stupid nor naïve. She had picked up on something when she saw me looking at the nameplate.

—You didn't like my full name?

—No. People with this surname are totally evil.

—Surely not everyone...

—They're unlucky for others too.

—Let's ask Rai Saahab.

—Is Vikas Narayan Rai our Supreme Court?

—Sirji, you never asked about my husband...

—I never ask my friends questions. I'm not in the CID.

They tell me what they want when they want. Listen Nidhi. Your husband was very suspicious of you, right?

She was very startled—He was. But how did you know?

—I find out many things. Just like that. You have no idea of the extent of my powers.

—Show me one that will make me attractive to you.

Nidhi did not say what she wanted to say. I understood. Warning signals began to sound.

—Deepakji, you engage with no woman. To remain undisturbed.

—Nidhi, if you had been born a few years later, you would have been my daughter.

On her lips, a coquettish girl's smile.

—Deepak Sir, had I been born a few years earlier, I would have been your wife.

The dangerous moment passed. She went to make tea. I thought: This evening I shall pray to Kamadeva to take his life-giving herb back. This girl, whose name was Nidhi, was beginning to attract me. Was it time again for my assassination? Possibly. You are not the tough fighter you once were.

As we drank tea, she suggested we have dinner there...

I agreed but said we should tell Vikas Rai. After all, I would be late returning.

KHATT! Nidhi banged the cup on the table. It did not break. She turned into a wild cat.

—Why do we have to tell DIG Saahab V.N. Rai? Am I a criminal? A call girl? Will I give you AIDS? Everyone feels free to give me lectures. Jagdeep says: Don't bother Sirji too much; what if something happens? Tony's advice: Madam, take great care of him. Vikas always looks at me with searching eyes. If I laugh, or tease, Soumitra won't look in my direction. When he looks at you, his eyes are full of worry. Why does everyone see me as an enemy?

She dropped her head on the table and wept silently. Her shoulders shook. I put a hand on hers.

—Nidhi, look up.

She raised her head.

—Look into my eyes.

She did so.

—Foolish girl. No one is your enemy. They all care for you a great deal. Vikas too. Govind Prasad and Harinarayan too. Soumitra also. You're one of us now...

She interrupted.

—You didn't mention one name.

—Sorry. Swadesh Deepak too. Something has been concealed from you so as not to hurt you.

—Tell me, Swadesh. Take me in confidence. I am very tough.

—I went mad. For seven years. Sometimes, I was cursed. Sometimes, I was a curse.

She caught my hand tight. First, there was fear in her eyes. Then a deep sadness. Finally, the wanderings of a darkling autumn. Then her voice became the voice of a mother.

—Oh Swadesh, my poor, poor Swadesh.

The crematorium bird returned. The stream stopped flowing. Mayavini's face was pale. I was King Lear. My clothes were rags. Lightning crashed. Rain pelted down. I went completely mad. Mad and roaring old Lear on the heath. Electric shocks. And me, swimming through the air.

Nidhi.

—Nidhi, I see with your eyes today.

—Nidhi, I want to sit on a swing with you.

—Nidhi, no one has any sympathy for me. People put their fingers to their temples behind my back and make signals, saying I'm mad.

—I cannot cross this river of sorrow.

—What a terrible curse. I could not say an ordinary line—Nidhi, how good you are.

Put him in a Museum of the Mentally Crippled. People will pay to see him.

—Nidhi, please help me to die. I am a leper. A social leper.

—Now I see everything through your eyes. Be happy.

—Once a successful victor. Look, I have thrown down my arms.

—I want to come out of the picture. I'm sick of living in a frame.

—Once Dennis the Menace went up on your wall; there he stayed.

—Will it snow tonight?

Nidhi put her hand on my mouth. My sorrows fled, abracadabra. Truly Sanjivni, the one Bajrangbali brought to the battlefield.

—Swadesh, I'll change my clothes and be back. Five minutes?

—If you have a thin, gold wire nose ring, could you put it on?

Is it my time for poetry?

What is that noise?
The wind under the door?
What is that noise now?
What is the wind doing?
Nothing again nothing.
Do you see nothing?
Do you remember nothing?
Those are pearls that were his eyes.* Are you alive or not?
Is there nothing in your head?†

Eliot, you never prayed for anyone. I will not pray for you. She came into the room. In the chiffon sari, her body was marble.

The nose ring reduced her age by ten years. Her nose was interesting now.

—Nidhi, do not cry again. A girl in tears frightens me.

—From today, an end to tyranny. If I hear of your pain, I will weep. Please don't order me, Swadesh.

---

* Shakespeare. From Ariel's Song in *The Tempest*.

† T.S. Eliot, a line from 'The Waste Land'.

She had dropped the ji from the end of my name. I closed my eyes to pray as children do.

—Oh Lord of the Bow, please order Bajrangbali to return the Sanjivni to its mountain.

Nidhi was also praying. For me? For herself?

9. Chal Khusrau Ghar Aapne*

A leaf flutters and a new eye opens
The sky fills with the flight of new birds
New fish are born in the rivers
And green spreads as far as the eye can see
In the dust, the fresh footprints of children.
—Rajesh Joshi

Their real colour was white. It was now the yellow of marble. They were thin at the top and at the bottom. Swollen in between. That paunch upset their symmetrical lines. Once they fall over, they can't right themselves.

The burnt flesh of my arm has liquefied. Maggots fall from the skin onto my bed. Chacha Harnam Singh's favourite word is 'tezi' (energy). When I said that my arm had been abnormally burning through the night, he would say that the medicines were infusing it with a new tezi.

All night, my arm jerks and throbs. The 'energy' in it keeps increasing. The burning increases, burns brighter, deeper.

Swadesh Deepak, externally hateful and dirty. Inside, a river of filth. Anyone might be revolted even to encounter him in a dream. Mayavini too is terrified. She has not come. The hostel for dream beings is empty. It is filled now with swollen worms who loiter there. Before it is morning Mr Shimla goes into the verandah to smoke a beedi. Seeing me moving constantly on the bed, he stops. He sees the worms crawling on my neck. He sees the worms

---

* Literally: 'Khusrau, it is time to go home.' From Amir Khusrau's lament on the passing of Hazrat Nizamuddin: '*Gori sove sej par, mukh par daare kes / Chal Khusrau ghar aapne, rain bhayee chahoon des.*' (Rough translation: The beauty sleeps on her bier / Hair spread over her face / Khusrau, it is time to go home / Night has swallowed this place.)

slithering and slipping over the white bandage on my arm. He sees the worms, swollen in the middle. He screams in Hindi. 'Behencho... The professor's crawling with worms.'

Even after his long shriek, she does not come. Sikandar drags him outside. The awakened patients sit in their beds like statues, looking in my direction. They cannot get up the courage to scream.

Sikandar uses his slipper to kill the worms coiling on the bed. Harnam Chacha gets me off the bed and onto the stool.

I feel no fear. By evening, millions of worms will be at work inside me. And then the last word of the play can be written: Curtain.

I am afraid of living, not of dying. I explained it myself: what else would a bastard like you get if not worms? How much pain you have inflicted. Nimmi, her face blanched, had said: This is no curse of mine. However cruel you were, you were as tender.

Soundlessly, I screamed—Take my memory away, please. Please kill my memory.

Message after message on the pager. Dr Vasantha on night duty. She gave me a glass of water to drink. She put a hand on my head. She asked: Are you in pain?

—I never feel any pain. I am a cold horseman.

—Deepak Sir, *aap kitna abhaaga hoti, dard nahin hoti.* (You are so unfortunate; don't you feel pain?)

—Please Vasantha. Don't speak Hindi badly.

She took off her glasses and wiped her eyes. She put on hers again.

She knew that when I speak English continuously, I have retreated to my secure country. No sorrow there, no joy. A limbo of the half-dead.

—Vasantha, Vasantha, please don't cry. I will never abuse you.

—*Main dar se nahin rota. Pita ki yaad aata.* (I do not cry out of fear. I am reminded of my father.) Tough, cruel like yourself, never crying. He didn't cry the day he was hanged. Sedition. Anti-national activity. I have terror dreams.

I no longer minded her bad language.

—*Agar Andhra nahin to Bihar ki jungalon mein maar di jaaoongi toh last moments mein aapko yaad karta.* (When I am killed in the jungles of Andhra or Bihar, in my last moments, I will remember you.)

—Vasantha. My child. My daughter. You have no right to die. You have to give birth to a hundred warriors.

At that time I did not know that Vasantha was Apoorva from *Sabse Udaas Kavita*. I was pregnant with her.

Looking carefully at the ceiling, the nurse tells Vasantha that Dr Naidu is on leave. Dr Shrikant is on his way from the Burns Unit. And I am to be shifted to the Burns Unit on Dr Chari's orders.

Harnam took off my choga* and dusted me down with powder. He put a new one on me. He did not know that neither the reek nor the worms would die with powder. Some stinks become a part of the soul.

As Swadesh Deepak's body now reeks of worms.

BURNS UNIT

Dr Shrikant is tall and his arms are proportionately long. His thin long fingers show he is an artist in the cutting of burnt skin. I did not verify this because I was sure he was Saratchandra's Srikanta.† He was not our kind of dwarf poet-leader. From my arm, the maggots fell, plop, plop, plop. There was a black cloth on the table. They wriggled madly on the black cloth on which they showed up clearly.

Tiny demons dancing.

Ma, illiterate, would invent new words. Yes, I remember.

---

* A loose shirt.

† Saratchandra's *Srikanta* (1917) was a love story between Srikanta and Pyaari, a child widow forced into dancing.

'Kulbul-kulbul' go the worms.* Shrikant asks Vasantha, 'What is wrong with him, Dr Vasantha?' Vasantha tells him that everything is wrong with Swadesh, Dr Shrikant.

Dr Shrikant has shared in the sorrows of many. He has understood everything. Now he will not ask anything about me. He looked at the mini-demons on the black sheet. He opened a bottle and sprinkled some powerful medicine over the worms. The swollen slugs died on the spot.

The nurse proffered a tray of instruments. The worms had turned her stomach. Her hand trembled.

Shrikant took the tray from her. He ordered—Go and call Sister Randhawa here immediately. Only she can assist on such a case.

Vasantha asked if there would be much pain.

—Not in the beginning. The skin is dead. But when I go deeper, it will be very painful. You can sit outside. I don't need you.

—I will stay. My father may need me. I need to get familiar with pain.

Shrikant fell silent. He was deeply sad. He understood that Dr Vasantha would not live long. In the flower of her youth, the police would murder her. And call it an encounter.

Sister Randhawa came. She would retire next year. Her self-confidence shows in her face. She knows me. She teases:

—Deepak, you're always up to something. Other people breed poultry. You breed worms. Whatever you touch makes a loss.

The scissors came forth. Shrikant cut the knot. He took hold of a loose end.

—Swadeshji, close your eyes now. You will ask nothing. I'm going to take off your bandage without wetting it. It

* 'Chulbul-chulbul karti aayi chidiya' (The birds chirp and chitter; chulbul-chulbul being onomatopoeic) is the usual song. It is unlikely that his mother, however illiterate, would have mistaken chidiya (birds) for keede (worms), so this conflation is probably Deepak's way of dealing with his body's betrayals. Or creating an alliteration.

will strip the skin off too but that will reveal the area where these worms have their nest. We call it 'Operation Search and Destroy'.

Dr Shrikant took hold of the bandage and yanked. I jerked an inch or two in the air. Sister Randhawa anticipated this reaction. She held my shoulders down.

Pain, waves of pain. Waves that flooded in and ebbed only to return.

Vasantha—Papa, you may talk to yourself. You are an actor of the silent era.

A strong medicine was sprayed over my arm. The stink became a reek and turned into a part of my body.

My lame memories beleaguer my crippled world. Was anything left unbroken?

Why are the heavenly forces my enemies? Pain of the kind to shake my dreams.

That night when I slit both wrists with a blade, I placed my hands in a tin. I did not let a single drop stain the sheet or the floor. I've always liked cleanliness. Parul goes to fetch a doctor.

Geeta keeps slapping me, a series of light slaps. She lights a cigarette and stuffs it into my mouth. I smoke it. She teaches science. Later she said that in such cases one does not allow the patient to fall asleep or else...

In my heart of hearts, I abused her viciously for that 'or else'. She could have let me go, she could have let me become an 'or else'. Dying is the most important task for me.

I tried three times and three times I failed. I lost my reputation.

My Bronze Age did not end. I should abandon myself.

Why does one always think of someone else's body while having sex?

In those days, I found thermometers very sexy. The movements begin.

Oh Krishna! You have said: Of the rivers, I am the Ganga. Why do you not give me my share of Gangajal? You have said: Of the seasons, I am the spring. Give me back my handful of spring, Krishna. Does Yamraj, the Comptroller and Lord of Death, no longer heed you? Krishna, you could throw Parthasarthi into the fire of war. Why did you stop me from burning myself to death?

In his last years, my father changed totally. Khadi clothes, for instance. He was, of course, a scholar of Urdu. But now he learned to write Hindi. Urdu translations of my stories began to appear in the government's Urdu papers. They would not publish the translator's name. I would get money orders for a hundred rupees at the Rajpura address which I would gladly accept. This was the reason why, until his death, I was thought of as an Urdu writer. The Hindiwalas would not accept me because I would not allow myself to take the protection of a school or an -ism by aligning myself with it. My father complained: Yaar, don't write such dark stories. When I translate them into Urdu, it hurts me.

He was smart. He was off before my years of darkness began.

My mother's around. No one had told her. She's almost deaf. Speaks in a shout. The old lady is a broken drum now. But her style is unchanged. If she finds out, she'll come to PGI. And then! First, she'll describe in gross detail the private parts of the doctor's mothers and sisters. Then she'll garland them with other abuse.

Next: a royal command—Take Kaka home. I will have prayers said for him. This is obviously some woman's doing.

The day before she died, I sat with her for hours. In her last hours, she mistook me for her brother Inder. She kept talking to me, calling me Inder. She was happy that Inder had come to visit. I was pleased that she died happy.

Someone came into the cutting room and ordered me to open my eyes. The pain spilled over from my eyes onto my cheeks. Vasantha dried my cheeks with cotton. Dr Chari pressed my shoulder. Shrikant kept cutting away, making sounds like someone chopping betel nut.

Dr Chari: Will you go deeper, Shrikant? You must kill each germ.

Dr Shrikant looked at him. His eyes asked: How much deeper?

Dr Chari looked at the nurse. She understood and brought the instrument tray forward. He picked up two pairs of scissors, one in each hand. For a moment, I saw his face. Such rage, why? His moustaches tremble. Why? I heard the cruel cold voice of death:

—Close your eyes, Deepak. Close your mouth. Vasantha, grip him. Sister Randhawa, Shrikant, grip his legs. Do not let him move at all.

The wrestlers put a forty-kilo man in a stranglehold.

One of the scissors sliced into the living flesh near the elbow. The other went to the shoulder.

—This deep, Dr Shrikant. This deep.

The scissors began to approach each other like dancers. Small pieces of flesh kept falling off. First flames began to flash across my entire body. They were followed by incendiary ice.

Now I was half-dead. Today I will not scream at all. On one side sat Colonel Surat Singh; on the other Vikas Narayan Rai. The flame and the ice kept switching places. I began to complain to Harnam Chacha's Ranchhodji.

Lord of my bodyscape, what sins have I committed in previous lives that you have ordained that I should be killed by Comptroller of Death Yamraj by inches?

Ranchhodji turned into a coquettish young girl. On her crooked lips, a crooked smile. She is silent now.

Around my heart, an atmosphere of terror. The birds fly from the branches of my tree and do not return.

—Your tree is cursed. Its very shadow is affronted by it. It has gone away. Now there are no birds in your destiny.

—I do not know you so I do not believe you. What does the word 'life' mean to someone deranged...

—Do not lament. It does not become you. You are a mind warrior. Why have you accepted that losing a battle is equal to losing the war? Has no one told you this truth: that a warrior must feel no pride? But the man who feels pride in his body cannot express himself. This is your tragedy, your curse.

—But someone, without being introduced, says, I have not seen...

—Now you will tell me what she said. That I have not seen Mandu. What terrible thing happened if she took a liking to you? If I were in your place I would have gone with her to Mandu. I'd have made some sweet memories and tied them up in a sweet little bag and hidden it away. Whenever I felt melancholic, I would take out one of those memories and talk to it and become happy again. But you? You Hindiwalas? Friendship seems to turn into sex and sensuality for you. Was I having a physical relationship with all the gopis in the myths? No. We were friends. We would fight and then make up again. Life is the sum total of these small joys.

—But Banalata Sen called me a coward to my face.

—Banalata Sen has been angry from birth. In her anger, she will say whatever comes to her mind. Is everything she says to be believed?

—But my salvation...

—How did the meaning of salvation become death? When you emerge from a river of sorrow, any experience you earn becomes salvation. How did you fall into this delusion that you are the only one in this state, the only one cursed? Keep these golden moments, handle them with care, treasure them; they become one's life experience. Strindberg in Sweden had the same illness.* For years he was without weapons, as you are. But from those deep waters he brought out pearls. He wrote about thirty plays, having seen the future. He understood the bitter truth of his time:

Perhaps there will come a time when we will be so enlightened, that we will view with indifference the brutal, cynical and heartless spectacle that life has to offer.†

—And what about Swadesh?

From an actor, he became a warrior. In his eyes, a wind from December.

—I will do nothing for you. One must never forgive those who are unworthy of forgiveness. Instead, I make them fight a Mahabharata and they destroy themselves. I will pray to my leading bowman for you.

Before he disappeared, he turned once again into a mischievous adolescent.

—A piece of advice? Treat the beautiful roughly. But first befriend them. A friend's abuse is sweeter than words of love.

As he vanished, he smiled sweetly. That smile was on my side.

The two pairs of scissors met in the middle. My eyes had turned into a cyclone from the pain. First, I saw Dr Chari's moustaches. They were still quivering in anger. He lowered his head to look at my arm. It was a cut of meat hanging in a butcher's shop. The blood had not been wiped away yet. Sister Randhawa brought the instrument tray forward. Dr Chari looked at it. The scissors fell to the floor. In his language he said:

—This man's destiny has become a mad dog.

* August Strindberg (1849–1912) also suffered from paranoia, exacerbated by alcoholism.

† From the preface to Strindberg's play, *Miss Julia*.

From Vasantha's mouth, the same word twice: Amma, amma.

She was leaning on the wall, her face white, her shoulders shaking.

She burst into tears, terrible tears. Dr Chari put a hand on her and said in a firm voice—Vasantha, your father was the most powerful warrior of all Kerala. First the Establishment drove him mad. Then they killed him. In moments like these, think of him.

Shrikant was cleaning my arm. Dr Chari gave an order.

—Deepak's operation at nine a.m. tomorrow. Dr Naidu will return from his holiday this afternoon. He will be in charge of the team.

—Deepak, I'm saying it for the first time: you will get better. Your arm has been saved. You will hold a pen again. You will fight the good fight. You are brave. Really brave. This surgery was painful, really painful.

They bandaged my arm. The blood seeped through the white cloth. Vasantha brought me out. My arm had been cut open; the pain was in my legs. My feet seemed alien to the rest of my body.

On the bench outside, Harnam Chacha, the nodding engineer Inder Singh and Kanta were waiting. Mr Shimla said they were going to amputate my arm. Kanta got up. She ran a hand over my intact arm.

—My little Kaka. My son. It must have hurt so much. Who knows why God is so angry.

I was made to sit down on the bench. Harnam Chacha distributed plastic glasses of tea. Vasantha fed me a small sip.

—Papa, Papa, when your arm recovers, we will play on a rope swing among the trees.

Then a long 'oh' emerged from my mouth and I began to cry. Silent weeping.

Vasantha dried my tears with cottonwool. It was wet. Dr Shrikant came out with a hand towel and put it over my eyes.

—Cry all you want. You will be relieved of the pain. I am Saratchandra's Srikanta.

Kanta—Kaka, stop crying. I cannot bear it.

Was I crying for the departed? Air Force friends, Army friends. Today it was my own pain. Vasantha beti swinging with me. My daughter. Where has she gone? How unlucky I am.

My son. Where is he? How unlucky I am.

My wife. Where is she? How unlucky I am.

Inside me, a scream. That internal scream became an echo. In every cell and pore, unbearable pain. I understood the truth. On a great journey, you must set out alone. She is hunting me, with jagged bones. For the king of spring, I am unworthy of mercy. Now I am empty-handed. The tiger died, falling from a tree. This night, the leopard will come closer. We can now smell each other. I am a walking corpse. Behind me, flying detritus. Why are the heavenly forces my enemies? I do not even know how to pray. The sea of pain is never still. I was in the deserts of the open sea.

ON MY BED, IN MY ROOM

I refused to speak. Even if I eat nothing, sleep does come in instalments; anger comes in instalments too. When speaking is meaningless, I refuse to speak. Mr Shimla asked my pardon for having abused me on the day I was brought into the ward. Harnam Chacha begged with folded hands that no one raise his voice. Dr Shrikant came. He moved my arm, turned it about. First, they cut you up. Then they pop by to look you up. Vasantha tried to feed me tea. I set my lips firmly together. Shrikant took the glass and brought a spoonful of tea close to my lips.

—Drink tea, please. Saratbabu commands it.

I drank half a glass of tea.

—Professor Kulhara, the head of psychiatry and Dr Chari were arguing about yesterday's operation. Professor Kulhara feels that once the shock treatment has begun, one can't take a break, leave a gap as it were.

Dr Chari had the last word—The infection would have

spread through the blood. In twenty-four hours, he would have been dead. Would you give shocks to a corpse?

The operation is fixed. Chari comes to my room, looks at me silently. Then, Dr Naidu, almost at a run. Very angry. Who dared to touch his patient? Chari explains.

Dr Chari: Deepak's arm developed an infection. It could have spread. Then no one could have saved him.

Dr Naidu: Yes, Sir. Thank you, Sir.

Dr Chari: If you're tired after your journey...

Dr Naidu: No, Sir. I will perform the operation.

I opened my eyes. Dr Chari teased: When I cut, it hurts. But when Dr Naidu operates tomorrow, you won't feel a thing. It will be painless.

As he was leaving, Vasantha asked: Sir, he's been completely silent. Some fear...

—It's not fear. Like a beautiful woman, Swadesh has this habit of offended silence. Who can coax him out of it? But Vasantha, it's not the same as anger.

Everyone left the room. I knew they would all return.

Professor Kulhara came next. He looked at me for a while.

Professor: As you lie there, take the name of God. It gives you strength.

Kanta: Kaka doesn't know how. He's never been to a temple or any place where pujas are performed.

Professor: Then read scripture. The sound of the mantras will have some beneficent effects.

It was time for Kanta to leave. She asked Suresh whether he would look after things.

—Mataji, do not worry, I will sit by his side.

Harnam Chacha brought tea. If I moved even a little, the pain erupted. Suresh fed me tea with a spoon. Harnam Chacha sat on a stool beside me.

—Chacha, your Ranchhodji is very angry. He says I cannot be forgiven.

—Bhagwan Krishna is often like a mischievous child. It's

his habit to tease, to annoy. But when he acts, you'll see a miracle.

Mr Shimla said I would be the first to recover.

—The doctors cut your flesh and you did not so much as moan.

Noddy Inder said that I had become a dervish.

—Neither happiness nor sorrow moves you.

A boy from Mother Teresa's home, nine or ten years old, has just been admitted. He stands near my bed. He knows nothing about himself. From time to time, he runs into the verandah. Hearing me speak startles him.

—Uncle. Me Michael. *Aap toh bol sakta. Phir chup kyon thhe?* (You can speak. So why were you silent?)

With my left hand, I gestured that he should approach. He did. I put my left hand on his head.

—Uncle, tell me a story. In the ashram, Sister told one every day.

I closed my eyes, stunned. All the stories had abandoned me.

—Michael, there was once a king.

Excitement transformed him.

—Michael, there was a queen.

I was silent. He was silent. Then he smiled—It's a lovely story, uncle. Tell it again tomorrow.

He went back to his bed, very happy.

Dr Naidu returned with a prescription which he gave to me.

—These medicines are not in stock. Get them from the chemist. It'll be about seven or eight hundred.

—I'll get them.

Dr Naidu was annoyed a little.

—How? Your sister isn't here. Your wife isn't here. Do you have any money?

I shook my head.

—Why do you hate yourself so much? Sister Randhawa told me that you didn't so much as squeak this morning. You should have hit the roof when Dr Chari was cutting with two scissors. As much as you try to be a hero, that much you will suffer. Deepak, I wish to see you dancing.

—Dr Naidu, when I get well my first dance will be with you.

He smiled. He wrote something on the paper and gave it to Suresh.

—Get this from the chemist. They'll bill me.

He went to the door and turned, asked: Have you informed your wife?

—No. What would she do here? Why bother her?

—It seems you like to hurt other people. I have many poet friends but none as cruel as you. You just want to hurt her. Are you a sadist, Mr Swadesh Deepak?

Suresh stepped in.

—Sir, I'll call my boss. He will tell Madam.

As he left, Dr Naidu pulled a sweet arrow from his quiver: Suresh, teach him some good things. Who knows why he thinks love is a weakness and an insult.

Dr Naidu left. Suresh went to get the prescription filled. Everyone was on their beds. My bed had been taken from me years ago. I was no longer a man. So no bed for me. Why has my integrity been taken as a fault in my character? I do nothing to make other people happy. Not even write.

How can I take dwarfs to be giants? The misery of that language is assured in which critics are held to be greater than poets. Everyone's last wish is to become famous.* They never consider their own stature.

Mayavini only comes at night. Is she a nocturnal species? One cannot trust one's eyes at night. I do not see what is; I see something else entirely. She had marked me with her

* Here Deepak uses the adjective 'naamwar'. This is a pun, I think, intended on Dr Namwar Singh and the desire of the belle lettriste to become noteworthy, famous (naamwar) and to attain the heights of Dr Singh.

musk. No one has the courage to approach me now. I have embarked on this long and perilous journey with the help of a few remaining memories. She is an expert at inflicting punishment. My burnt arm, neck and chest are enduring symbols she has left me.

My favourite outfit: the half-sleeved shirt. How can I wear it now? Up to this time, I thought that the hunt was of the strong. When she made me a citizen of the Nation of the Insane, I understood this frightening truth: hunting is a mental sport, not a physical one. One night she was taking my abuse. The next morning she was taking me home for breakfast. She distracted me and sank her teeth into my throat. And I became a blood-soaked thing forever more. Neither alive nor dead. I did not fall prey to her fatal attractions. So why do I spend all my leisure time thinking of her? I became Dr Faustus. He pawned his soul to the devil for Helen of Troy.

The prayer he should have made to Jesus Christ, he made to her.

Oh sweet Helen, give me a kiss and make me immortal.*

Vasantha came in and sat down on the stool. She took my hand, the burnt one, in both hers.

—Papa, *neend nahin aata*? (Can't you sleep?)

—Vasantha, I am going to teach you to speak. Will you stay in my home?

—Nahin, Papa. *Aapse Hindi seekhne ka samay nahin hota. Next month MD ho jaata. Idhar se chalaa jaataa. Phir kisi bhi din police ke haat, maara jaata.* (No, Papa. There is no time to learn Hindi from you. Next month, I get my MD degree. Then I leave here. And some days later, I die at the hands of the police.)

Vasantha is lucky. Her life and death are neatly plotted. No suicide attempts, no seductresses, no burn scars.

—Are you taking revenge for your father?

---

* The line from Marlowe reads: 'Sweet Helen, make me immortal with a kiss:'.

—No. No. No. We do nothing for revenge. There is no place in the sphere of the political for a personal agenda.

When Vasantha leaves here, I know, she will seek refuge under the roof of the jungle. There is no better way to elude predators.

—Vasantha, do you remember your father's last words?

—Very clearly. He was on death row. He was shouting at me—Why does it take so long to make coffee? The ruling class and the police have strange ways of inflicting torture. Before they killed him, they drove him mad. Whenever one of his revolutionary comrades was killed, they would place the dead body in his cell at night. They would say only one line—Look at your revolution. They had bloodied his warrior-soul long before they killed him. He was completely mad. When they were covering his head with a black cloth, he came out of his world of madness for a moment—Vasantha! Vasantha! Come to me quickly. We will swing together, on a swing that reaches the sky.*

I have no idea how I received this revelation of truth: women with the name Vasantha never die natural deaths. They are always fully armed. They die in real or staged police encounters.

—Vasantha, aren't doctors supposed to keep a mental distance from their patients? But you...

—Papa, I saw you and was reminded of my father. He had the same volcanic temper. Like you he would lie in wait, his belly to the ground, a crouching tiger. At any moment, the fatal spring would come. Papa! Papa! Write a play about me. I will be dead by then. But I will definitely come for the first show.

How could I tell her the terrible truth that I could no longer write? I am barren. I am a wasteland. I am cursed. I am a bastard. I am no man. A man slain by a woman, unmanned, that's Swadesh Deepak.

---

* These lines are in standard Hindi.

Before I fell asleep, I thought of Punjab's favourite poet son, Shiv Kumar.* From a life of ugliness and exile, he managed to pluck some images of beauty and turn them into poems. In the spring of his life, he lost all sense of joy in the world. Before dying he wrote:

Joban rutte jo vi marda, phool bane ya taara

(Who dies in spring becomes a flower or a star.)

Very soon now, Vasantha would become part of the flowers and the stars as those who die young... Vasantha will become a star. A star of cool light.

My eyes were closed but I was not asleep. Someone came into the room without the sound of footsteps. My heart stopped beating. Was it Mayavini? Next to the bed, someone with a terrible face was standing. One eye was destroyed. His nose was broken and twisted. His ears were torn. Seeing that I was shivering with fear, he said:

—Do not fear. I am a peace-loving demon.

—Demons do not have beards. Your face...

—A million little wounds. Thanks to the blessings of Pitamber Prabhu, I grew a beard and it concealed the wounds.

—But Ranchhod is very angry with me.

—The Lord of Seasons gets very angry at the sight of injustice. He is as hot as the sun, quick as the wind. When he flies past, he scoops up the fragrance of the flowers in his shawl. When he shakes it open and the scents fall to the earth, spring arrives.

—And yet he did not have mercy on me.

—Yes. You sent your plea to the chief Lord of the Bow. He read it and teased:

* Shiv Kumar Batalvi (1936–1973) was the youngest person to receive the Sahitya Akademi award for his verse play *Loona*. He is known for his romantic poetry, most recently popularized by the soundtrack of the feature film *Udta Punjab* (Abhishek Chaubey, 2016).

—Krishna, how can we separate punishment completely from mercy? Swadesh is unchivalrous. But how can the right to devastate his soul belong to someone else? Give him something. Not a long life. Give him your gift of being happy. He has to write a play about Vasantha.

The peace-loving demon put his closed fist upon my body. Seeing the question in my eyes, he said:

—My Lord Krishna, he who is the Ganga among rivers, has sent you a fistful of spring.

He opened his fist. Fragrances began to play over my body. The stagnant smell of the hospital left by way of the windows. The peace-loving demon vanished as suddenly as he came. That small share in Ranchhodji's spring! Now no revenge can be wreaked upon me...

THE FUTURE

Winter. Evening tea at the Shri Ram Centre. Today Piyush Mishra is with me. He loves me greatly, respects me deeply. He is Colonel Surat Singh off stage as well as on it. Bold, energetic and without compassion. He did not like Nidhi from the very beginning. When I went to wash my hands, he spoke to her. Nidhi told me about it later.

—How did Swadeshji become your friend?

Nidhi lets no opportunity to tease pass her by.

—Piyushji, he's no friend, he's my yaar. When two hearts are bound up in a relationship, it's no longer a friendship.

—He is a most cruel man. When he hurts you, he will leave a deep wound. Be careful.

—I am sure the wound he leaves will be redolent of him.

Annoyed, Piyush left.

We got into the car. She did not turn the key in the ignition. She does not ask useless questions.

—You will eat with me.

—No. Vikas...

—For a change, listen to what I say before you speak. I called Rai Saahab and told him. I have my orders: I have to get you back by ten p.m.

—Dinner with you...

She started the car. The engine's heart began to beat. She got angry.

—If you have dinner at my home, what am I going to do? Rape you? Your friends keep giving me dire warnings. What am I likely to do to you? How am I going to hurt you? I am your enemy, right? Everyone hates me.

She put her head on the steering wheel. I turned the key off.

The engine had a cardiac arrest. I took her hand and brought her out of the car. I sat her down next to me on the footpath.

—Listen, Nidhi. Listen to what I say, listen carefully. I won't say it again. The Lord of the Bow, whose eyes are full of elan, sent you to me. For years, everything has been dry inside me. And then Ranchhodji poured a fistful of spring over me. An empress from the animal world proved her existence with me. I had no armour, no shield to protect myself from her. Like a python, she is an expert at creating a dangerous stillness. First, she digs her nails into your soul. And she is an expert at squeezing the life force from the body.

My breath was coming in gasps. I fell silent. She lit a cigarette for me and put it to my lips.

—Tell me everything. Tell me all about it, Swadeshji, tell me the truth.

—For me she was Helen of Troy, she was Draupadi. Two dangerous beauties, two fiery heroines who ended the two eras in which they lived. I was fooled by her.

I had no idea that she was thirsty for my blood. She knows how to use her fatal charm to kill. She was not a woman to accept defeat. She was a lover by profession. But no one can frighten Swadesh into defeat. She took my refusal as an insult. And this turned into a curse.

Nidhi took both my hands in hers. She lit another cigarette.

—She made me into a resident of a horrible Hell. I tried

to kill myself three times. She saved me each time. How could she let me out of her control? Now my blood had a permanent lustre. I was in a constant state of excitation. All around me, a desert. Cactus too. And spiders as big as my palms. Her effect was devastating. My memory failed. My strength left me. My rage disappeared. Now I was a chunk of meat.

Her grip on my hands strengthened.

—Nidhi, Nidhi, I know the words you want to use. Don't say them. Both of us will be cursed. She's twisted those words and destroyed them. Nidhi, Nidhi, you don't know. Whatever life has taken from me, you're giving it back. Nidhi, Nidhi, if you were not with me, I would find it difficult to breathe. Listen Nidhi, the medication has made me impotent. Nidhi, listen. My disease seems to run in cycles of four or five years. Again I will take the jump. But this time I will take the final jump. To keep you at a distance, a safe distance, is sorrow, a burning sorrow. But when my head gets disturbed, even a little, I return to that terrible Hell. My luck is a mad dog. Dr Chari said this in Malayalam.

She put her palm on my lips. When she spoke, each word vibrated.

—Now be calm, Swadesh. As long as I am around, you will not take that final leap. How will you go into that tunnel of darkness? I will be there with you, a lantern in my hands. I will always be with you. You have no idea how strong the power of my prayer is. I am a stupid woman but I am a very good woman. And from today, I am your doctor. Now we will never risk the whole venture of love.

She helps me to my feet and then helps me into the car. My fears begin to evaporate, one by one. Today, she is driving fast. I am smoking. Murari Bapu's picture is staring at me.

—Jagdeep was saying that your face is as it was ten years ago. This long illness could do nothing to change it.

—Jagdeep is a rogue. He can't breathe if he doesn't tease.

—He was saying, when you were young, you got up very early and very hungry. You opened the bread box and ate up the morning sun. Which is why a small sun has made its home in your face.

—Nidhi, please don't tease.

She gave me a sweet stern warning:

—I haven't even started. Wait and watch.

The car stopped at her place. As soon as I got out, she put out the light.

She parked it at a special angle, turned on the lights again. They illuminated the nameplate. It said—Apoorva Nidhi.

—Whose name is that?

—Mine. You didn't like my surname. So I changed it by court order. Now to change it on my bank account and other important papers. Tell your friends to address me as Apoorva now.

I took her hand and said—Mad girl.

She caught hold of my hand and said—Mad boy.

Now she would forget to use the -ji even when we were with others. Vikas called. It is nine-thirty, Deepak hasn't returned.

Nidhi said we haven't eaten yet.

—Then don't. It's his bed time.

—Rai Saahab, we'll be done by ten-thirty. Sorry for the delay.

—Okay. Should I come to pick him up?

—No. He will get back.

—Do not send him by auto.

—Please, Rai Saahab! I'll drop him back myself.

She hung up. On her face, a beautiful annoyance.

—I tell you! Why does he feel he controls you?

—Listen Nidhi, that's not control, that's worry. Concern. He has been the only constant witness to my seven years in Hell. He gave me an invaluable gift: the will to live. He took my hand and led me from the Nation of the Ill. Now I am in a jungle of flowers. I have found my feet. Vikas knows that

I am in perennial exile. I cannot spend too much time in one place, even in my own Heaven. Which is why he tries to hold me to a time-table.

Apoorva's face became understanding.

—What patience Vikas has.

—I went with Vikas to Allahabad. To his house. His mother knew a little about me. One day she said, while we were talking about something else—I have four sons. They are all good men but Vikas is a god!

The food was delivered. When she got up to get it, she went inside and came out with a large bag. Seeing my inquiring look, she said:

—It's for you. You liked half-sleeved shirts, didn't you?

—How can I wear them now? My burned arm…

—Don't say these hurtful things. Why would anyone look at your burnt arm? What was that Hindi film song—*Tere chehre se nazar nahin hat-ti* (I can't take my eyes off your face)…

—It's a big packet. How many shirts are there?

—Just four.

—Is this a gift or a dowry?

—First agree to the marriage. Listen, put on the navy blue one tomorrow. You will blossom in that colour.

—You're saying the things I should say.

—For a dumb fool like you, one has to give it all in writing.

When Nidhi talks like this, I get signals of the sorrows to come.

---

8 a.m. The phone rings. Apoorva.

—Tell me.

—When a beautiful girl calls in the morning, one says Ram Ram, good morning or Namaste.

—Ram Ram, good morning, Namaste.

—Arvind Gaur* called. Mahesh Dattani† will talk to some people. He has invited you and me.

—What time?

—Eleven a.m.

—So you call at eight a.m.?

—It will take you an hour to get ready. I'll come for you at nine a.m. We'll loiter for a couple of hours.

Then her tinkling laughter:

—Will you take Rai Saahab's permission or must I?

Before I could snarl abuse at her, she had hung up.

When I came down the stairs, she was in the car. I was wearing the navy blue shirt she'd given me. She got out quickly. I was standing under the shade of a tree. She came up to me and put her hand on my shoulder. No rings on her fingers. No bangles on her wrists.

Now there was a deceptive silence. Were my times of trouble coming?

Nidhi's eyes filled with tears. I was not scared. Now I was adamantine.

The branches of the trees were bare. One cannot wish flowers onto them.

—Deepak, Deepak, I will kidnap you. You are mine.

Tears began to fall. I abandoned all caution. I dug an elephant prod into my head.

—One does not cry on meeting. One cries on parting.

She took my hand and led me to the car. This time we did not dawdle. We raced down the road.

—We can talk more if you don't drive fast.

She slowed down. I touched her small ear. The creases on her forehead evaporated.

---

* Theatre director (b. 1953) known for his political and socially relevant theatre. He is credited with having directed a version of *Court Martial* that has run for more than 450 shows.

† English-language playwright (b. 1958) of plays like *Dance Like a Man* and *Final Solutions*.

—Arvind Gaur loves your novel *Mayapot*. He gave it to me. I didn't like it.

She looked at me for a reaction.

—Go on. Say it all. Without hesitation.

—The hero of *Mayapot*, Santosh, is a parasite. He does no work. His friends love him and so they pay his way. Dr Radha wants to marry him. Who could love a useless fellow like that?

—Apoorvaji! You are a thirty-year-old child. We do not always think with the help of logic and reason. Being a parasite is not a criminal activity. He is an understanding and sensitive man. He does not claim his rights as other men do. If he is told not to meet you again, he does not come again. He has a unique rhythm to his life. Look at me. For the last five years, I have been idle. Unemployed. A parasite, and yet Vikas, Soumitra and Rajendra Yadav love me and look after me. And a mad girl called Apoorva wants to kidnap me. Do we look at someone's bank balance before we love?

She looked at me, wordlessly. Then she asked the impossible question of possession:

—If I settle down abroad, will you come to me?

—You're nuts. My mad Apoorva. You should find a man your own age. Not a middle-aged and half-bald Swadesh.

—I like the middle-aged and half-bald Swadesh. I desire him only.

And one day, mad Apoorva did go abroad. I remained here. In my country, I have grown tough again. But parasites are almost always tough.

THE PAST

The skin-grafting operation: Dr Naidu, Shrikant and two other doctors. Vasantha near my head.

—Papa, *aapki right arm theek ho jaayega*. (Papa, your right arm will get better.)

—Vasantha, 'jaayega' nahin, *jaayegi*.*

* Deepak corrects her use of gender.

I look at the round light. Broader than the table. I was terrified.

Dr Naidu: Don't be frightened. This won't hurt like Dr Chari's operation. You are, after all, my friend.

Me: This chandelier frightened me. If it falls, I'll die.

Dr Naidu: We will all die, but it won't fall.

Me: Vasantha, my river has dried up. But I want to swim.

Vasantha: The God who sent you spring will send you water.

I did not feel anything as they grafted skin from my thigh onto my arm. I was under sedation.

When I opened my eyes, I was back in my room, on my bed. Sikandar squeaked.

—Bossman has woken up.

They were all standing by my bed.

Mr Shimla: Sir, was it painful?

I shook my head.

Inder: It took five hours. I got worried. I was praying all the time.

Harnam Chacha: Kalgiwaale (Guru Gobind Singh) was protecting Professor Saahab. What man can harm him?

Kanta: Talk to me, Kaka. Geeta, Savita and I sat on that bench for hours. Five hours. Who knows what they were cutting?

Geeta came close. She had a cup of tea and a spoon in her hand.

—Open your mouth, Deepak.

I opened my mouth. Geeta fed me a spoonful of tea.

The nurse came with a thermometer. I shook my head. Geeta took the thermometer from her. I opened my mouth. Geeta put it in and sent the nurse back. She left. In a low voice I said to Geeta.

—Today, the thermometer is very sexy.

First she was startled. Then she gave a crooked smile.

—The scoundrel Deepak is well again.

The sedatives bore me off once more.

Mayavini came. The three cheetahs had left her. She was formless today. She had left her body behind in my murderous city. Today I want to speak.

—You are my judge. When do I get my punishment?

—You have set those dwarf corpses on the branches of trees. We are both our own murderers.

—How long do I have to live on the point of a dagger?

—Why do I sneeze when I look at the sun?

—A lioness will have sex nearly three hundred times on her honeymoon. When one lion tires, another is called in to service her lust.

—The bitch-goddess soon tires of a single lover. She needs a new man to tame and domesticate.

—I have measured your boundaries. You are an astonishingly lusty monkey.

Is this the end of the most difficult period of my life?

She stood up. Now she had a form again. She turned to leave.

—Swadeshji. Banalata Sen came! I am frightened of her.

She left. Her footsteps were unsteady.

Vasantha has a plate in her hands. Sweetmeats. I don't eat sweets. I ate them.

—Papa, MD passed. *Ab jaata.* (Now I am going.)

—My child, not jaata, *jaati*. Stay with me for a little while and you'll learn Hindi well.

—Papa, this is our last meeting. I will not return from where I am going. My end is a police encounter.

I was shocked to see my little daughter make life-and death decisions so easily. I could see her fate clearly written on her forehead: a police bullet or the noose. Girls named Vasantha do not die of natural causes.

—You will not cry, Papa. Please bless me.

—I thought I would arrange your marriage and bless you then.

—I do not want blessings. I want a boon. I want to be tough and cruel like you.

—Vasantha, Vasantha, I am not tough. A woman frightened me. Now I whine like a puppy, day and night.

—You will get well. Dr Chari says so. He never lies. Your powers will come back. You will write a play about your child Vasantha. Tell me the name of the play. Papa, tell me now.

The monsoon broke inside me. The rains of June, long wet hair. Sleeping words turned over in their sleep. Give us life. We will speak on the stage to our audiences. The wind began to blow through the rain, sharp knives constantly touching me. I was sure spring was not far away. For my daughter Vasantha who could choose her own death, I would take a creation myth and turn it into a Vasantha myth. The power of creation came over to my side. Decide what you want to do. You will be able to write.

How could I know then that even three years after release from the hospital I would still be dry? That each drop of blood would still be burning? That my head and my consciousness would not work together. Like a barren woman longing to be pregnant, I would struggle on. My first book for my daughter. Or else I would write nothing. My stubbornness came back. It was a welcome sign. I had begun to look for good luck.

—Vasantha, Vasantha, your play will be called *Sabse Udaas Kavita*.

Vasantha's face immediately grew stern. She put a hand on my head.

—Papa, Papa, Vasantha will go now. *Vasantha ab nahin aata.* (Vasantha will not return.)

For the last time I wanted to correct her language. But I didn't. Would correct language protect her from the bullet?

This was our final parting. No news ever came of her, nor did she ever come.

THE PAST

The electric shocks began again. Again I was deeply sad. I have no faith in past lives. What I have left of my memory tells me that in this life I have done no evil to others. So why are the forces of Heaven arraigned against me? Now I will depend on medication for the rest of my life. Psychiatric medicines are blunt instruments to the head; you are left in a state of half-unconsciousness.

Dr Partha Choudhury sat on my bed. We do not even have a silent conversation.

He has endless patience. I have a strong will. I am good at turning away from others. I am even better at it than Queen Kaikeyi in her House of Rage. I have been a lone wolf from birth, an expert at conversing with myself.

These people are testing my strength. I drink water constantly. I am parched. Geeta has gone to the Red Cross canteen to get tea. The doctor and I are alone.

In this moment, my guard was down; a cat with eyes half closed, warming itself in the sun.

Dr Partha Choudhury: After seeing *Court Martial* in Calcutta, she said this to you, right: 'I have not seen Mandu'!

At this strategically planned moment, he declared war. I came out of my House of Rage—Yes, that's what she said. Who told you?

Numberless times, Kaamna has presented herself to me. M.F. Husain and Jehangir Sabavala must have made her together. Draupadi must have been just like her. This frightened me. What if, like Draupadi, she could make a vow—Until I have washed my hair in blood, I will not dress as a queen again. The beautiful is also the terrifying. I could smell her; not her perfume, but her aromatic blood. A foolish urge was born: I will have her at all cost. Pride won. Attack. Such a beautiful woman must be given pain. I got bestial pleasure out of this. In those days, only I knew the shlokas of the body.

THE FUTURE

Nidhi called. Her Maruti car had collided with a Tata Sumo. I had often advised her not to talk on her mobile while driving, not to change the music cassettes. She would say with a pure smile—You worry too much.

Now an accident had happened.

—When the accident happened, I was talking on the phone.

—Yes, but the Tata Sumo halted abruptly…

—Shut up. You think I'm mad. I'm giving you advice…

—Please, Deepak. Nothing happened. Forty small bumps and bruises. Ask my mother if you want. She's right here.

—I have nothing to say to her. Idiot, how were you saved? Why didn't you die?

—Just before it happened, you came and sat down on the next seat. You shouted at me to slam the brakes. Before dying, I saw your face. Now I do not fear death. I managed to brake in time.

—A good-for-nothing like you should have died.

—How much you abuse, Deepak!

—It's a family thing.

I could hear crying. I exploded.

—Let me die first. Then you can cry your eyes out.

—I'm crying because you're abusing me so much. It must be lo…

—Don't say the word. We'll both be cursed. I'll come tomorrow.

—No. Not now. My nose is as big as a…

—The other bits?

—They're all the way you like them.

—You're a hussy.

The sound of water flowing over stones.

—Robert Browning's lines: You smile. My painting is complete.*

* The line from Browning's 'Andrea Del Sarto' read: 'You smile? why, there's my picture ready made, / There's what we painters call our harmony!'

She laughed. The stream flowed on.

The geranium in the window will definitely flower this year.

The seventh psychiatric session with Dr Partha Choudhury.

I have thrown down arms. Whether I am angry with him or I do not speak to him, it makes no difference. He has become my alter ego. His single-minded vision is now to discover all my terrifying and life-threatening secrets.

This was the pre-determined end of my dark journey.

I am a crippled submarine desperately trying to break the surface of the deeps.

Despair and decaying darkness sometimes decrease and sometimes expand. Last evening, I saw the golden thigh of a cloud in the setting sun's rays. It was very sexy. Kaamna. That morning when you bent over to give me the book on tantra, I remembered the curve of your back. I could have encompassed your waist with my interlocked fingers. You have a deep friendship with fire. You are living proof of the impossible. Proof of improbable.

—That night she said she wanted to visit Mandu with you. Why did you turn violent?

—Seeing me awakened her sleeping dreams. They yawned and stretched luxuriously. You cannot dream such juicy dreams with an ugly husband by your side. She loves beauty. She must have thought: Swadesh can be the instrument that will make these dreams come true. But she did not know one thing: I am never available on rent.

The doctor working on his MD was taking notes all the time.

—But when you insulted her, abused her in front of everyone, why did she come the next morning to your room to take you to her home for breakfast?

—When you were in London, did you meet Sylvia Plath?

Partha Choudhury was totally silent. Also alert. Perhaps I had tried another mode of attack.

—She had killed herself before I reached London. She put her head in a gas stove. Ted Hughes was having an affair with a model, I believe. Sylvia could not take this. Her third attempt was successful. She became a cult figure. Swadeshji, why are you asking about Plath?

—She has taken birth in me. I also made three attempts. Do you know why Mayavini came to my room? About women who have unquenchable desires, Plath wrote:

> Every woman adores a fascist,
> The boot in the face, the brute
> Brute heart of a brute like you.
>
> ('Daddy')

First, Partha Choudhury's ears went red. Then angry colour leapt into his eyes. He half rose from the chair. His strong arms on the table. Burning embers on his face. In a voice that sounded as if he were pronouncing a death sentence he said:

—Swadesh Deepak! I have not met a person more deserving of hatred. You remember everything you need to know that will come to your defence. You put your own construction on Plath's words. You change their meaning. With all the dirt inside you, it's a wonder that you write. I feel ashamed to call an animal like you a writer.

I could feel no anger. From Arjun I had turned into Brihannala, an impotent dancer. But I was surprised to see Partha Choudhury smiling. He seemed to be happy, having done damage to my image in my own eyes.

—Swadeshji, after being abused that much will you come to my house? I'd like you to come for breakfast one day.

—In the old days, I would have murdered you by now.

—You're right. So why did a respectable woman come to your guesthouse after you had abused her in front of so many people? Why does she take you to her house for breakfast? I'll tell you. In our Bengal, writers and poets are given the status of gods. Ordinary homes have pictures of Tagore and Saratchandra on the walls. Small shops too. They are worshipped. At book fairs, the poor will go without food to buy books. This is the wealth of culture they have. Which is why Golden Bengal—Shonar Bangla—has become Poor Bengal. Do you know why your abuse did not count with her? Because it was a necessary part of Swadesh Deepak, author of *Court Martial*. The entire essence of his character—the limitless rage of his protest. Stop thinking in this petty fashion; break out of these petty notions. Such a woman could not possibly have evil intentions. Give me her address. I will write to her. She will come to PGI, Chandigarh. She will come. She is certainly not evil. Shall I call her?

—What need to call her? Kaamna visits every night.

And my secret was out. Partha Choudhury knew all. Who I spoke to, who I spoke to in English. My imagination had imbued someone with flesh and blood.

In the Palace of Magic, a Road for the Generals had begun to be built. A road out. Small scenes began to wing their way back to me. The shape of her back as she bent over to retrieve a book. Skin like velvet. Ignoring all basic decencies, I touched her with my fingertips.

She turned to me and I said:

—I want to touch you properly.

She looked at my face and began to laugh.

—You're blushing, Swadesh.

She opened the book, put on her spectacles. And she turned into a veritable manifestation of the desires of the flesh.

—You look really sexy with spectacles on.

—Then come to Mandu. I'll wear spectacles all the time.

—Doesn't my abuse offend you?

—I'm surrounded by sycophantic men twenty-four hours

of the day. Including my husband. He begs to sleep with me. I looked at you. You have only to say the word and the doors of myth fall open for you. You are Kartikeya, the warrior son of Shiva, the angry one. He laid a curse upon his mother—If a woman comes to pray at my temple, she will be a widow in the next seven lives. Okay, Swadesh, tell me what do you think would happen if we were together?

—After bed tea, we would make love.

—Sex so early in the morning?

—The day should begin well.

She looked at me; first silent, then sad. She knew it was not in our fate to visit Mandu. The gods had cursed us. The Calcutta scene broke up. I was with Partha Choudhury, in my room.

First I thought of Krishna Baldev Vaid. At first, a good friend. Then like illiterate and fractious women, we fought. It's been about fifteen years. His Harvard thesis topic came back to me—Twist in the Tales of Henry James. Coleridge's long poem—'The Rime of the Ancient Mariner'—came back. Henry James's *The Turn of the Screw* came back. Krishna Baldev Vaid sees this as the world's greatest work of the supernatural. Vaid's rages beggar mine but he thinks with acuity and he writes well.

I start walking in the balcony. My feet were strong. Swimming in the air. *The Turn of the Screw* came back in full. The screw set in my head turned. It kept on turning and then opened. The light went on. The window opened. I was bathed in a flood of light. The scenes are settling into place. The regrets of the body are ceasing. The shadows of despair vanish in the sunlight. My first prayer—When will I become a part of blank pages?

The river of the body begins to flow. Images, symbols and metaphors return.

My fear is a dwarf woman, the carnivorous bird flying behind her became flesh and blood. I begin to see a safe road.

My primordial terrors began to diminish.

Mayavini took off her tantra-soaked clothes. Now she is Kaamna. I am Swadesh. Once I replied late to a letter. A complaint arrived—Swadesh does not remember me. I told her—I have placed all your memories in a fixed deposit called Kaamna. This FD is in the National and Grindlays Bank, Calcutta, in your name. Whenever you want, you may draw a few memories.

Animal stories cease forming in my head. The sharpness of my fear ceases. Now in the days of heat my place of residence was no longer the North Pole. I stopped hunting for safe roads.

I began to measure my boundaries.

That night she came to me for the last time. Completely silent. Deeply sad. Her clothes the kind you wear for a puja.

—Kaamna. You've learned my bad habits. No Namaste, no good morning.

—Good evening, Swadesh. You are going to be released from hospital.

—Whose hand will I take as I leave?

—Why should you need a hand to hold? If you so desire it, hold your own hand.

—Kaamna, I have become a desert. How will I write?

—With the help of your limitless life force. Recognize it. Swadesh, you can go from being a cemetery to being a garden.

—My strength. Pray that I get back my moral strength.

—I'm off then. I have to send my little one to school. I will not return.

—Kaamna, I have not yet asked your pardon for the unseemly...

She stood up.

—Stop living with these regrets and apologies. I liked the unseemly Swadesh Deepak. My dream of a complete man. I have had enough of seemly men who crawl and squirm. They are worms in body and mind.

All night I thought good thoughts. All night, I made good decisions. I liked Kaamna. Now I can pray for T.S. Eliot. On his grave is inscribed: 'Pray for me'. He knew that words and language cannot give us deliverance. Only prayer can save us.

Now I will not speak English. Some people will say it is pride. They do not know that the cursed belong to every nation. International passports. I could speak Spanish, Russian too. Italian and Dutch as well. Not German. It is too difficult. In the state of being cursed one transcends nation, time and language. We are international citizens.

Now when sorrow comes, I shall proclaim it from the rooftops, share it with my friends. That one wishes to hide sorrow is itself a sign of sickness.

I will write to Jehangir Sabavala. I will write to Rajendra Yadav. I will write to Soumitra Mohan. But I will not write to Krishna Sobti. She does not like ill friends. I will go to Sheila Sandhu in Delhi. I will tell her all my secrets. She never ridicules anyone. She will give me advice as before—Deepak, go to her. She wants you. Why should she be your enemy? Then she will be angry—Don't get so angry. Actually when I do get angry it hurts inside, causes a terrible pain.

I will not call her a woman but a lady. I will not shout. I will not correct anyone. I will stand there with hands tied.

And I will write a play for Vasantha. What name did I tell her? *Sabse Udaas Kavita*? It is possible that my daughter Vasantha is already a sad poem. But enough. *Iske baad hoton par Khuda ka naam hai, saqi.* (After this the name of God will be upon my lips, cup-bearer.)

In the evening, Dr Pratap Sharan said:

—Deepakji, tomorrow we will discharge you.

I sat down abruptly on the bed.

—I'm staying. I won't go home.

—It is dangerous to get fond of a hospital. We don't

keep patients in the psychiatric ward for more than three months. Your case was different. You were here for five months. No one will hurt you. You must try. Think positive. Rehabilitation is a difficult time.

I was silent. Was the list of my sorrows set to increase?

—Your family, your friends will assume that you've been discharged and so you've recovered, you're fine. But a psychiatric condition is never fully gone. In this country, every man is an expert on every disease. They will tire you out, they will enrage you. Just get these irritating do-gooders out of your home and heart.

Dr Sharan smiles his infrequent smile and says—Now smile; abusing, shouting, these are not difficult for you. You don't even forgive women. You will have to become a Durvasa* to deal with these irritants. If you get angry, walk out.

—Will I be able to write?

—Not now. But choose an idea. Think about it. Right now, you will feel scared. The fears you have are linked to racial memories. Do not struggle with them. You must accept them. Come and see me every week for a chat. Do not travel too far without telling me. Keep yourself fit. Clean your room yourself. Tend the garden, watch TV. And if you feel like it, go out.

—Am I not completely normal?

—No man is completely normal. And you're a writer. You can change your way of thinking simply by trying. But don't be in a hurry. Take it easy. Very easy.

When Chacha Harnam Singh returned after taking Sikandar for a walk, they were the first people I told. He closed his

* The son of Atri and Anusuya, the sage Durvasa was known for his legendary short temper.

eyes, folded his hands and offered a prayer to Kalgiwaale. He opened his eyes and smiled.

Gori sove sej par, mukh par daare kes
Chal Khusrau ghar aapne, rain bhayee chahoon des.

I took his hand and said—Chachaji, how much suffering I've inflicted on you. You even washed my used utensils.

In my eyes were tears. Holy tears. Chacha Harnam said—Service to the learned brings spiritual merit. With your blessing, Sikandar will be discharged day after tomorrow.

Sikandar's advice—Bossman, when you want to cry, eat a banana.

Khusrau, it is time to go home...

THE PRESENT

I came home. The house had forgotten me. I had to make friends with it afresh. I am in my room. Everything is in its place. Geeta had not allowed anyone to touch anything. Who thought I would ever be back with my books? Geeta and Sukant kept peering in, past the screen door. When a man or an elephant goes mad, they can never be fully trusted again.

There was something that was irritating me. My thinking was now in slow motion mode. I could not sleep. From some dark corner of my mind, the information arrives—The sky's colour is white. The room in the hospital was all white. I came out. Geeta asked—What happened? What do you want? You could have called.

—I'm going for a walk.

—It's three o'clock now. Wait a little.

—Where is it written that no one may walk at three o'clock?

She was now sure this disgusting person was well.

—Let Sukant go with you.

—I don't need any bloody help.

Our paint seller Amod Joshi's shop. First, he was shocked to see me. Then very happy. We've been friends since our

Adimanch Theatre Group* days. My work is never delayed if he can help it. I told him about the colour of my room.

—We'll make it white. I'll send two men right now. But until then have a cup of tea.

He told some friends about my return. They came. The stories began to flow. Darkness fell. And my fear erupted.

—I'll take you back on my scooter.

—Take a rickshaw.

—No, I'll walk.

I began to walk. There's only one route home. I have to turn left. The third gate. I turned right. No gate. Where did it go?

I thought hard. I should scream loudly. Someone will hear and come. Then I can ask who took the third gate. Don't be frightened, sissy. You're on Mall Road, not in the jungle. And then I wanted to pee.

Then my memories attacked. The three cheetahs tore into me. Vasantha, Dr Chari, the scissors, the maggots, Lukman Ali, electric shocks, Partha Choudhury, Kanta and...and... and...twenty-six times Mayavini.

Was it time for me to go back to the hospital? To ask for my home address?

Who can protect me from this great fear?

In this life-threatening cold, an unquenchable thirst.

For the rest of my life, there will always be these danger warnings.

Who is testing my strength? My diseased thinking. My Mayavini.

You will not understand the meaning of her name. It is without happiness.

All my terrors fresh and alive. The shortcomings in my personality begin to show up. My courage is imaginary.

---

*Adimanch Theatre Group, according to its Facebook page, was founded in 1976 in Ambala by the director and actor Milkhi Ram Dhiman who died in 2014 while directing a play by Vijay Tendulkar.

Will it always be this way: that my sorrows will keep increasing?

A rickshaw stopped. He took me for a fare. He was smoking a beedi.

—Give me a beedi, bhai. Light it for me. Come here.

He got down. I took a long drag. A fit of coughing.

—Saahab, first you puff. Then you draw deep.

—Do cheetahs live here?

He stepped back and took a long sniff to check if I had been drinking.

—Saahab, where do you want to go?

—Where is 108 Mall Road?

—You're standing in front of it. Go in now. You'll catch a cold.

—Thanks a lot. You are an angel.

He hopped into his rickshaw and vanished. When he heard English, he probably thought I was an officer. They're the sort who will arrest you for no reason at all.

Geeta and Sukant were on the verandah. In attack mode.

—Where were you? What took you so long?

—You should be home before dark.

—I was about to send Sukant to the police station.

Now I was sure this was my wife.

HOSPITAL DAYS AT AN END, NOW DAYS OF INSULTS HAD BEGUN

Every Hindustani is a doctor. Every disease has a cure that he knows of. The elders of my family and Geeta's relations several times removed, all came to visit. They would call Geeta out of the kitchen where she was working while Parul was studiously addressing the newspaper.

—Bhainji, here's the cure you can depend on. Seven glasses of water. In two days, he'll be right as rain or I'll shave my moustache.

Not that he had moustaches.

Geeta: Deepak drinks that much water every day.

—No Bhainji, you're getting it wrong. When he gets up, he has to sneeze and drink seven glasses straight. Believe me, on the third day, he'll be leaping and hopping about.

He left. I know he reads the Urdu newspapers where you get these tips.

Parul: The old and the foolish. You should have reacted.

In the old days, I would have caught him by the collar and thrown him out of the house.

Geeta: React? Your father? He wouldn't react if someone kidnapped me.

Parul: Mama, you can be sure no one would kidnap a woman of your temper.

Mrs Singh, a friend of Geeta and mine, came to visit. In good times, she was a regular guest. She saw me lying down and let off a poisonous barb.

—Geeta, some people have all the luck. They can lie down all day and still eat.

When you hear something that pleases you, you are going to be happy. Geeta did not object to her words. Mrs Singh left.

—Papa, I should have slapped her. You react...

—Parul, it doesn't register. I'm in neutral gear. Wait for some time. All these people are on my hit list.

—I remember my father: the roaring man. Oh God. How long? How long, God?

But I know in my heart I have lost the battle.

I am the warlord of a defeated army. I can only dream of a false victory now.

Every day a sordid play is enacted around me. The cast includes family and friends. I have stopped dreaming of a miracle. I live in a house with an offensive armistice.

I bathe early every morning out of habit. I change my clothes and sit in the verandah. My helpmeet and life partner stops on her way to work.

—Are you on your way to work?

I shake my head.

—So why are you all dressed up? Don't wear such good clothes at home. You can wear them when you go out.

—When am I going to go out?

—Of course. When you're sitting on a throne. Listen, you should look for a job.

—I don't know how to work. I can teach literature. I can write.

—Oh God, why did I ever set eyes on you?

I did not have the courage to remind her of those days. On the day you saw me, you stood there as if rooted to the ground—he is a living volcano.

I called Dr Avneet Sharma. Could he admit me again? How can a fallen king live in his own palace as an outcaste?

Looking at God's works, even a mountain can turn to ash. My magic tongue had burned up. I was a marked man. In Shakespeare's words—the branded forehead.* On my forehead, a mark that anyone can read—Mad. This gives them license to say anything they want. I can't take them on. Fear. I fear no one. I do not respect anyone either. When will your last scene be played out? Curtain. The end of all chaos.

My college colleague Indrajit came to visit. In the seven years of my illness, he has never shown his face.

—Deepak Saahab. I want to impose on your good nature.

* Perhaps Elizabeth's lines, 'Hidst thou that forehead with a golden crown / that should be branded, if that right were right / The slaughter of the prince that ow'd that crown…' *Richard III*, Act IV, Sc IV.

I have to teach American poetry at the MA level. You know I'm not very good at poetry. If you could guide me...

I wanted to say something. The words got stuck in my throat. Oh my God, is he a monster? How can he be so cruel? Words were born.

—Professor Indrajit, I've forgotten everything. Now please do not ever come to my home again. Nor will you call me. Please go.

The winter was in full bloom and in the sky, pregnant clouds. It seemed necessary to prepare for the change in season. Umbrellas to be bought. Rajesh Varma alias Raju is in Sadar Bazaar. Friends with every shopkeeper. I phoned him. He took me on his scooter to Singh and Sons. He's an old sardar from Rawalpindi. A sweet talker. He saw me and asked:

—Saahab Bahadur, it's been a long time since you've graced my shop.

The assistant kept showing me umbrellas. I kept refusing each one. Finally the Sardarji opened an umbrella himself. It was a good one. I refused it. He was shocked, he asked:

—Saahab Bahadur, what's wrong with these umbrellas.

I explained—They have wires in them.

He almost fell over in surprise and looked at me with astonished eyes—Umbrellas are going to have wires in them.

—Okay, you should have told me that in the first place. Give me one.

Raju: Deepak Sir likes to joke.

This very Raju would travel with me to Bombay and Calcutta. When I was not allowed to travel alone.

After I return from hospital, my security cordon becomes weak.

When my wife goes to work, I am in the verandah. When she returns, I am still in the verandah. Her standard question—Did anyone call?

I say no. I do not tell her that I do not hear local calls.

I know that after the guerrilla battalion, the infantry will follow. She uses my illness as a weapon against me.

—Look at my luck. I work, you lounge. I have never seen such a shameless man. You wouldn't bathe for weeks, until your body would reek, and I was the only one who was there for you.

My disease is the kind you can insult at will. No one is grateful for small mercies.

If a man is no longer an earning member, why is he a parasite? I don't know. Why are old tigers banished from the pride? I don't know. Now, I am a branded, stained person. When someone is abnormal, you are allowed to say anything you want. There is always a spy following me.

People, my family, would be busy frightening me. All activity stopped. And yet life was not peaceful.

My play was stillborn. What would Vasantha be thinking? Is she dead? Chaos. The days of hospital were better than these days of being insulted.

Vikas Rai does not need to be told anything. He came. He understood. He took me to Delhi. I spent a long time with him. In Ambala, I was a guest for a few days.

Vikas never preaches. If he thinks it's important, a signal will suffice. He has stayed with me. He began to fix me to my old time-table. I began to meet people and talk to them. I began to become part of the flow of life. My weight began to increase.

In my own house, I had become a pet dog, now past its prime. I could not be put out of my misery nor could I be thrown out of the house. My food was almost thrown into my thali as if to say: eat it if you want; if not, have fun. I have become an outcaste. I was warned:

—If I die before you, don't you come to light my pyre. I won't find room even in Hell. Sukant can light my pyre.

—I have no desire to do such ridiculous things.

She was startled. The eunuch was talking back.

—I didn't know that. A leopard never changes his spots. How long will you pull on with this fake drama?

I have no other reliable way to live. I don't even have a full-blooded roar.

Soumitra came from Delhi. He does not have the habit of asking lawyer-like questions.

I kept talking. He kept taking pictures. When he sent the pictures a few days later, I shivered in disgust. I had become a worm.

—You can use these pictures to frighten children.

—One can only feel revulsion for this man. My family was right.

—You see a cockroach in the kitchen, you reach for a chappal. Fataak. Splat goes the roach. You see Swadesh and you have a shoe in your paw and a shloka in your maw. From my head, a hundred pigeons take flight every second.

Two days into Soumitra's visit. Late in the evening, he and Sukant were having a small celebration of my release. We get a trunk call. My elder sister says it's all over with my mother—*puri ho gayi* (It is finished). That's how we say it in Punjab—*pura ho gaya*.

I did not tell Soumitra. There was no reason to. He had never set eyes on her.

In the morning I told him that my mother had died. I would have to go to Yamuna Nagar and return by the afternoon. Soumitra said he would go back too. The atmosphere had changed. Then he said softly—Deepak, your powers are coming back. Now you will be able to write.

In Yamuna Nagar when Ma's body was lifted to be borne off to the cremation grounds, my maternal aunt made the spiralling motion with her finger at her temple—the lowest and most naked way of calling someone mad.

—A madman shouldn't light my elder sister's funeral pyre.

My younger brother lit the pyre. I did not feel any sorrow.

—Am I rising above sorrow, above joy?

—There is no meaning in living or in dying.

—The rule of the tides has ended. Life will go on as before.

From Delhi, a visitor. His name: Arvind Gaur, director of the Asmita Theatre Group. I had never seen him before nor his work. In his eyes, the light of commitment.

Geeta sat nearby. She knows I can no longer hold discussions. I can only say 'yes' or 'no'.

Geeta says Ranjit has already done a production so what...?

—My *Court Martial* will be different from Ranjit Bhai's. I plan to use flashbacks.

Geeta looked at me. I signalled: Let him do it.

Arvind said—You must come to Delhi for the first show.

We were both silent. Geeta's face fell. If I refused, we'd have to say why, which would be demeaning.

—Deepak doesn't travel much these days. But I'll talk to his friend Vikas Rai. He will go anywhere with him.

Arvind Gaur knew that I had some diseased secret. He's smart. He said nothing. I do not know why I gave him this unimportant information.

—Ranjit Kapoor has come to Ambala twice.

Arvind Gaur has done over a hundred shows of *Court Martial*.

Midnight and I am awake. I sleep in snatches. My naughty lover comes and goes at will.

Vasantha came and sat on the chair by the bed. I was delighted. My daughter has come home.

—Papa, my play? My *Sabse Udaas Kavita*?

I have learned many reasons for not writing.

—Vasantha, the play is about armed revolution. I know nothing about this.

—*Aap jab* Court Martial *likhti toh sena ke bare mein kya jaanti? Khoj-khabar karti. Tab likhti.* (What did you know about the Army when you wrote *Court Martial*? You did research and then you wrote.) Then write. Papa, do your homework. I want my play.

—Vasantha, I only write tragedies. Your death will be certain in the play.

Vasantha caught my hand. My eyes filled. It is time for a daughter to tell her father some terrible news.

—Papa, Papa, *Vasantha toh mar chuka.* (Papa, Papa, Vasantha is dead.) They shot me in both knees. They threw me in a field. Papa, Papa. It took me hours to die. I was thinking of you. No pain. No tears.

—My mad daughter. Come for the first night. I will know that you are there.

—Papa, I won't come alone. I'll bring the full war group to see it.

—Vasantha, pray that I too may die. My passport for all countries has been cancelled.

—First write *Sabse Udaas Kavita*. Then die.

I walk and I think. I talk to trees. I return from the walk. Geeta puts tea on the table. She looks at me. She is startled. And very happy.

—Deepu, your face has that old gleam on it. You're writing...

I nodded.

—Thank God. Now you'll be fine.

Geeta will now establish a curfew. No one will be allowed to come over. I will be at home but I will be 'not at home'.

I began to draw into myself. Outside scenes and people began to withdraw from my life. I began to conduct a silent conversation with myself. No one came to me in my dreams.

I was being continuously purified. I knew my priorities. The name of my heroine. I also knew that my heroine would be the union of two women. She would have Vasantha's clear political thinking. She would also have Nidhi's playfulness. They would complete each other.

Renu Mittal, much loved by Geeta and the family, came over. In her arms, a baby only a few months old. Renu is immersed in Hindi literature. I asked her the child's name. Renu smiled, her eyes shining with happiness. Apoorva.

I went into my room. On a paper I wrote in big letters—Apoorva. The other characters emerged onto the page from the stage of my soul—Dr Sukant, Naren, DSP Ahuja, Retired Judge, Jailor, The Zamindar, Jagmal Singh.

In a day, I had burgeoned into a pregnant woman. I was happy, contented. I don't know why I decided that the play should begin with a poem. And it should end with a poem.

I had written my fill of harsh and adamantine words. This play about revolution would begin with the gentle language of poetry. Of my own accord, my eyes opened at two-thirty. When I am writing, I have an internal alarm clock...

I always write the last scene first so that I will never stray out of the frame I have set myself.

With no conscious decision, I concluded that Rajesh Joshi would write the poems for the play. It's not as if he is a poet of slogans. He is excellent at investing words with new meanings. But I had never met Rajesh Joshi nor had I ever corresponded with him.

From the floor, I rose to the roof. From the roof, I flew to the moon. My self-hatred vanished. The fear of night visitors vanished. My grip on the pen was solid. The family was no longer angry with me. My grip on myself was solid. I stopped looking for acceptance in other people's eyes. Now I was writing. I was a creator. A small god. I was the author of the final sunset.

Gyan Chaturvedi came from Bhopal. First I told him my bodily fears—Gyan, I'm impotent now.

—Tell your women friends. They will feel safe.

Then he explained.

—This is one of the side-effects of psychiatric medicine. Do not make the mistake of taking something for this condition. And especially not from those sex specialists who have those men handing out little slips of paper, promising to make you a young man again.

I told him about the play. I told him about wanting to ask Rajesh Joshi to write poems for it.

—Don't worry about that. Rajesh Joshi lives in Bhopal. He's a friend. I'll put some other writers and poets after him. Manzoor Ahtesham will pester him to death. Bhagwat Rawat will hound him. He will have to give up and write the poem. Write down something about the play. I will personally hand it over to him. After all, poets have a healthy fear of doctors.

Fifteen days later, Rajesh Joshi sent the poem. In Apoorva's cell on Death Row, the sun rose.

The experiment of starting and ending the play with a poem was a success. The credit goes to Rajesh Joshi.

THE FUTURE

Sabse Udaas Kavita got written.

Arvind came to Ambala. I read it to him. He was silent for a while then:

—It is a dangerous play but I will do it.

Shashi Prakash said—You've never been to Bihar, you've never been to Andhra Pradesh but the play is correct in every detail.

Most delighted was Dr Pratap Sharan. That I could write

again was a personal victory for him. He knows that those who suffer from the illness never recover fully.

Apoorva-Vasantha, as she exited the final scene of the play. She took my dangerous and fatal yellow colour with her forever. Now I had total faith in the season of spring which had returned to me. I threw away my blind disability medal. The poison returned to my gaze. The people sleeping inside me woke up. I will give them life. For I am a powerful warrior. I will give life and I will take life too. Now I was no ordinary seer. My end shall not be in silence.*

The evening of *Sabse Udaas Kavita*'s first show in Delhi. I was in an unspeakable rage. I cannot remember the reason. I told the director, my friend Arvind Gaur—Nidhi is not to sit near me.

Arvind was first shocked, then sad.

—Nidhiji called. She wants to see the play with you. She'll take it badly if I stop her.

—If you're so worried about upsetting her, let her see the play. Alone. I'm off.

That evening I pushed Nidhi away in front of everyone.

Gagan Gill, Vikas Rai, Sukant, Piyush Mishra, Misha and Swadesh sat together and watched the play. The Karan-Arjun of Hindi letters—Rajendra Yadav and Nirmal Verma—were not present. They were not in the city.

In the last scene when Apoorva-Vasantha is about to hang, she reads out the poem written specially for this play by Rajesh Joshi. And then she will take her final step out of this world.

* This could be a reference to the famous last lines of *Hamlet*.

I became one in soul with Apoorva-Vasantha. I was outside Rajesh Joshi's poem and inside it too.

The light on Apoorva's face. She pulls the ribbon off her hair and shakes it free over her shoulders. It was an act of defiance of death. Apoorva was free of fear. Swadesh was being freed of fear too. Rajesh Joshi was free of fear in the first place.

Come and enfold me in your shawl, spun from the yarn of darkness
Come, sleep that will close my lids forever, come
Come, broker of my last breaths
Come, evil woman, intent on wiping the slate
of my life clean of every last scene, come.
Come, for you may take nothing but this body
Come, for this body has completed every vow required of it.
Come, for every file is filled.
Come, for every letter has been answered
Come, for injustice has been protested
And revenge taken
Come, for I may have no love of you
But come, for now I have no fear of you.

DARKNESS

I can cry. I can abuse. I can rage. Vasantha caught my hand, raised me up and said:

—Papa, papa, jump out of your dusty history.

The blood ran quick and fizzy, reaching the pores of my fingers.

I took a mighty leap. I came out of my world of cowardice.

Kaamna's beauty, as expansive as her body, was no longer an illusion. No more a hallucination. Now the flowers were free of fantasy. The stones began to dream again. Your camouflage shines. In these clothes, all your beautiful lies are hidden. The light falls on hair soft as the moon. Now I will touch it and see. I do not have a single picture of her. But I have her with me. And my armoury is filled up again with my lost weapons.

At the time of need, I will choose the right weapon to attack. Offence is the best defence. I fought my own case and left that seven-year-long hateful country. I had won a victory over myself. I am no longer a translation of myself. The fish have become blood-thirsty. The wind was no longer dry, no longer without enthusiasm. The wind was no longer a cold woman, a frigid woman. The wind is my old ally. My stalwart guard. It has returned as a weapon. Now I will no longer be anyone's prey. For seven years, I was Brihannala; male dancer, impotent of mind, castrated in body.

I began to take on my real identity. Swadesh Deepak: the angry one, blind with rage, who neither forgives nor asks forgiveness, no longer a little boy, in the world of Rajendra Yadav, the low one, who will not turn away from private injustice nor will be silent when he sees social injustice. He writes *Court Martial*. He has no pride. What he has written amounts to a handful of dust. Now, every woman is a goddess to be worshipped. I will not share my joys or sorrows with a woman. I will not refresh both bodies by sharing mine. I will talk of women's issues and like the editor of *Hans*, I will rejoice in the applause. However, I must ask myself: am I becoming a clever prick?

When I was being released from the hospital, Dr Avneet Sharma said to Geeta—Madam, here's your third child, Deepak. You'll have to re-learn your maternal skills.

FACE TO FACE AGAIN

It was 1991 when I first came to this city. Ten years have passed. Even the name of the city has changed: Kolkata. Usha Ganguly has completed 250 shows of my play. She wants to read *Sabse Udaas Kavita*. A small Swadesh festival. Usha isn't just my friend, she is also Geeta's true friend.

Before I came, I met Dr Pratap Sharan. His advice:

—Do not go if you are terribly afraid. But there is only one way to deal with this internal fear, this psychic fear, which is to confront it. This is the last thing preventing you from getting well. The last hurdle if she comes to meet you; be as ordinary, as normal as possible.

Talk to her but do not get angry. Do not tell her anything about your illness. It's possible that she might not even hear of you being there.

I could not tell Dr Sharan that Kaamna knows everything.

The fifth day in Kolkata. Usha had put us up at the Circuit House. I know you don't like staying at hotels. I came out of the room and went into the dining hall for my first cup of tea. The young men at the reception stopped me with:

—Sir, your photograph is in *The Statesman.*

He showed me the page in the newspaper. It was a listing of the day's plays and my photograph. Seeing my face turned to stone, he decided that I must not know Hindi and said:

—Sir, this is your photograph in *The Statesman.*

It was as if millstones had been tied to my feet. Dragging them to my favourite place, I sat down. The window opened outwards and a breeze, soft and wet with lake water, came in. It tweaked my nose and moved on.

Today the Royal Bengal Tiger would come.

Today, the confrontation. Already her frightening scent was manifesting itself.

Today, blood calls to blood. One more leap into the pit?

—Today, the Lord of the Body would not take back his fistful of spring, would he?

—Today, the tragedy of this unexpressed pride of the body would be completed, right?

—Today, will I be thrown to her?

—Today, will she come with her three white cheetahs or as a sleek young cheetah herself?

—Today, all your strategic tricks will fail. Your carriage wheel will stick in the mud. You will forget how to use your weapons. Then certain death. A slow language death. You, fucker Swadesh Deepak, and the psychiatric ward!

—Today I will meet my judge. Not my judge but an unjust judge from some Arab country who will give you seven years for a single expletive.

—Today, you understand, do you not, Seed of Shame? There is no author in any language as lightweight, raddi and mentally crippled as you are. You are not a swine, you are the son of a swine. You should be stoned in the town square. You should be spat upon. Your family finds you repellent and yet you wish for the love and praise of your audiences. And that too without writing!

You took a woman and her beauty and turned it into a myth. Into a Puranic tale. Into an imaginary story. When a beautiful woman turns into a myth, she wreaks havoc. Sometimes as a beautiful Draupadi she becomes the cause of a bloody internecine war. Like some jungle animal she promises that she will not adorn herself again until she has washed her hair in blood.

As soon as beauty becomes a myth, its home becomes the jungle. Animals outside. Animals inside.

I return to my room. I take out a Larpose. I'm supposed to take it at night. It takes doctors months to adjust psychiatric medicine dosages. They're not supposed to be changed randomly. I put the Larpose back. People who have bipolar disorder sometimes find themselves at the North Pole and sometimes at the South. That's when a man loses all dreams, all imagination.

I won't shave. I won't bathe. I won't change. My night clothes—kurta and tahmad—will do. I want to appear helpless and unarmed. What should I beg for? What if she gives it? When did you become that fucker Devdas? You need two women to die.

I suddenly thought of the maggots. The blood running from my wrist. The flesh smouldering after the fire raged across my upper body. Sometimes I'd be frightened of my sixteen-year-old son, as I lay there in my stink. When Geeta gave me milk to drink, she was my enemy. Hospital. Psychiatric ward. Bananas. Sikandar. Harnam Chacha. Kalgiwaale Maharaj. Electric shocks. The sour smell of my body after five months. Eunuch. Coward. Dog.

Wretch! Are you still not whole? Confront the bitch.

Before I got this message, the scent of her body reached me. My senses were on full alert. The doors of my soul opened.

I got down the stairs. On the last step, I stopped. Let me look my fill first.

My yogini. Unchanged since I first saw her.

A white sari. White blouse. Her hair damp. No ornaments. On her wrist, a red thread. Will she take me for breakfast again in order to cast a spell over me? The intervening years slipped away. My Maya Bakhshi. My morning sun. I would like to die again at her hands.

My soul threw open its arms. She saw me and came to me, her footsteps hasty. Her fatal beauty was accentuated by beautiful spectacles. I have always wanted a woman in spectacles. One has to try very hard to find a quiet corner where her spectacles won't break.

She reached me. Dr Pratap Sharan reminded me—Keep a safe distance. I folded up the arms my soul had flung open. The entire hall was watching this meeting, its collective breath suspended. She was naked. She let out a sad sigh.

I took both her hands in mine. I brought her to her chair. It was the chair near the window that opened on the lake. The water stopped breathing. So did the wind. Her damp hair did not stir. Had she forgotten her mantra?

She kept looking at me, shocked.

—Swadesh. You had such great colour in your cheeks. How come you're so pale?

I thought: I should tell her. They're not pale, they've been drained. The woman who had decreed that I should die by inches was right in front of me but I said nothing.

—I heard you were ill. That you had to leave your college job.

This woman was, without doubt, a soul hunter. If I were the old Swadesh, armed and dangerous, I would have grabbed her by her wet hair. I'd drag her face up to mine and shoot off a fire-arrow—You bloody bitch. Those aren't things you heard; they happened.

My brain's control room stopped working; the administration of my body stopped. I could not frame a complete sentence. Tea and veggies all over my clothes. My pyjamas always wet. A swine floundering in the muck, whose full name is motherfu...Swadesh Deepak. I feel like spitting when I see my own face. Children look for stones with which to pelt me as I pass.

But my old days had been stolen by Kaamna. I said nothing.

—You stopped answering my letters. If you had said something, I would have come.

—I do not share my sorrows with anyone. It is something personal and private. I remember William Faulkner—*Between grief and nothing, I will take grief.* If you had come, do you know what would have happened? You would have seen a long worm stretched out on a bed. You would hear words that had dried and had begun to decay. No doubt you would have hated...

In a stern voice, she interrupted me.

—Nothing like that would have happened, Swadesh. You seem unable to look beyond the body. Do you know what would have happened if I had come? I would have given you a great big scolding and you would have hopped off your bed. You have no idea of my power. But what did happen?

In the old days I would have said you are my nemesis, the Goddess of Vengeance, a sworn enemy. You are my judge. You inflict punishment and then ask: what happened?

With both hands, I beat my breast. Kill me, kill me. Kill me. Who would? I had made three attempts myself. The coward must always fail. The most severe curse: I would forget my Hindi. What can be worse than that: The loss of one's language? Not one dream from a single book was left to me. My end did not come as Mishima's did, not as Kawabata's did. Because my body was impotent, because my mind was impotent. Always a whining puppy. There was a secret terror too. My sorrows were untold. I was always flinching, curled up. For a moment, the fire would flare up. And then in the next minute it would turn to ice. I could not bear to stay alive.

But I told her nothing. I knew nothing about her cult, her following, her community. Her secret expertise. Her mysterious skill.

She suddenly realized that I was afraid of her. She became sad; she went off to the Sunderbans to search for her Royal Bengal Tiger. The breeze, having touched the water of the lake, blew into the room. Like some naughty adolescent, it coquetted about and vanished. Her hair curled around the left side of her white neck.

She used two fingers to push it back. She was very sad.

—Did you never even once want to tell me?

Who knows where the old Swadesh, rich with words, surfaced from!

—Once I wanted to call you to me. I wanted to marry you in court.

She felt the old Swadesh was back. She burst out laughing.

—You should have. What court marriage! I would have kidnapped you. We would have gone somewhere else and had a fine old marriage. And do you know what would have happened after that? You would have been raging every day and I would have to calm you down in my citadel.

I thought I should say: You bloody bitch. I want you in total. You are my destiny. I did not say it. I remembered a line from a letter by Keats:

If you are not in a room, I cannot breathe in it.[*]

I thought I'd tell Kaamna. I didn't.

Because we both understood that we must keep our personal dreams to ourselves. We are not fated to meet.

We knew this was our last meeting. Neither of us were sad at all. Perhaps we had both abandoned our stubbornness. We had gained nothing from it.

I saw a delicate tremor run through her body. This is the sexy way in which the bodies of many beautiful women signal that they have come alive.

—I will not come this evening to listen to *Sabse Udaas Kavita*.

—Nothing worth listening to.

—I've seen it on stage. I've read it too. Listen, Swadesh, where did you develop this habit of belittling yourself? You were better as an aggressive person.

I came out to see her. She knew I would not come to the car. She looked at me for a few moments. She had discovered the secret: that Swadesh was now a lost soul, never to be found. With quick steps, she went to the car, stopped. And just as quickly, she came back. My breath stopped.

She stood right in front of me. I don't know why she asked me, I don't know why she said:

—Swadesh, was it my fault?

---

* The line might be: 'You are to me an object intensely desireable—the air I breathe in a room empty of you is unhealthy.' This is from a letter to Fanny Brawne, written somewhere during May 1820.